Tourism Organisation

TOURISM ORGANISATION

Saurabh K. Dixit
(B.H.M.& C.T., M.T.M. & JRF-NET)

Reference Press

4831/24, Ansari Road
Darya Ganj
New Delhi-110 002
Phone: 51563444
Fax: 51563334
E-mail: info@essessreference.com
url: http://www.essessreference.com

First Published 2005

ISBN: 81-88583-86-3

Rs.750/-

Published by:
Reference Press
4831/24, Ansari Road, Darya Ganj,
New Delhi-110 002.
Phone: 51563444
Fax: 51563334
E-mail: info@essessreference.com
url: http://www.essessreference.com

Printed in India at:
Mehra Offset Press, New Delhi

Contents

Preface

The success of any sector or organisation largely depends on its foundation management. Management is considered to be the 'soul' for any sectoral or organisational development. Lacking proper management might be accountable to crumble the whole edifice. There should be proper knowledge about the detail and pros and cons before moving towards venturing in a specific field.

This book, titled : 'Tourism Organisation' reflects a vivid comprehension of management tools to be adopted to make efforts, towards creating a niche. This book is endowed with diverse sorts of facts and guidelines comprising proper staff-training, working with proper channel system, employee's direct interaction with management head, advertisements, providing basic facilities to tourists, care about their securities, trained, educated and soft spoken guides, smart field boys, proper infrastructural system, proper knowledge of public dealing, unity of command, hierarchical system, span of control etc.

For someone who is serious about entering the arena of tourism, the present book must prove to be a recourse to ensure success. The book divulges the basic guidelines, a successful organisation looks for.

All kinds of suggestions are cordially solicited.

Author

1

Introduction

For any industry to develop, an organization is a must as it plays a vital role in its planning, development and growth. Organization consists of individuals whose primary role is the achievement of the objectives for which it has been set up. Administration as a general field may be divided into two constituent areas: (i) administrative organization, which deals with the internal structure and arrangement of the personnel of the agency, and (ii) administrative management, which is concerned with the direction of the personnel, fiscal control and other techniques related to operation. The aim of the organization is 'to arrange people into working groups, associating those with similar functions or purposes in order to move efficiently to obtain a desired result from their combined action. In other words, organization means combination of a group of individuals whose main purpose is to achieve through group action the objectives for which it has been set up. It is the framework within which an industry works. It relates to the structure of the industry, and is concerned with the issues involved in, and the approaches to it. This could be any industry including the tourism industry.

The basic determinants of success in the field of tourism can be threefold: (i) attractions, e.g., climate, scenery, historical and cultural features; (ii) accessibility, i.e., distance of destination, their location and transport facilities; (iii) amenities, e.g., accommodation, catering and entertainment facilities. An appropriate mix of all the above three components is necessary for the success of tourism, and it is the task of the organization to achieve this success. The organization of tourism may be divided into two parts. First, there are sectors of tourism, i.e., the various providers of tourist services—the hotel and catering services, the transport services and the entertainment services; second, there are the levels of tourist organization—national, regional and local. The organization of tourism can therefore be horizontal as well as vertical. It also varies widely from country to country as there are a number of considerations which influence the nature of organizational setup.

Today almost all the countries have a tourist organization. Rapidly growing awareness of the economic, financial and social advantages of tourism development, together with the recognition that such advantages can best be achieved through systematic efforts to expand tourism, has led many states especially after the Second World War to extend and enlarge their direct interest in tourism. To manage tourism on scientific lines, many nations have set up organizations to deal specifically with the subject of tourism. However, the pattern and nature of these organizations differ widely from one country to another.

Factors that Influence

The type of a tourist organization in a particular country is influenced by a number of factors in that country. The political, economic and social system in a country will have an important bearing upon its tourist organization. In countries where there is a centralised government, this is likely to be reflected in the tourist organization, as is the case, for example, in Spain and the Russian Federation. In these countries the tourism industry is centralized and dominated by the government. By contrast, in countries such as Switzerland, Austria, Germany, Great Britain, with a federal state organization, the tourist industry is decentralised with a minimum of governmental interference. In these countries, the tourist organizations consist of one or more cooperative bodies at the national level and there is also a high degree of devolution to individual states or regions in various matters concerning tourism.

The importance of tourism to a national economy is another factor which influences the character of an organization. In countries where tourism is very important in relation to other industries, or conversely, where tourism is well developed and of substantial economic importance, the tourism organization is likely to be well developed and the government actively concerned with tourism. This type of organization is functioning in large number of countries. In Italy, it is a dual Ministry of Tourism and Entertainment, which is concerned with tourism as also with historical monuments, theatres and other forms of entertainment. Similarly, in Spain the dual ministry controls the press, radio and television along with tourism, while in France, the dual ministry controls tourism and entertainment.

The stage of tourism development is yet another important factor likely to have a considerable influence on the organization. For instance, in countries where tourism is not yet fully developed or is just beginning to develop (as is the case in many developing countries including India), better results can be achieved if the industry is centralised and under direct government control. In such countries direct government intervention would seem to be not only desirable but indispensable. Also as these countries would require huge sums of money for the development of infrastructure, these would come from the state as the private enterprise may not be in a position to invest because of lack of resources at their disposal. On the other hand, in countries with highly developed tourist industries, it is common to find flexible, decentralized tourist organizations, which have evolved over many years as is the case in Austria, Germany and Switzerland. Switzerland has a long history of tourism and as such there is a highly developed tourism organization which is decentralized and also reflects the federal character of the state. The organization of tourism, therefore, is complex and involves many forms and is influenced by a variety of factors. A study of tourism organization should logically begin with the official tourist organization called the National Tourist Organization followed by other semi-official or private organizations which together serve the objectives of tourism.

UN Conference Recommendations : The United Nations Conference on International Travel and Tourism held in Rome in

1963 considered the role of organizations in the development of tourism. The resolutions and recommendations of the conference are contained in the third part of the documents, which deals with tourism development. In a general resolution on the organization of tourism, it states that the conference.

- (i) considers it incumbent on governments to stimulate and coordinate national tourist activities;
- (ii) is convinced that this task can in the main be carried out through the medium of national tourist organizations;
- (iii) recommends that national tourist organizations should be granted the authority and resources necessary to enable them to take effective action, as desired by governments, for the development and promotion of national and international tourism.

The conference was unanimously of the opinion that national tourist organizations having governmental or semi-governmental support were an essential foundation for building up a prosperous tourist industry. Various forms of a national tourist organization were considered during the conference. In some countries the organization was in effect a government department directly responsible to a minister; in others it was a section of a government department. In many countries the tourist organization was a separate government agency. The conference noted that the degree of direct government control over such agencies varied a great deal from one country to another. In yet other countries the organization, though wholly or mainly financed by the government, could properly be described as non-governmental. Some non-governmental tourist organizations also received financial contributions from various sectors of the travel industry.

The conference was of the opinion that it was necessary, especially in developing countries, that the government should leave the organization responsible for tourism—whether a governmental or semi-governmental organization or a government agency— complete autonomy in the exercise of its functions. The conference considered it desirable that, in the case of national tourist organizations which did not include representatives of the principal administrative and private (producer and consumer) activities related to tourism, those activities should be represented by an advisory body with, if possible, spokesmen for organized labour in its membership. The conference also agreed that government should make adequate funds available to enable the national tourist organizations to carry out their work effectively. In view of the fact that tourism was an important social, economic and cultural factor, and recognising that, in the interest of their peoples, governments should assume their responsibilities in the field of tourism, the conference considered that such responsibilities should be delegated so far as possible to national tourist organizations.

The conference was of the opinion that the activities of the national tourist organizations should not be restricted to promotional questions alone, but should also cover the establishment, improvement and development of tourist equipment through either direct or coordinate or consultative action, as might be appropriate in each specific case. In developing countries, private enterprise was often unwilling or unable to invest in hotels and other enterprises connected with tourism because it lacked resources. In such cases, the conference felt, the state should lend assistance. The conference also believed that in order to be able to carry out their proper functions, national tourist organizations should be endowed by the government with the necessary authority and resources.

The conference expressed the opinion that where no national tourist organization existed, the government cognizant of its social responsibilities should take the initiative in setting up such an organization, which would aim at the development of both domestic and international tourism. That should be done in consultation with the private sector of the industry and where that sector was not sufficiently developed, the government should take action to stimulate its development.

The conference recommended that national tourist organizations should be awarded wider competence, increased responsibility and larger resources, so that they could promote the development of domestic tourism and thus assist in the development of international tourism. It recognized that in certain cases international tourism can encourage the rise and development of domestic tourism.

In every country governments are concerned about the tourism industry. There are several reasons for this. The important and obvious reasons are related to the economic impacts of tourism, e.g., employment generation, balance of payments and the contribution of tourism to the country's gross domestic product (GDP). Tourism also has social, cultural and environmental impacts which may be positive or negative. Governments are generally concerned in maximising the benefits and minimising the costs.

Governments are also responsible for framing the overall tourism policy. Policy is a guideline for the future or a course of action to meet defined goals and objectives. Tourism policy refers to guidelines and decisions designed to assist in meeting tourism goals and objectives. National, regional, state or local governments formulate tourism policies concerning their respective regions. At the national level, governments have an important role in influencing tourism. They can influence tourism both on demand and supply sides. Tourism is influenced on demand side to maximise net income and minimise costs. This can be achieved by

(i) removing the requirements of visas to stimulate demand;

(ii) promoting and marketing by way of funding tourist organizations which advertise at home and abroad;

(iii) exchanging controls on outbound tourists;

(iv) exchanging requirements on inbound tourists;

(v) levying entry/departure taxes;

(vi) providing subsidies to tourists; and

(vii) taking any action affecting disposable income/free time.

On the supply side the governments can influence tourism with a view to protecting the consumer and obtaining quick economic benefits. This can be achieved by (i) providing infrastructure like roads, airports, wayside facilities, etc.; (ii) improving level of public services like water, sewage treatment, medical facilities etc.; (iii) manpower development including education and training; (iv) providing range of investment incentives by way of granting loans, subsidies, grants, tax holidays, etc.; (v) planning permissions zoning building regulations; (vi) Legislation regarding protection of resources like national parks etc.; and (vii) framing rules regarding flow of foreign investment.

Tourist Organization on National Level : The National Tourist Organization (NTO) is the body responsible for the formulation and implementation of national tourist policy. It is the proper agency and instrument for the execution of the national government's responsibilities for the control, direction and promotion of tourism. All countries which are engaged in tourism have a national tourist organization which plays a leading role in both the formulation and the implementation of the government's tourism programme. This organization is also responsible for coordinating the different activities of all the bodies interested in tourism development. The national tourist organization may be a full-fledged ministry, a directorate general, a department, corporation or a board.

There is, however, no set formula as to what constitutes the most satisfactory constitutional arrangement for the national tourism body. Tourism ranks as a full ministry in some countries with a minister enjoying a cabinet rank. Another arrangement in many countries is for tourism to share a minister with information or with arts, sports and culture. Yet other possibilities include attaching the tourism office to the presidency of the council, putting it in the charge of an official of the rank of a deputy secretary with an occasional voice in the council of ministers. In others, it has semi-autonomous status of a corporation and functions not as an organ of the government but rather as a professional body outside it. It will be apparent that the arrangement and the constitution for the national tourist organization vary widely. It depends on factors like political structure of the country, the level of economic development, of potential value of tourism to the economy, the level of tourism development and also availability of capital for tourism development including infrastructural developments.

Functions of the National Tourist Organization : The National Tourist Organization is primarily concerned with control, direction and promotion of tourism. The object and functions of the NTO are therefore to ensure that the maximum possible value from international tourism accrues to the country for its economic and social benefit. The functions of the NTO, however, will vary quite widely in relation both to (i) the degree of the direct intervention that the government desires to exercise and (ii) the level of development of tourist industry in the country concerned.

At the Estoril Seminar in 1966 in England, it was agreed that the NTO would normally undertake the following functions.

(i) Research,

(ii) Information and promotion within the country,

(iii) Regularisation of standards of lodging and restaurants,

(iv) Control of activities of private travel agencies,

(v) Publicity overseas,

(vi) Technical and juridical problems,

(vii) International relations,

(viii) Development of selected areas, and

(ix) Overall tourism policy and promotion.

Research is a basic function of a national tourist organization. A concomitant of institutional promotion is research into the tourism potential of the, principal markets and investigation into the marketability of the country's tourist product. This is an important direct responsibility of NTO.

Information and promotion within the country helps not only the actual international tourist but also the domestic tourist. The information offices located at important tourist centres serve as a facility to the tourists. These are a major aid to tourists both overseas as well as local. These centres provide accurate and up-to-date information to tourists visiting various places. In most countries, NTO has its own branch offices in strategic places throughout the country. These offices are responsible for information and reception services for visitors and liaison with the local tourist interests. It is also the responsibility of the NTO to encourage and promote tourism consciousness among the government agencies and the public so that they will realise the benefits that a country can derive from tourism.

Regularisation of standards of lodging and restaurants is very essential for tourist satisfaction. Since the growth of tourism depends directly on consumer satisfaction, the NTO, in its role of administrator, manager and promoter of the tourist product, acts as the government watchdog to ensure the maintenance of appropriate standards of quality and service of lodging establishments. This supervisory role has been enlarged and strengthened because of the complex problems arising from the growth of tourism and the expanding needs for safeguarding the interests of tourists. The degree of tourism development, and of the travel sectors' maturity, naturally determine the extent to which the travel industries are self-regulating and the scope of NTO's supervisory role.

Control of activities of private travel agencies is another important supervisory role of the NTO. More and more tourists are utilizing the services of private travel agencies. It is essential that the tourists should get good and efficient service and protection. NTO should be responsible for the maintenance of appropriate standards of quality and service of the travel agents. Travel agents should be regarded as having professional status and this could best be brought about by introducing appropriate legislation.

Publicity overseas is a major function of the NTO. One of the most important activities of any national tourist office is promotion of the country as a destination for tourists. Among other activities, promotion includes advertising, publicity of all kinds, public relations, the provision of information and the distribution of printed sales material. Planned publicity and promotion on behalf of the country are among the basic functions common to all NTOs.

Normally no other government agency exercises this function. The NTOs cooperate with other governmental departments and the travel trade in promoting tourism for their country.

Technical and juridical problems are those which are related with the administration of law. This is very crucial as on it will depend the quality of various services provided by various sectors. NTOs have to be very cautious while administering law. Technical problems on the other hand are concerned with the development and maintenance of various services. Continuous detailed assessment has to be made of the extent to which the infrastructure, superstructure and organization plans are likely to meet future tourism demand. It is imperative that the NTO should take part directly in each of these stages. The optimum development of tourism in any country implies a close knowledge of the attractions of the country; acquaintance with the motivations and the needs of the market; the processing and presentation of the country's attractions in the manner most favourable and acceptable to the market; action of the market to create effective demand; and the provision of adequate facilities, amenities and services to ensure the maximum satisfaction of tourists. All these areas are of technical nature and the NTOs have to take proper care for their efficient maintenance.

International relations are also a very essential part of tourism. International contacts resulting from tourism have always been among the most important ways of spreading ideas about other cultures. Tourism can be a vehicle for international understanding by way of bringing diverse people face to face. It has been cited as a major contributor to international goodwill and as a prime means of developing social and cultural understanding among all people of the world. The interaction of a large number of people with the local population of a country visited results in making friends. It is the responsibility of the NTO to deal with aspects of tourism development that have a bearing on relations with foreign countries. It maintains offices and representatives abroad for the promotion of tourism traffic to the country, and has close relations with foreign tour operators, travel agents and carriers. It cooperates with NTOs of neighbouring countries in mounting joint regional travel promotion programmes. Governments also empower NTOs to represent the country's tourism interests in international organizations and, wherever necessary, to join with other government agencies in negotiations for the conclusion of agreements in the field of tourism with foreign governments.

Development of selected areas to attract tourists is necessary. In every country there are hundreds of areas of tourist potential. However, due to various constraints it is not possible to develop all these areas. It is important to identify and select certain areas which have the maximum potential for tourism development. A detailed scientific survey of these areas will help in avoiding wasteful expenditure. To the extent permitted by its economic resources, the NTOs should encourage development of selected resorts. Existing possibilities of attracting tourists—mountaineering, winter sports, beaches, national parks, game sanctuaries, national monuments, sites and shrines, pilgrim centres, folk traditions and customs, festivals and sporting events—should be developed and protected. In a developing country the NTO should consider obtaining a preliminary survey in order to assess clearly what positive tourist attractions the country already had, what potential tourist attractions existed, and how they could most effectively be developed within the limits of the resources available.

Overall tourism policy and promotion is very essential as it helps in the optimum utilization of resources. In calculating returns from investments in tourism, the national tourist policy cannot restrict itself to limited considerations of immediate financial and economic profitability. It has to consider the beneficial effects of tourism on general national development where considerations of non-economic character may be equally or even more important, than purely economic returns, viz., cultural considerations, social considerations, political considerations, etc.

The NTOs should take all these factors into consideration while formulating overall tourism policy and promotion. They should not consider tourism from its balance-of-payments aspect alone, but should take into account the contribution which tourism makes to international trade by developing the national economy and enhancing social values.

Work of NTO : The National Tourist Organization is likely to be concerned with four broad areas:

(i) administration,

(ii) production,

(iii) marketing, and

(iv) financing.

The administration will be concerned with the personnel of the organization, with the part to be played by tourist in the overall national developmental plan; with effective liaison with concerned government departments like finance, home, planning, health, transport, communications, education, culture, public works, labour etc.; regional cooperation and legal matters and advisory services, etc.

The production part will be concerned with all those elements and activities which make up the tourism product. Production will include the inventory and assessment of the country's natural attractions and the development and protection of these assets; the listing, assessing and forecasting the country's tourism plant, the requirements in infrastructure where tourist development is planned, the drawing up of plans for regional or area development, the establishment of close relations with the hotel, catering and transport sectors of tourism, the recruitment and training of personnel for the tourist industry, etc.

The marketing area will be concerned with research into the principal and potential tourist markets, their size, socio-economic characteristics, preferences of tourists for food and accommodation, spending power and the like, with sales promotion, public relations, advertising, maintenance of overseas offices, etc.; and collaboration with other countries in the same region.

Finally, the financial work will involve investment in and financing of tourism in the country. It will, for example, provide financial assistance for approved tourist projects, approve loans or grants for hotels, seek and encourage private investment in various tourism projects and, where these are not enough, seek funds from international agencies such as World Bank, or International Bank for Reconstruction and Development. The role of foreign participation in tourism development is important in many of the developing countries which have not the necessary capital available for investment.

Another important area of the work of a national tourist organization is its role as the spokesperson for private tourism industries, to communicate their needs to the government and to strive for the most satisfactory solutions. The NTO has to ensure that the expectations and operations of the private tourist operators are consistent with the aims and objectives of the national tourist programme and policy. With the recognition of tourism as an industry through the formation of large integrated travel enterprises and the development of package travel, NTOs are experiencing the need to foster the integration of their country's tourist industries (travel agencies, tour operators, hotels) so as to enable them to become more efficient and effective partners in promoting tourism in the country.

Whatever the tasks that the national tourism body is called upon to do, what is most important is that it should have the full powers necessary to carry them out. The NTO can carry out its task most effectively and satisfactorily only when it has broad powers and adequate resources. The governments should make adequate funds available to enable the national tourist organizations to carry out their work effectively. The NTO must, above all, have authority. It must be able to present effectively and forcefully the case for tourism among the claims of other sectors competing for government support and finance. Lastly, it is essential that the tourist organization maintains a close and harmonious liaison with all other interests that may be involved in tourism development. To sum up, the national tourist organization has to mobilize all potential national forces and resources available for stimulating the growth and development of tourism.

Indian Profile

Tourist Organization : Tourism as a separate organization was set up rather late in India.

Prior to the formation of a separate organization, tourism was a part of the Ministry of Transport. The government, had, however, started devoting considerable time and attention to the development of tourist traffic immediately after independence. By that time it was recognised that tourist traffic was an important source of earning foreign exchange as well as promoting international understanding.

The first step towards the development of the tourist industry in India was initiated in the year 1945 when the Sargent Committee was appointed. This committee, set up by the then Government of India under the chairmanship of Sir John Sargent, the then educational adviser to the government, submitted its report in the year 1946. The main recommendation of the committee was that a separate tourist organization should be set up at the Centre with regional offices in metropolitan cities of Bombay (now Mumbai), Delhi, Calcutta (Kolkata) and Madras (Chennai). The committee also recommended setting up of tourist publicity cells in Indian embassies and consulates all over the world. As a follow-up, an adhoc tourist traffic committee was appointed in 1948. This committee was entrusted with the job of suggesting ways and means of promoting tourist traffic to India.

Temporary Committee : It was in 1948 that the independent Government of India took the first step towards promotion of tourism in India. The Ministry of Transport constituted an ad hoc tourist traffic committee consisting of representatives of the concerned ministries and of tourist, transport and hotel industries. One of the major recommendations of the Sargent Committee appointed in 1945 was that the work of development of tourist traffic in India should be undertaken on a "methodical basis by a separate organization". As a result of this recommendation, a separate tourist traffic branch was set up in the Ministry of Transport in 1949 with the main objective of development of tourist traffic in India. The subsequent years witnessed an expansion of the branch and its activities in various directions. In 1955-56, its headquarters establishment was increased from one branch to four branches, each having wide- ranging duties.

The four sections looking after various subjects were :

(i) tourist traffic section

(ii) tourist administration section

(iii) tourist publicity section and

(iv) distribution section.

The tourist traffic section was to look after a larger number of travel trade subjects which included development of both internal and external tourist traffic, legislative matters, five-year plans, travel agencies, hotels and rest houses, facilitation, tourist statistics and monthly reports. It also dealt with international conferences on tourism and conferences relating to United Nations and its agencies, coordination with railways, establishment of tourist bureaus in States and development of tourist centres and the training of guides. The *tourist administration section* was to deal with administration work relating to tourist offices both in India and abroad, budget, delegation of financial powers to tourist offices, opening of new tourist offices in India and abroad and periodical inspection of tourist offices. The *tourist publicity section* was to deal with publication of tourist literature such as pamphlets, guidebooks and posters, issue of advertisements and participation in exhibitions and fairs. The *distribution section* was to deal with the distribution of tourist publicity literature in India and abroad.

Within a short period of time there was manifold increase in the activities of the Tourist Traffic Branch. The four branches as they developed during the years 1955-56 performed a variety of duties covering almost all the important segments of tourism. These branches were functioning under one deputy secretary and two under secretaries. At this stage there was a proposal for the creation of a directorate general of tourism. One reason advanced in favour of this proposal was that the policy making and executive functions were combined in the existing staff of the tourist division of the secretariat and that these should be separated. However, this proposal did not find favour as it was felt that the subject of tourism had not yet developed to an extent as would justify an immediate separation of these two functions.

Information Offices : Another important step during this period was the opening of a chain of tourist offices both in India and abroad. Steps were taken to establish regional offices at important ports of entry. Tourist offices were opened in Delhi, Bombay (now Mumbai), Calcutta (Kolkata) and Madras (Chennai). This was followed by the establishment of a chain of information offices all over the country. By the year 1955, nine such offices were opened. The staff in the regional offices in India consisted of one regional officer, one assistant regional officer, one receptionist and two clerks. The staff in information offices consisted of one information officer and one clerk. Regional tourist officers and the information officers had to perform wide-ranging duties. The duties of the former included liaison with State governments, the local tourist agencies, the railway authorities, airlines, shipping agencies and hotels with regard to travel trade of the region. Other duties were as follows:

(i) making suggestions for improvement of tourist traffic facilities in the region,

(ii) assisting Ministry of Transport in the preparation and distribution of publicity material,

(iii) selling tourist literature supplied by the Ministry of Transport and State governments and the Publications Division,

(iv) issue of permits and cards to foreign tourists holding tourist visas, issue of tourist introduction cards, distribution of embarkation and disembarkation cards to the airlines, travel agents and security control for observance of frontier formalities,

(v) attending to the complaints of tourists and travel trade regarding lack of amenities and bringing the same to the notice of the Ministry of Transport and the local authorities.

The duties of the information officers included :

(i) surveying tourist resources in the region and maintaining an up-to-date record of available facilities,

(ii) organizing tourist promotional activities,

(iii) attending to all enquiries regarding tourist amenities and tourist attractions which may be made at the Tourist Information Office whether personally or by correspondence,

(iv) receiving parties of tourists at aerodromes and railway stations and rendering assistance to them, and

(v) keeping close liaison with the travel trade and local authorities.

The details of the functions of the tourist offices are as follows:

(i) Attending to personal and postal enquiries of Indian and foreign tourists.

(ii) Collecting and compiling of detailed up-to-date information for dissemination to tourists.

(iii) Preparation of handouts containing information on places of tourist interest for distribution among tourists.

(iv) Assistance in expeditious clearance of travel formalities of tourists arriving by air and sea.

(v) Issue of liquor permits, tourist introduction cards, railway concession forms, etc.

(vi) Making various arrangements for departmental guests consisting of travel agents, writers and film makers including booking of accommodation, airline seats, arrangements for sight-seeing, transport, entertainment, etc.

(vii) Rendering non-financial assistance to important tourist groups, individual tourists, travel writers, journalists, etc., who are on tour of India.

(viii) Publicity and tourist promotion by contributing articles to press and travel magazines, organizing film shows, talks on radio, lectures, club meetings, etc.

(ix) Taking up problems of various sections of the travel trade in order to ensure that tourists face no difficulty whatsoever.

This involves liaison with various Central and State government departments.

(x) Enquiries into the complaints of tourists against shopkeepers, taxi drivers, etc., and getting them refund wherever necessary.

(xi) Liaison with archaeological department, State government tourist departments and other local bodies for the maintenance and improvement of tourist facilities.

(xii) Arranging regular film shows at airports for a large number of tourists.

(xiii) Distribution of tourist literature to travel agencies, hotel counters, airlines, etc., as also publicising tourist centres through display of posters at focal points.

(xiv) Allotting guides on rotation basis for tourists and travel agencies, supervision of the quality of services rendered by guides, and conducting periodical training courses for guides.

(xv) Inspection of hotels from time to time, screening shops, shikar agencies, travel agencies and car operators for approval, and generally supervising the services of all branches of the travel trade.

(xvi) Organizing special programmes for tourist cruise ships such as cultural shows, fashion shows, etc., and arranging sight-seeing tours for tourists from these ships.

(xvii) Arranging meet-the-people programmes and Indian home visits for foreign tourists.

(xviii) Assisting foreign journalists, TV and radio publicists, film producers, etc., in getting facilities so that the country gets maximum publicity abroad through such media.

(xix) Maintaining a statistical section for compiling tourist statistics.

(xx) Promotion of sight-seeing tours and inducing tour operators/agents to start new tours where necessary.

(xxi) Supervision of the working of tourist bungalows/youth hostels, etc., put up by the Department of Tourism.

(xxii) Participation in meetings and conferences related to tourism promotion like Pacific Asia Travel Association (PATA).

Tourism Organisation on Global Level : In short, the functions of the tourist offices in India include supply of up-to-date information on places of tourist interests after tourists had arrived in India, keeping in touch with all the segments of travel trade, assisting the tourists in clearance of various travel formalities, distribution and display of tourist literature and periodic inspection of various facilities available for tourists. Tourist offices were also to ensure that the various amenities are developed and maintained in each region. In addition to attending to foreign tourists, the tourist offices were also to cater to the needs of domestic tourists.

Overseas Tourist Offices : The Central government decided to open a chain of tourist offices overseas with a view to attracting foreign tourists to India. The first step in this direction was the establishment of Government of India Tourist Office in New York in the United States of America in December 1952. The reason for opening an office in the United States was that as an affluent country its people had enough money and leisure to afford a holiday in India. Nearer home, special staff was also provided in the offices of the High Commissioners for India in Sri Lanka and Australia for tourist promotion work in these countries. To arouse interest among Europeans to visit India, a chain of offices were also opened in the continent. The first office in Europe was opened in London in July 1955. Two more offices were opened, one in Paris in February 1956 and the other in Frankfurt in September of the same year. In order to promote tourist traffic from Australia and New Zealand, a tourist office was opened in Melbourne in September 1956. Also in 1956 an office was opened in Colombo on the occasion of the 2,500th anniversary of Gautam Buddha. The office in Colombo was responsible for helping and promoting a large Buddhist traffic from Sri Lanka.

Functions : The functions performed by the tourist offices abroad were more or less similar to those performed by the regional offices in India, with the difference that while the regional offices in India mainly assisted the foreign tourists who had arrived in India, the tourist offices abroad furnished preliminary information to tourists intending to visit India. Their duties included publicity and public relations, sales promotion and reporting to the Department of Tourism about the trends in the tourist travel abroad. The details of the functions of the tourist offices abroad are as follows:

(i) To establish and maintain continuous contacts with travel agents, airlines, shipping companies, professional clubs and international tourist promotion societies.

(ii) To establish and maintain continuous contact with heads of national tourist offices of the other governments, tour promoters, travel writers, film and TV producers, etc.

(iii) Tourist publicity and promotion by way of sponsoring articles in press, by television and radio programmes, by advertisement campaign and through participation in exhibitions, etc.

(iv) To supply up-to-date information about tourist facilities in India through various channels to the potential visitors.

(v) To supply information to Central government's Department of Tourism about current trends in tourism in the area of their respective jurisdiction.

(vi) To organize film shows of tourist documentaries and other films of tourist interests for various groups.

(vii) To organize and supervise the advertisement programmes geared towards promotion of tourist traffic to India.

(viii) To attend to various personal and postal enquiries made by potential tourists and to assist in preparation of itineraries.

(ix) To prepare a monthly newsletter giving all the information of tourist interest.

(x) To distribute tourist literature to travel agents, wholesalers and other agencies responsible for promoting tourist traffic and maintaining a mailing list for distribution of publicity material.

(xi) To participate in social functions, conferences and meetings with a view to acquainting the potential visitor about India and its tourist attractions.

In short, the functions of tourist offices abroad include acquainting the potential visitor about the various tourist attractions and facilities available in India through publicity, public relations and sales promotion.

The Criteria for Opening Offices : The most effective way of developing tourist traffic from abroad is to establish direct link with the countries concerned by opening tourist offices there. The tourist offices set up in other countries work for the promotion of tourism traffic to their home country. Although the main criteria for opening new offices abroad is the number of tourists coming from the country concerned, factors are also taken into consideration. The following are some of them: (i) The potentiality of the tourist market in the area. (ii) The spending capacity and the travel consciousness of the population of the country. (iii) The need to develop a particular area from the foreign-exchange point of view, e.g., hard-currency areas. (iv) The cultural and/or historic affinity between India and the country concerned. (v) The importance of the place from the international tourism point of view. An office at such a place can persuade the transit tourists to include India in their itineraries.

Setting up of Department of Tourism : It was on March 1st, 1958 that a separate tourism department was created in the Ministry of Transport to deal with all matters concerning tourism. Thus a long-felt need of such a department was at last met. The new department was put under the charge of the director general who had under him one deputy director general and four directors each in charge of administration, publicity, travel relations and planning and development.

By a presidential order dated 14 March, 1967, the Department of Aviation and Tourism, which was under the Ministry of Transport and Civil Aviation, was formed into a separate ministry designated as the Ministry of Tourism and Civil Aviation, with two constituent departments:

(i) Department of Tourism and

(ii) Department of Civil Aviation.

The ministry was under the charge of a full-time minister. It was after nearly eighteen years that subject 'tourism' was accorded a separate entity and became independent of transport. With the formation of the new Ministry of Tourism and Civil Aviation, tourism got the importance due to it and thereby achieved all-round expansion in its activities.

The Department of Tourism now became an attached non-participating office of the Ministry of Tourism and Civil Aviation headed by the director general of tourism. The director general of tourism carried an ex-officio status of an additional secretary to the Government of India. Although an attached office, the department is both a policy-making and an executive organization and corresponds directly with the other ministries and departments of the Central government and State governments.

Recently tourism has been accorded the status of a full-fledged ministry and is designated as Ministry of Tourism and Culture. It is headed by a minister who is assisted by a secretary and a director general. The Ministry of Tourism is both a policy-making and an executive organization and corresponds directly with other ministries and departments of the Central and State governments. The functions of the Ministry of Tourism are both promotional and organizational which are conducted by the following divisions:

(i) Planning and Programming;

(ii) Publicity and Conference;

(iii) Travel Trade and Hospitality;

(iv) Accommodation

(v) Supplementary Accommodation and Wildlife;

(vi) Market Research; and

(vii) Administration.

The activities of the ministry have since increased manifold and cover a wide range of subjects. The various activities fall under the following broad heads:

(i) Collection, compilation and dissemination of tourist information in India and abroad and attending to enquiries from international tourists, tour operators and travel industry such as airlines, steamship companies and hotels.

(ii) Cooperation with international travel and tourist organizations at government and non-government levels.

(iii) Development of tourist facilities of interest to international tourists.

(iv) Publicity at home and abroad with the object of creating an overall awareness of the importance of tourism.

(v) Simplification of frontier formalities in respect of international tourists.

(vi) Regulation of activities of the various segments of the travel trade such as hotels, youth hostels, travel agents, wildlife outfitters, guides, tourist car operators and shopkeepers catering to tourist needs.

(vii) Compilation of statistics and market research on international tourist traffic to India and their utilization for more effective tourist promotion.

The ministry has a chain of twenty-one tourist information offices established in important cities in India. Four of these offices (regional offices) are located at Mumbai, Delhi, Kolkata and Chennai which are major ports of entry. The remaining sub-offices are functioning at focal points of tourist interest in Agra, Aurangabad, Cochin, Jaipur, Khajuraho Varanasi, Bangalore, Bhubaneswar, Hyderabad, Panaji, Patna, Port Blair, and Thiruvananthapuram. With a view to attract tourists to the north-eastern region, offices have been opened Guwahati, Shillong, Imphal, Itanagar and Naharlagun (Arunachal Pradesh). The tourist offices in India furnish information to the tourists regarding travel and tourist attractions in India and also render assistance of non-financial nature. These offices help the department in exercising some measure of control over various segments of travel trade and try to ensure that the foreign tourists get various services at reasonable cost and are not inconvenienced in anyway during their period of stay in India. All these offices work in close collaboration with State governments, travel agencies, excursion agencies, hoteliers, carriers, 'shikar' out fitters and tourist car operators.

For overseas promotion, the ministry has eighteen offices. The offices located at New York, Los Angeles, Buenos Aires and Toronto cover USA, Latin America, Canada and the Caribbean Islands. The regional director, with headquarters in New York, supervise the functioning of these offices. In Europe the offices are located at London, Paris, Frankfurt, Brussels, Moscow, Amsterdam, Stockholm, Vienna and Milan. These offices cover Continental Europe under the directions of a regional director stationed at Frankfurt. The offices in Sydney, under the supervision of a regional director, cover Australia, New Zealand and Fiji Islands. The tourist office in Tokyo covers Japan, Philippines, Hong Kong SAR and Thailand. The office in Singapore, which is also under the guidance of Tokyo office, covers Singapore, Malaysia and Indonesia. West Asia is covered by the tourist office located in Dubai. Two more offices in Tel Aviv (Israel) and Johannesburg (South Africa) have been opened. The overseas tourist offices form a direct link between the department and the travel trade in foreign countries. Their functions include handling of enquiries, dissemination of accurate information, advertising, publicity, public relation with press and travel trade and supply of up-to-date information to the department about current trends in tourism in the area of their jurisdiction.

From a small beginning in 1949, the tourist organization as it stands now has passed through various facets. The recognition given to tourism as an industry paved the way for its standing as an independent discipline. In between 1949 and today there has been a tremendous amount of work which has helped in strengthening the organization. The appointment of various expert committees, advisory commitments, councils and boards from time to time has helped the organization grow tremendously.

Example of Italy : Italy, like India, is one of the oldest countries where civilization and culture have enjoyed a long history. Both Italy and India are endowed with ancient traditions, art, architecture, religion, philosophy, etc. Italy is a long, narrow peninsula and lies at the foot of the European continent. It is a beautiful country with numerous picturesque lakes, rivers and mountains. The northern mountains and lakes and the southern seas, forests of fir trees and Indian prickly pears, the fog of the lagoons, Gothic cathedrals and Greek temples, the rationality of the Renaissance have combined to make Italy a country where nature and culture blend superbly.

The warm Mediterranean climate and the protection afforded by the Alps make Italy a land of sunshine where pine trees grow at the foot of snow-capped mountains and a deep blue sky spans equally over the cliffs of the Riviera, the soft hills of Tuscany and the historic monuments of Sicily. It is because of the magic spell of its scenic splendours and artistic grandeurs that Italy today is one of the most sought-after eldorados for tourists all over the world. It is truly a tourist paradise and the tourist trade in Italy has become an economic and social factor of enormous importance. The tourist arrival figures in Italy are simply startling. The foreign visitors to Italy have grown from two million in 1931 to over 36 million in 1999. The yearly increases are far beyond those registered in other European countries attracting foreign visitors.

The Italian authorities, considering tourism as an economic and social factor of enormous importance, have created special agencies and departments to manage and organize tourism in the country. These special agencies and departments operate under the overall supervision of the Ministry of Tourism and Entertainment. Earlier it has been discussed that organization of tourist industry in any country varies very widely and depends upon a number of considerations which influence the nature of organizational set-up. One of these factors is the importance of tourism in a national economy. This factor is likely to influence the character of the organization. Where tourism is developed and is of substantial economic importance to a country, the organization is also likely to be well developed and the government actively concerned. Tourism organizations in such countries may have a government department wholly or substantially concerned with tourism. In Italy it is the dual Ministry of Tourism and Entertainment, which is concerned in addition to tourism with historical monuments, theatres, and other forms of entertainment. The following paragraphs will discuss how tourism is organized in Italy.

At the top of the organizational pyramid lies the Ministry of Tourism and Entertainment (Ministero del Tourismo e dello Spettacolo). This is the central authority. It was created by the Legislative Act of July 1959 absorbing the former Commission for Tourism created in 1947. The Ministry of Tourism and Entertainment has two departments (general directorates): one for tourism and the other for entertainment. The Directorate General of Tourism has six main divisions:

(i) tourist organization inside the country,

(ii) reception and tourist resources,

(iii) tourist aids,

(iv) international relations and festivals,

(v) professional training and tourist industries and

(vi) legal and technical affairs.

In 1969, the country was divided into 20 regions. There was a shift to decentralization of the administration which involved the reorganization of regional administration and the creation of regions. Fifteen new regions, besides the other five which existed for several years with special statutory provisions, came into existence. The ministry's functions before the formation of these states as a result of shift to decentralization were much wider in scope and covered a wide range of subjects. However, since 1971, with so many fields of competence in tourism transferred to the regions, a decree was enacted limiting the ministry's field competence mainly to the following:

(a) International relations,

(b) Creation and managing tourist offices at the frontiers;

(c) Tourist promotion abroad through the National Italian Tourist Organization; and

(d) Guiding and coordinating regional administrative activities.

Planning of tourism within the framework of overall national development plans remains with the ministry through its consultative capacity to other ministries concerned. The implementation of those plans at a regional level is now entrusted to the regional boards [Ente Provincial del Tourismo (EPT)]. Such matters as tourism policy, the administration of loans, the grading of hotels and the general coordination of tourist services all come under the control of the Directorate General of Tourism, which is the tourist part of the Ministry.

Central Tourist Council : The Central Tourist Council (Consiglio Central del Turismo) is created within the Ministry of Tourism and Entertainment to exercise functions of advisory and research nature. The council is called together twice a year by the minister and may address itself to any question or questions relating to tourism in general and criteria of tourist publicity in particular. The council's recommendations become binding in certain cases, namely, measures necessary for creating cure, sojourn and tourist resorts and their revocation.

Presided over by the minister, the council is composed of 59 members, some of whom represent ministries such as tourism, the interior, foreign affairs, finance, public works, education, defence, civil aviation, transport, industry and commerce, agriculture and forests, health, etc. Besides there are the representatives from National Italian Tourist Organization [Ente National Italiano per il Turismo (ENIT)], the national committee for the Olympics, automobile club, etc. Representatives of the employees in industries or enterprises concerned with tourism, workers in these enterprises and specialists in tourism are also represented in the council. The council is formed for a term of four years. It has a secretary who is usually a high official of the ministry. The Central Tourist Council was reorganized by a presidential decree of August 1964.

National Italian Tourist Organization (ENIT) : The chief function of the National Italian Tourist Organization [Ente National Italiano per il Turismo (ENIT)] is propaganda and promotion. This organization is responsible at the national level for the Italian tourist promotion overseas. ENIT has 26 tourist overseas promotion offices. It has also correspondence offices abroad in collaboration with Alitalia Airlines. The main functions of this organization can be summed up as promoting and developing the foreign tourist movement to Italy. In order to achieve this task the ENIT has to perform the following functions:

(i) carry out tourist promotion abroad through its overseas promotion offices;

(ii) create and administer overseas tourist offices;

(iii) collect and analyse statistical data pertaining to the international tourist movements;

(iv) carry out tourist marketing research and studies; and

(v) within its terms of reference, perform any other duties entrusted to it by the Ministry of Tourism and Entertainment. ENIT is a public law body created in 1923 and reorganized by a presidential decree in August 1960. It has an autonomous legal status and is subject to the control of the Ministry of Tourism and Entertainment. The chief executive of this body is the president who is appointed by the Minister of Tourism and Entertainment. The president presides over the board of directors and the executive committee. In the case of his absence or inability to attend the board meetings, he is replaced by the seniormost official among the three representatives of the Ministry of Tourism on the board. Following the president in the administrative structure of ENIT, the director general is the chief professional officer. Other senior officials are the inspector general, the chiefs of divisions and the directors of tourist offices abroad.

The ENIT supreme authority is invested in a council of administration which is nominated by a ministerial decree and comprises, in addition to the president, 28 members among whom

16 represent various ministries, regional boards of tourism, the autonomous bodies for cure, sojourn and tourism of whom four represent employers and four workers in the tourist enterprises. The executive committee comprises the president of ENIT and four board members to be nominated by the council. The committee adopts the necessary measures to implement the programmes of tourist activities laid down by the council of administration. ENIT has an independent operational budget which is financed by allocations put at its disposal by the ministry.

Regional Tourist Boards : The Regional Tourist Board (Ente Provinciale per il Turismo) is an intermediate level between the national and local levels. The boards were created first by the law decree of June 1935 and were reorganized by the presidential decree of August 1960. They have administrative autonomy and a public law status. The boards are situated in each regional capital and are subject to the ministry's supervision in carrying out their functions. The boards cover almost all activities in the region concerned with tourism. The following are the specific functions with which the regional tourist boards are concerned:

(i) to promote and develop the foreign tourist movement to the region;

(ii) to study tourist problems in the region and take necessary measures towards the growth of the regional tourist economy;

(iii) to take action aiming at exploitation of tourist attractions and resources;

(iv) to coordinate, within the region, all activities of a touristic nature and those activities exerted by various organizations concerned with tourism;

(v) to maintain relations with the regional, provincial and local authorities, with industry, chambers of commerce and other such organizations or associations having any tourist impact;

(vi) to collect and analyse tourist statistics;

(vii) to carry out inspection and classification of hotels and other types of accommodation and judge their rates; and

(viii) to carry out other duties which may be delegated to them by the minister of tourism and entertainment.

Each regional board is managed by a president, an administrative council and an executive committee. The president of the board is nominated by a ministerial decree for a term of four years. He is a political nominee and is the legal representative of the board. The president presides over the administrative council and the executive committee. The board is technically managed by a director who is usually a professional from a tourism field. The regional boards are financed through public funds by way of allocations by the ministry in its annual budget, and also partly through subsidies and contributions of organizations, associations and various bodies directly or indirectly interested in tourism. Close scrutiny of the functions of the boards will reveal that these are chiefly concerned with the development and growth of tourism in a region. The product development is the key function of the board in a particular region. A region often becomes a separate main destination within a country for a foreign tourist. As such, regions provide a basis for the formulation of tourist products which can be promoted in appropriate markets and which call for information services.

Autonomous Bodies : The Autonomous Bodies for Cure, Sojourn and Tourism [Azienda Autonoma de Cura, Soggiorno e Turismo (ACST)] were instituted by the state in 1926 with the scope to promote tourism in their respective territorial zones under their competence. These were reorganized by the Presidential Decree of August 1960. These autonomous bodies, working on a local level, have the task of exerting all necessary efforts to expand the visitor traffic to the locality. They have administrative autonomy and public law status and are subject to the supervision of the Ministry of Tourism and Entertainment. The recognition of such a status is conferred on localities comprising the whole or part of the territory of one or more adjacent towns of the same province where the visitors' traffic constitutes an essential element of the economy of that locality. There are certain conditions specified pertaining to the minimum amount of sojourn tax required, availability of sufficient accommodation capacity, appropriate hygienic installations, satisfactory public services and sports equipments, etc. Each autonomous body for cure, sojourn and tourism has a president and a council of administration.

The foregoing description of the tourism organization in Italy shows the interest which the country takes in development and promotion of tourism. Although the ministry exercises a strong directing and controlling role, there appears to be a great degree of decentralisation in the organization of Italian tourism. Not only local promotion, but also the whole of the tourist administration in individual regions, districts and towns is in the hands of local bodies with a substantial degree of autonomy, which are in turn represented at higher levels.

2

Significant Features

Accommodation facilities constitute the most important item in the package of facilities offered to the tourists. The success of tourism industry depends to a great extent on the availability and quality of accommodation facilities. Modern tourists are becoming progressively conscious of greater comforts and conveniences and as such comfortable accommodation is a deciding factor for growth of tourism. The Estimates Committee of the Lok Sabha in its report for 1975-76 has stated that "since the hotels constitute the most important and, in fact, a basic element of tourism infrastructure, the various measures taken and efforts made to tourism promotion will not produce the desired results if the hotel accommodation in the country lags behind." "Accommodation facilities are the places where tourists stop (cease to be) travellers and become guests. The level of guest satisfaction achieved by an area's accommodation facilities will, in a large measure, determine the total success of the tourism programme."

Various Types

Accommodation facilities can be of many types, viz., hotels, motels, inns, guest houses, private hotels, establishments with bed and breakfast only, holiday camps, holiday and conference centres, paying guest accommodations, choultries, youth hostels, etc. Among them hotels are the most important. Almost all foreign tourists stay in some hotel or the other. The other types of accommodation are mainly used by the domestic tourists in addition to hotels. An attempt was made during the enquiry to find out the relative importance of these different types of accommodation for the domestic tourists.

It could be seen from the table that out of 500 respondents, 323 (65%) used hotels, 134 (27%) choultries, 75 (15%) stayed with friends and relatives, and so on. Hotels being the most important type of accommodation, a large number of tourists use them. Next to hotels, come choultries because they are free or cheap. Till recently most of the pilgrim centres in India had only public choultries meant for the devotees. Now the situation has changed. The concerned authorities are providing fairly comfortable paid accommodation, which is mainly meant for the masses. A survey conducted by the Indian Statistical Institute in 1982-83 revealed that 76.8% of foreign tourists preferred hotels. The relevant figures for youth hostels, host family accommodation, rent-free places and other categories were 4.3%, 12.5%, 1.5% and 4.8%.

As majority of the foreign tourists and about 65% of the domestic tourists, as seen above, use hotels, this class of accommodation is studied in detail.

Different Categories

With a view to maintaining standards and enforcing control, the Department of Tourism, Ministry of Tourism and Civil Aviation, Government of India, has a system of categorising the available accommodation as per certain criteria. Accordingly, the hotels could be either approved or unapproved. When a hotel comes in the approved list it presupposes that it is of international standard. Normally a foreign tourist would prefer only an approved hotel because it has the stamp of official recognition. This is an important aspect as far as a hotel is concerned because approval itself is sufficient advertisement. So though not at the initial stages, all the hotels above a particular standard try hard to get this recognition at least in due course. Most of the new hotels constructed as per standards stipulated by the Government automatically come in the approved list. The classification of hotels as per the above stipulations came into effect from 1963 and consequently data on hotels as per the classification are available from that year.

The number of approved hotels and the rooms therein are given for a period of time. It could be noted from the table that the number of approved hotels which stood at 186 in 1963 had come down to 166 in 1968 and to 152 in 1971 and steadily increased thereafter. It is not clear how the number of hotels could come down. The Hotel Review and Survey Committee, 1968, has also noted the reduction in the number of hotels but no explanation is given for the reduction. Perhaps it may be due to closure or sometimes due to derecognition. Yet another possible reason for the decrease could be that there might have been differences in the criteria adopted for approval over the years due to changing circumstances. However, there has been continuous increase in the number of hotel rooms. It has risen from 7,085 in 1963 to 29,332 in 1982 as seen from the table.

Over the period, the number of hotels has doubled and that of rooms more than trebled. This high rate of growth is certainly attributed to the patronage given by the Government in terms of some tax incentives and the creation of a Hotel Development Fund in 1968. During the recent years, 1978-1982, by and large the growth rates are lower, both in the number of hotels and in rooms in absolute terms. According to the Federation of Hotel and Restaurant Associations of India (FHRAI), this trend is attributed to reduced incentives. It may be added that during 1982-83 there has been considerable increase in hotel capacity particularly due to the construction of many large hotels on the eve of the Asiad.

It would be ideal if the rate of growth in hotel capacity keeps pace with the rate of growth of tourist arrivals especially when the existing hotel infrastructure is not sufficient. Data reveals that during 1963-82, the increase in the number of hotels and rooms was about 100% and 300%. As against this, the increase in foreign tourist arrivals was 500% during the same period. This shows the wide gap between the demand for and supply of hotels.

It could be seen that throughout the period in question, there has been shortfall in hotel accommodation, which has been very acute since mid-1970s. However, by 1985, the gap between the demand for and supply of hotels, on the basis of projected room capacity and tourist arrivals is likely to be completely wiped out.

1. The foreign tourists stay in hotels for about 70% of the time of their stay in the country. (This percentage is worked out from 'statistical evidence that the average stay is 14 days, of which 10 are in hotels.') But, according to published evidence, the average stay of foreign tourists in India works out to 33 days in 1963, 20 days in 1968 and about 25 days each for the subsequent years. Hence, for the purpose of calculating the hotel requirement, the average stay is taken as 25 days throughout. With the assumed 70% stay in hotels the number of days of stay in hotels per tourist works out to 18 days.

2. The foreign tourist arrivals in a year is taken to be 1,000. Then the total visitor-days (foreign) for which hotel accommodation is needed works out to (1,000 x 18) 18,000.

3. It is estimated that 'the ratio of foreign to Indian guests in 5 star hotels is 73 : 27'. In respect of other approved hotels, this ratio is likely to be lower. The survey of tourists given in data would reveal that the ratio of foreign tourists to domestic tourists staying in luxury class and medium class hotels is 249 : 164—roughly 3 : 2. We have already seen the hotel requirement for the foreign tourists alone to be 18,000. Then the total requirement of hotel accommodation would be (18000 x 5/3) 30,000 visitor days. It would mean that when 18,000 beds are needed for 1,000 foreign tourists, another 12,000 beds have to be provided for the domestic tourists.

4. Normally the occupancy in approved hotels as would be seen later is 72%. If that is so, the total number of beds to be provided would be $\frac{30.000 \times 100}{72}$ = 41,660 in a year.

   This works out to 114 beds per day.

5. From a sample of 50 hotels, the room-bed ratio is calculated for finding out the hotel room requirement for the 114

beds. The ratio works out to 1: 1.87. From this ratio it could be found that for 114 beds 60 rooms are required. Taking the foreign tourist arrivals for different years, the requirement of rooms is worked out for these years. The researcher is aware of the limitations in this calculation, namely, the room-bed ratio may not be truly representative for all the hotels and for all the years.

6. The estimate is conservative as we have assumed uniform demand pattern which is not very realistic.

The available figures in would give the impression that a large number of the tourists did not have any accommodation. But it is not so. Such of those who did not get accommodation in these (approved) hotels would have gone to the unapproved hotels which are not included in the above analysis. While analysing the occupancy ratio, it would be seen that some of the hotels have an occupancy ratio well exceeding the average and it is learnt that in some hotels, which are not covered in the survey, the occupancy ratio is over 100%. This indicates that some of the rooms would have been let out to more than one customer during the day depending on the time of checking out or in extraordinary cases extra beds would have been provided.

In addition to the approved hotels, there are a large number of unapproved hotels. There are as many as 324 such hotels (as per the *Hotel and Restaurant Guide: India,* 1983). Perhaps, the figure would be even more as the *Hotel and Restaurant Guide* includes only those hotels which are members of either the FHRAI or/and the regional hotel and restaurant associations. One would think that these hotels are substandard in terms of facilities and comfort. But they are not and in fact some of them are awaiting approval by the Department of Tourism. On enquiry it was found that their applications for recognition are pending with the Government. Their recognition is a question of administrative procedures and consequent delay and not one of quality of these hotels. "According to Government sources, applications for star classification from 171 hotels are still awaiting clearance with a room capacity of 14,003."

Even foreign tourists, who normally prefer approved hotels,

stay in these hotels as "many of these hotels are clean and those who spend money from their own pockets naturally prefer inexpensive accommodation".[1] That is to say, inexpensiveness coupled with comparatively good services and facilities makes these hotels suitable for the middle income and low income classes of tourists—foreign and domestic. As seen already, all along the shortfall in the approved category of hotels has been partly met by these unapproved hotels. Hence while taking an inventory of hotels, it would be realistic to include these hotels also.

Many hotels are under construction or on expansion. "The Ministry of Tourism and Civil Aviation has approved another 205 hotel projects which are in various stages of completion with a room capacity of about 16,765". In Delhi alone 12 new hotels were under construction with an envisaged capacity of 4,358 rooms. Of these about 2,500 rooms were completed in 1982. The pace of construction is beset with many problems like lack of infrastructural facilities and essential inputs and inevitable bureaucracy.

By the next year, when all on-going projects would be completed, there will be about 60,100 hotels rooms, calculated as under.

Approved hotel rooms	29,332
Unapproved hotel rooms (Awaiting classification)	14,003
Hotels under construction—expected to be ready by next year	16,765
Total	60,100

These projected 60,100 hotel rooms would be just sufficient to meet the demand, at the rate of 60 rooms per 1,000 tourists, for about one million expected foreign tourists. (As noted earlier, the projected demand for hotels include an appropriate fraction of the domestic sector also.)

"The criteria for classification have been set by the Department of Tourism and include everything from the size of the room to qualifications of the staff. Initially hotels are classified into 1 star, 2 star, 3 star, 4 star and 5 star. Recently yet another class, namely 5 star deluxe, is added. 1 and 2 star hotels may be referred to as economy class used by budget tourists. 3 and 4 star hotels are referred to as middle class hotels and 5 star and 5 star deluxe hotels obviously come under luxury class.

It could be seen that 2 star hotels outnumber the other hotels throughout. Next comes the 3 star hotels followed by 1 star. The number of 5 star and 5 star deluxe hotels lagged behind the 4 star hotels till 1979. From 1980 the same rose up. But in respect of growth, 1 star hotels have reduced in number, while the growth rate of 2 star hotels is not steady. Perhaps these could have been upgraded consequent on improved facilities. Regarding the rest, there has been significant growth though not uniform. During the 22 year period, the number of 5 star hotels has increased by 586%, 4 star hotel by 158% and 3 star hotels by 208%. The growth in hotel rooms as against the number of hotels would give a more realistic picture. It could be seen from the table that the number of rooms in 5 star hotels has increased faster than that of the other classes of hotels, followed by 3, 2 and 4 star hotels.

A considerable hotel capacity is in the unclassified category of hotels. In fact about 50% of the approved hotels and rooms during 1978-80 remained unclassified. It only signifies the inordinate delay in getting a hotel classified. A hotelier is anxious to get his hotel approved and classified as quickly as possible. It would be in the best interest of the hostelers, if this could be expedited. Things have started moving in this direction. The unclassified hotel capacity is reduced to 30% by 1984 from 50% in 1978-80.

At this stage it would be of interest to study the user pattern of the different classes of hotels. It could be noted that fewer tourists use luxury class hotels compared to medium class and economy class hotels. Only 10% of the foreign tourists use luxury hotels while about 40 and 70% of them use medium and economy classes of hotels respectively. Out of the 500 domestic tourists interviewed, only 343 used hotels of one class or the other. Of these 343, only 17 used luxury class hotels, 157 medium class hotels and 310 economy class hotels. Evidently, it could be concluded from the above, that both foreign and domestic tourists mostly favour the medium and economy class hotels. Hence the need for more of these hotels. But presently over 30% of the hotel rooms are in the luxury hotels. However these luxury hotels are not mainly intended for the tourists. In fact their clientele are mostly from the business and Government.

Supply of and demand for each class of hotels cannot be equated. Yet, the study of the extent of the tourists getting the class of hotels of their choice would indicate the gap. As, per data the availability of different types of hotels as stated by the foreign tourists is given. (This study is not extended to domestic tourists.)

Out of 48 tourists who used luxury class hotels, 42 (85%) could get this particular accommodation in most cases as indicated by a high percentage of availability, namely 60-100%. Similarly 75% of the tourists who used medium class hotels and 70% of the tourists who used the economy class hotels were able to get the particular class of hotels of their choice to the extent of 60-100%. Such of those who do not get hotels of their choice would naturally go in for other classes of hotels within their reach. From the table it could be seen that the demand for middle and economy classes of hotels is more than the supply, indicating the need for more of such hotels.

The availability of hotel accommodation in terms of number of hotels or rooms is an important factor in the context of tourism development. Equally important is their geographical location/ physical distribution. But there cannot be any hard and fast rule in this regard because normally hotels come up at places of demand and it is not realistic to expect equal distribution. However, it would be of some interest to study the existing position in India regarding the regional distribution and concentration of hotels in metropolitan cities.

The Federation of Hotel and Restaurant Associations of India (FHRAI) has divided the country into 4 regions geographically, viz., northern region covering Delhi, Uttar Pradesh, Rajasthan and all other northern States; Calcutta region covering Orissa, West Bengal, Bihar and other eastern States and eastern Union Territories including Andaman and Nicobar Islands; western region covering Maharashtra, Gujarat, Madhya Pradesh and Goa, Diu and Daman; and southern region covering Andhra Pradesh, Karnataka, Tamil Nadu and Kerala, and the Union Territory of Pondicherry.

The more conspicuous aspects seen from the table may be

highlighted here. The regional distribution of the approved hotels is lopsided with 119 hotels in the southern region, 111 in the northern region, 99 in the western region and 41 in the Calcutta region. This would give the impression that Calcutta region is very much lagging behind compared to other regions. This is so because most of the areas included in the Calcutta region, particularly Assam, Tripura, etc., are not conducive for development of infrastructural facilities. Besides there would not be enough demand for accommodation in these areas due to non-accessibility. Even basic transport facilities are being developed only now. Such developments supplemented by the extension of Vayudoot services to this region would improve the tourist flow into the region.

The southern and northern regions are better placed than the other regions in regard to hotel infrastructure. This incidentally reflects the relatively more and increased tourist traffic in these regions. The situation with reference to the northern region would be slightly better when the 12 large new hotels constructed in connection with the Asiad are also taken into account. The position is not much different with reference to the unapproved hotels.

As regards the star-wise distribution of hotels, the northern region stands first in terms of number of all categories of star hotels. With respect to 1, 2 and 3 star hotels, the northern region is followed by the southern region, western region and Calcutta region. On the other hand, the relative position of the regions is different in respect of 4, 5 and 5 star deluxe hotels. Here the northern region is followed by the western region, southern region and Calcutta region.

It is of interest to note that the southern region with the largest number of approved hotels occupies 2nd place with regard to 1, 2 and 3 star hotels and 3rd place in respect of the other star hotels. This is partially explained by the fact that almost 50% of the approved hotels in the region are yet to be classified. Similar is the situation with regard to the Calcutta and western regions also. Perhaps when the classification process is complete, the star-wise distribution of hotels would be different. It also emerges from the study that there is a case for speedier classification of hotels, once they are approved. In respect of unapproved hotels the pattern of distribution is the same.

The distribution of approved hotels in the major 4 metro cities, namely, Delhi, Calcutta, Bombay and Madras, reveals that out of a total of 128, 37 are in Delhi, 12 in Calcutta, 50 in Bombay and 29 in Madras. The relative position of the 4 cities with reference to the unapproved hotels is more or less the same. A casual look at the distribution of hotels in these four cities vis-a-vis their respective regions reveals that 33% of the approved hotels and 30% of the unapproved hotels in the northern region are in Delhi alone. The corresponding figures for Calcutta work out to 29% for both approved and unapproved hotels. Bombay accounts for 50% of approved hotels and 53% of the unapproved hotels of the western region. In the case of the southern region 29% of approved hotels and 9% of unapproved hotels are in Madras. These figures speak of the degree of concentration of hotels in these four cities. This situation should not be explained away by saying that these cities are predominant. The point of interest is that there are other cities in the different regions, but they have not grown as big as the metro cities though most of them have fairly known for the tourist attractions. So a case may be made for extra effort to decentralise the hotels in the less developed cities in the respective regions.

It is of significance to study the position of Tamil Nadu in this context. From the table it could be seen that there are 48 approved hotels, including 23 star hotels and 25 unclassified ones. In other words, 13% of the approved hotels in India and 40% of the approved hotels in the southern region are in Tamil Nadu. These figures are quite encouraging as far as Tamil Nadu is concerned. This is partly due to locational advantage as the major city in the southern region, *viz.,* Madras, is in Tamil Nadu. This natural advantage is supplemented by the more encouraging steps taken by the Government to develop tourism.

The study is further extended with reference to total number of rooms in the four major cities to give yet another dimension to the analysis. It could be seen from data that in respect of the rooms in approved hotels, Bombay stands first with 4,054, followed by Delhi with 3,875, Madras with 2,032 and Calcutta with 1,135 rooms. It may be noted that over 50% of the rooms in the approved hotels are in these four cities, though in terms of number of hotels, these four cities together account for only about 35% of the total number of approved hotels.

It is not intended here to make out a case for equitable distribution of hotels in the different regions/cities or creation of hotels standardised capacity. The differences are bound to exist. This pattern of distribution of hotels would change in due course with the changing emphasis and with the development of new and more tourism centres.

It is of academic interest to know the ownership pattern of hotels. This is studied with reference to 364 hotels, both approved and unapproved, taken at random from 16 cities/tourist centres with eight or more approved hotels each according to the *Hotel and Restaurant Guide,* 1983. The data are presented data.

It could be noted from the table that out of 210 approved hotels with 19,801 rooms, 24 hotels with 941 rooms are owned by sole trading concerns, 40 hotels with 2,221 rooms by partnership concerns, 80 hotels with 5,444 rooms by private limited companies and 60 hotels with 10,678 rooms by public limited companies.

It is of significance to note that a large number of luxury hotels are owned by corporate undertakings while a few such hotels are owned by the non-corporate sector. In the case of 3 star and the luxury class hotels the corporate sector owns 60 while the non-corporate sector owns only 16. Out of the 12 one star hotels 3 each are owned by partnership and sole-tradership concerns, 5 by private limited companies and 1 by public limited company. The non-corporate sector owns 20 two star hotels while the corporate sector owns only 11 such hotels.

In terms of rooms, out of 25,325 (approved and unapproved taken together) 10,768 are owned by public limited companies, 6,170 by private limited companies, 5,165 by partnership and 2,123 by sole tradership. In a nutshell, in respect of approved hotels corporate sector claims a major share. In the case of unapproved hotels the non-corporate sector predominates.

This position is not due to any special treatment to the corporate sector in the matter of granting approval, but due to the fact that the corporate sector by and large are financially well off, construct hotels according to standards and stipulations for the grant of approval, while the hotels in the non-corporate sector usually are not of international standards, perhaps due to less favourable financial position.

Number of rooms per hotel is taken as the measure of size. Size of hotel depends on a host of factors such as location, class and ownership of the hotel and so on. A hotel in a metropolitan city would normally be big. Similarly higher the 'star' of the hotel, bigger is the size. Further, eventually hotels owned by corporate undertakings tend to be big while those owned by non-corporate undertakings tend to be small as mentioned earlier.

The average size of hotels in Bombay, Calcutta, Delhi and Madras and the all-India average are given. It could be seen that the average size of hotels in these four cities is comfortably higher than the all-India average. The table (last column) also gives the average size of hotels, star-wise. It could be seen that the average size of 5 star hotels works out to 240 rooms, 4 star hotels to 81 rooms, 3 star hotels to 52 rooms, 2 star hotels to 42 rooms and 1 star hotels to 33 rooms. Average size of unclassified hotels works out to 55 rooms. The Hotel Review and Survey Committee reported that the average size of hotels star-wise was 170, 72, 46, 36 and 31 rooms for 5, 4, 3, 2 and 1 star hotels respectively in 1968. Over the years there has been significant growth in the average size of 5 star hotels, i.e., from 170 rooms in 1968 to 240 rooms in October 1982. In the case of other classes of hotels also the size has increased but only marginally.

It could be seen that by and large, hotels owned by soletraderships are small in size compared to others. The average size of approved hotels owned by sole tradership is the lowest with 39 rooms per hotel and is the highest for those owned by public limited companies with 178 rooms. In the case of partnership and private limited companies the average size works out to 55 and 68 rooms respectively.

The average size of hotels, all hotels approved and unapproved taken together, given in the last column reveals that the hotels owned by the public limited companies are the biggest with an average of 174 rooms per hotel. This figure is roughly 3 times, 4 times and 5 times the average size of hotels owned by private limited companies, partnership and soletradership.

Fixing the hotel tariff is just like pricing any product or service. It is beset with many problems. The price should be affordable to the public and remunerative to the owners. In the case of hotel industry, the problem of price fixation is more pronounced because of the highly perishable nature of its service, seasonal spurt and slag in the demand and unadjustability of supply to demand in the short run. Further, the cost of construction, operating cost, locational factors, the degree of competition, etc., are also to be considered.

It is said that room tariff normally is not determined by market forces of supply and demand. It is true that tariff quoted by the hotels concerned has to be approved by the Department of Tourism. "But practically every year early in September hoteliers represent to the Department of Tourism for a 10 to 15% increase in their room tariff. Their applications are rubber stamped by the Department and hotel charges go up annually in early October." Why should this be approved? The Department cannot act otherwise. The hoteliers have a better bargaining power because of sellers market prevailing in this industry due to the heavy shortage in hotel capacity.

But, if the market conditions change the pricing mechanism also would change. What has been happening in New Delhi since the Asiad is an example in question. To meet the anticipated short-term increase in demand on account of the Asiad, as many as 12 new and large hotels were constructed. But the anticipated increase in demand did not materialise. The sudden increase in the hotel capacity has changed the market condition from sellers market to buyers market. Many hotels are now selling rooms at cut rates. "Some of them like Samrat of the ITDC Chain have officially announced off-season discounts of 30% but others are doing so under the counter. Two of Delhi's posh hotels are selling rooms to single occupants for as little as Rs. 300 against the listed tariff of Rs. 750 or Rs. 775." This may be an isolated instance but it certainly proves the point that market forces have a definite say in price fixation, apart from regulatory measures by the Government.

The room tariff quoted by the different hotels are normally for a day. Some hotels take 24 hours' stay as a day while in others there is a particular check-out time, usually 12.00 noon. The latter practice is certainly against the interests of the inmates. The hoteliers may have their own good reasons. However, it may be suggested that the Government would do well if it tries to maintain uniform and standardised procedure in all hotels. Incidentally this would create a better goodwill among the tourists. It may be added that the hoteliers are seized of this matter and have made a beginning in this direction.

The room tariff are of three types, namely, the American, plan, Modified American plan and European plan. "American plan includes three full meals and room. Modified American plan includes the price of the room, breakfast and dinner. No meals are included in room rates under the European plan." The European plan is adopted in most of the unapproved hotels in India. In the case of a sample of 50 approved hotels, 20 offer all the three plans, 15 offer European plan only and the rest either the American plan and/or the Modified American plan.

These different plans are good as far as they go but in passing it may be mentioned that it would be better if the tourists are given the freedom to eat anywhere they like. The American plan and the Modified American plan give the impression that there is an element of compulsion attached to them. This should be avoided. However, in practice almost all the tourists eat from where they stay unless they are on the move. It is important to give the freedom to the tourists because invariably most of them will be on the move on sight-seeing during day time and it would be too much to expect them to come back for their noon-meal and sometimes even for the supper. Perhaps there would be some valid reasons from the point of view of the hoteliers, because they should have an assured demand to justify their investment in the restaurant section of the hotel which is not usually frequented by the general public as much as in the case of economy class hotels.

A comparison of room rates in India with those in other countries shall help in assessing the competitiveness of Indian hotels. In the case of deluxe hotels, Indian rates are the lowest. In the case of 1st class hotels Indian rates are the second lowest, the lowest being that of Colombo. Again ours are the lowest in respect of standard hotel rates and of the economy class. This is confirmed from the survey. It was found that 385 out of 500 tourists have opined that Indian tariff is relatively lower their own countries.

About 80 have stated that the tariff is equal to theirs while about 35 stated that the tariff is higher than theirs. It could be concluded from the above that Indian hotel tariff, by and large, is lower. This is a favourable factor and could be effectively used as a promotional incentive. But care must be taken to see that we are not underquoting ourselves. In our eagerness to earn foreign exchange, are we in effect attracting and subsidising the middle and low income foreign tourists at the expense of our own people? It may be suggested that there should be a more pragmatic and realistic approach to the tariff policy.

There may be a temptation to quote lower rates thinking that it will attract more custom but in all probability it will create a psychological feeling among the international tourists that Indian hotels are of a lower standard. They may not appreciate a lower rate for better comforts and services and so as a matter of caution it is necessary to keep a watch on the tariff movements elsewhere and try to keep pace with them. It may be added that the above line of argument/suggestion has been made with respect to tariff prevailing in hotels which are frequented by foreign tourists, who are mostly relatively affluent. As regards the tariff in hotels frequented by domestic tourists, especially the middle and low income group, the need for lower and cheaper rates can rarely be overemphasised.

Apart from the listed tariff, some hotels charge sales tax, luxury tax, service charge, etc. There is no uniform code or procedure. These charges and taxes also vary from hotel to hotel. It is officially stated that in hotels which charge service charges, tipping is prohibited. But in practice how effectively this prohibition is done is anybody's guess. In this context, it is suggested that efforts should be made to standardise the procedure and practice with respect to these sundry charges. With the practice there is a psychological inhibition in the minds of the tourists that they are fleeced. An all-inclusive rate would certainly create better goodwill and confidence.

The user psychology and behaviour should always be kept in mind in tariff fixation. There are tourists who are extremely sensitive to price levels and for them reduced rates would be a stimulant. Yet reduction in tariff must be very cautiously done so that it does not lead to customer suspecting the quality of the hotel. Another category of tourists are willing to pay for quality though price remains the important factor. The third category is the luxury group tourists. "Service has traditionally been a distinguishing, often famous, feature of the hotel. Customers from high income brackets are attracted by the comfort and status of such establishments. Price must be used to reinforce this image rather as a competitive device. These are 'status symbols' for their guests; then they have to ensure that they remain one of the most 'expensive' hotels." That is to say that high tariff sometimes will be a stimulant for the luxury class tourists as much as low tariff will be for budget class tourists. This is an important point to be borne in mind in making tariff policy decisions.

In passing it may be highlighted that there is need for providing enough physical comforts and services commensurate with the tariff. It is seen from the survey that out of 235 foreign tourists staying in star hotels, 152 have stated that the tariff is commensurate with the services rendered. The rest felt that though there are enough physical comforts, the services provided are not satisfactory. This certainly points out that there is greater need for trained personnel at various counters.

By occupancy ratio is meant the ratio between 'sold rooms' and 'installed rooms'. It means the extent of utilisation of hotel capacity. Hence higher occupancy ratios would mean greater utilisation and *vice-versa.* An unduly high occupancy ratio would indicate a short supply of rooms. Hotel industry on the whole with its 'perishable product' and diverse demand pattern due to time and locational factors cannot hope for 100% occupancy of all its units at all times. There are bound to be differences in occupancy ratios of different hotels for obvious reasons. Hence a study of the occupancy ratio for different types of hotels would help in ascertaining the extent of utilisation of hotel infrastructure and also in deciding upon the priority to be adopted in the development of different classes of hotels.

The all-India average occupancy ratios for different categories of approved hotels are recorded for five years for which complete data are available. It could be seen from the table that the occupancy ratios over the years have come down for almost all classes of hotels, with the exception of 2 star hotels. (No satisfactory explanation can be ascribed to the increase in the occupancy ratio of 2 star hotels. It may be quite accidental.) The average occupancy ratio for all hotels taken together has decreased from 75.8% in 1978 to 70.2% in 1982 and to 64.2% in 1983 and 65.5% in 1984.

The decrease could be attributed to increase in total capacity without corresponding increase in demand. In the four-year period the increase in foreign tourist arrivals is only 15% while the number of rooms in approved hotels has increased by 34%. Category-wise the occupancy ratio for 5 star hotels has come down from 87.3% in 1978 to 79% in 1982 and to 66.6% in 1984. The decrease in occupancy ratio of the 5 star hotels is the steepest. This could be due to substantial increase in the number of rooms, to the tune of about 170%. Considering this increased capacity, the decrease in occupancy ratio is only marginal. Similar trend is found in other classes of hotels too. In respect of unclassified hotels there is decrease in both the number of rooms and in occupancy ratio, the latter decreasing steeply. One possible reason for this steep decrease could be that most of such hotels when compared to the star hotels are in places other than the 4 major metropolitan cities where the demand for hotels is comparatively less. It could be seen that out of the 28 unclassified hotels in the northern region only 2 are in Delhi, of the 19 in Calcutta region only 5 are in Calcutta, of the 45 in western region only 17 are in Bombay and of the 59 in southern region only 10 are in Madras.

Now certain questions pose themselves. Whether the present occupancy ratio is normal or otherwise? Whether new hotels should be commissioned or not? If yes, what class(es) hotels are to be commissioned?

Whether the present occupancy ratio is normal or not is a matter of opinion. All approved hotels in India fix room rates according to the modified Hubbert formula. Accordingly, the excess of their operating expenses over income from other sources (restaurant, etc.) has to be recovered from room income, at 60% occupancy ratio. Normally a hotel with 60% occupancy ratio would break even. The approved hotels have 65% occupancy ratio which is certainly very encouraging.

Since the demand for hotel rooms has always been on the

increase, more hotels are to be developed. In doing so it should be remembered that foreign tourists prefer medium class hotels and domestic tourists prefer economy class hotels. That means emphasis should be laid on 3, 2, and 1 star hotels and economy hotels like the Janata hotels.

Accessibility refers to the relative location of a hotel with respect to the nearest city proper, railway station, bus stand, airport, etc. Normally, except the airport, all other important places, including trade centres, bus stand and railway station, are within the city. Till very recently it was thought that hotels should necessarily be within the city proper or as near as possible to the places of activity. That is why almost all the hotels, except the new ones, are located within the city proper. On an analysis of the physical location of 100 hotels, both approved and unapproved. It was found that 94 hotels were within a distance of 10 km from the downtown area, 89 hotels were within 10 km from the nearest railway station and 91 hotels were within 40 km from the nearest airport. 10 km to the railway station/downtown or 40 km to the airport should be considered normal. Now it is clear that the already established hotels are very much within the city complex. Some of them are located even in the most congested and uncomfortable places.

Of late the trend is changing, perhaps not out of choice but out of necessity. Sufficient and convenient land for a new hotel within a city is almost a luxury today. From the tourists point of view, perhaps they will like to have sprawling hotel complex far away from the polluted, noisy and sometimes maddening atmosphere. They will like to have a comfortable hotel with clean and fresh air, extensive gardens, lawns, natural setting, etc. All these could be relatively easily provided if new hotels are located away from the already congested cities. This would initially appear to be an unwise proposition with respect to 'sales'. But with the improved transport and communication facilities and established 'brand image' proximity of hotels to the heart of the city has only limited significance.

The latest thinking on this aspect is the establishment of hotels in semi-urban and rural pockets. "Land is fairly cheap in non-metropolitan areas, so hotels can be built out; they don't have to be built up. Natural light, ventilation and renewable sources of energy can be tapped far more effectively out in the country than they can be in towns. Further such settings lend themselves to the village-hamlet atmosphere, thus attracting domestic tourism from the cities. So if these complexes are effectively planned, they can have a built-in flexibility, responding to quick changing tourist patterns, catering to a wide cross-section of travellers." Such a hotel is referred to as condominium hotel or shortly 'contel.'

Experts consider that there is enough and more scope for 'contels' in India. But the practitioners must be convinced about the new concept. A beginning in this respect is already on the anvil. It is held that with the introduction of travel circuits to develop tourism in a most integrated manner, major hotel chains are thinking in terms of setting up their units at strategic halts so that the groups travelling under their sponsorship could be easily accommodated in their own 'net.' In this regard, the Tamil Nadu Tourism Development Corporation has a place of pride, in the sense that most of its hotels are located *en route* of its weekly conducted coach tours, providing accommodation to its clientele under one roof and at the same time getting an assured business. Thus the 'contel' concept is basically a strategic marketing technic. It is held that 'contel' could rectify the imbalances in hotel industry like too much concentration, too many luxury class hotels, too many large-sized hotels, etc.

Hotels provide a vast range of services and facilities. Though originally conceived as a place where a temporary sojourn is provided, over the years the basic feature of a hotel has changed very much. With the emergence of status-symbol consciousness, hoteliers started playing to the expectations of the public by providing a variety of facilities, some of which are highly sophisticated. The facilities provided by the chosen approved and unapproved hotels are given.

It could be seen from the table that as many as 35 distinctive facilities are provided by hotels apart from accommodation. To ensure competitiveness and to meet the user demands, hoteliers have added a host of services to the 'basket' they sell.

Most of the approved hotels offer varieties of facilities compared to the unapproved hotels. Precisely that is why these hotels come under the approved category. However, in certain respects the hotels have to gear up their services such as own transport facilities, tour arrangements, etc., for the benefit of the tourists. To meet the increasing demand of the business tourists, secretarial and similar services need to be extensively provided.

Normally one would think that this is the way it should be, but there are strong views against this kind of tendency of providing a host of ancillary services. The travel writers, Hugh and Collen Ganzter, opine that "A hotel is a hotel. It is not a restaurant... not a shopping arcade... not a health club, beauty parlour, office centre or convention hall. In other words, we must return to the concept of a hotel as an inn, a hostel and a lodge... Hotels have been forced to engage numerous specialist organisations under their umbrella because their status-conscious guests wanted to be cossetted. That age is passing fast."

However, from what we see around us with respect to the nature and varieties of facilities provided by most of the modern hotels and also the attitude of the so-called elite tourists, it is doubtful whether such change would set in so sooner what is important is the attitude of the tourists and guests and not that of the hoteliers. The possible extent of change in the attitude of the tourists is anybody's guess. After all money increases the craze for luxury. Businessman would cash such human nature.

It is but natural that in the case of industries dealing directly with people, there would certainly be complaints by the users as to the quality, range and price of facilities and services rendered. The industry should welcome users' complaints and suggestions and try to do the maximum to eliminate their recurrence.

An attempt was made to ascertain the broad areas of users' (foreign tourists) complaints about hotels in the country. It could be seen that poor maintenance of even available facilities was the major complaint followed by poor sanitation, lack of sufficient physical facilities and the like.

Most of these complaints are real. A day's stay in a hotel would reveal how poorly the installed facilities are maintained. The shortcomings of Hotel. The hoteliers would do well to bestow more attention to the areas of major complaints.

Quality of Service

The essence of the long run success of any economically based enterprise is its ability to survive and prosper, which ultimately depends upon its net profitability. The main items provided by a hotel are rooms, food and beverages and services. The most important among this set is the service element, which determines the guest's attitude towards hotel, which ultimately affects the profitability. Hotel industry is very much a "people-industry" which produces intangibles. The service aspect particularly personalised services cannot be mechanised or automated. Quality, care, facilities are very vital than the quantity or numbers.

The profitability of hoteliering firms largely impinge on the amenities and quality of its services, which is the crucial determinant of the volume of sales. If a hotel organisation aims to seek out a specific portion of the guest market and to maintain a high occupancy level, then it must pay close attentions to modifying the products and improves the quality of services it offers . In this chapter an attempt has been made to apply the service quality model in order to examine the gaps in services of the hoteliering establishments. It is tried to unravel the mysteries of why some firms are successful and others are not. Hopefully the issues raised here will stimulate the interest of both operators and researcher concerned in this type of tertiary activity.

The technology of most service organisations especially in hotel concerns, is conceived as "knowledge technology", as opposed to manufacturing technology where output quality is physically measured. In this regard service technologies tend to consist of the ideas, goals and rationale for the methods adopted. Furthermore services do not tend themselves to physical controls relating to quality factor and therefore should rely on intangible process of controlling . In addition to produce the hotel services, the customers and the service worker must interact. This interaction process can be seen as a situation where workers not only produce the output but are simultaneously involved in delivering it as well.

The hospitality industry seems to be a relatively successful one, although in many developed countries the boom in tourism and the hotel business is over. Especially in the coming decades it will be necessary for the industry to emphasise quality not merely quantity. The hotel industry in developing countries should actively market its product. Marketing its product is simply attuning the hospitality offer to the wishes and expectations of the potential demanding consumer of hospitality. This marketing process can only be executed if one knows the needs and expectation of the guests and what can be offered. The principal factor that determines the guest's attitude towards a hotel is the quality of service received. Automation and mechanisation has helped in ruling out the human element in a number of industries but the human element is the determining element of the hotel business.

The architecture of a hotel, the decoration of the lobby the furnishings of a room are examples of hotel attributes that may be the reason behind a benefit, or tangible surrogates for intangible benefits, but they are not the benefits. The benefit is what they do for the consumer e.g. gives a sense of security, a sensation of prestige, or a feeling of comfort. And the credibility of these benefits tends to diminish rapidly if an expectation is not fulfilled. Decor is soon forgotten, if a room service takes an hour or so. A sense of security is not credible if slovenly characters are seen in the lobby or met on the elevator. It is this fulfilments of expectations, or lack of it, that creates the perception of deliverability for the consumer. The competing hotels may be seen as providing the same sense of security, grandeur, prestige and comfort. The tangible surrogates attributes their ability, to differentiate and at the same time, are no longer deterministic in the consumers choice of a hotel.

The definition and measurement of quality is no small matter for the growth and performance of hoteliering firms. These factors have been found to be particularly elusive with regard to services and almost undefinable at least in consistent terms, in regard to hotel services . If quality per se is 'elusive and indistinct' and often mistaken for impressive adjectives and not easily articulated by consumers then added intangibility of services certainly compounds the difficulty of definition and measurement. Yet as quality measurement and improvement has become so vital to managers and marketeers of the hotel services, and when, as has been pointed out, quality is the single most important consumer trend of the coming decades then it becomes imperative, both theoretically and empirically to analyse the factors and suggest measures to improve the quality of hotel services.

The search for quality trend has prompted some researchers to begin to develop various definitions of service quality models. A basic consistency and consensus seems apparent among these numerous studies. Essentially concerns rests on largely abstract dimensions, such as perception, expectations and satisfaction. This communality leaves apparent need, at least at this stage, to debate over such a framework. Rather it gives an opportunity to test these dimensions and to seek empirical confirmation.

Empirical verification of abstractions, however is no less elusive than the definition of quality itself. It seems, in fact, that the frustrating attempts at definition may be preventing, rather than facilitating, successful efforts towards empirical confirmation. But the difference between the abstractions can be measured. For example if quality is measured vis-a-vis expectations, and perception is the level of satisfaction derived, then it seems only logical that if the difference between the two can be measured then not a definition of quality, but a measurement of its existence or non-existence can be obtained. This measurement in fact may just, be a more significant marketing tool. It also has the advantage of being somewhat less of an abstraction, although not totally, to deal with, and this considerably eases the task. Many research investigators , have termed these differences between abstractions as gaps. Others have referred to the measurements of these differences as 'disparity analysis'. The analysis presented here is based on the service quality model . After a brief review of the conceptual foundations of the exercise, the findings from the present study of gap analysis in hotel services are presented.

How to Maintain Standard ? A concept called "missing service quality" was developed by Gronrops in his model. His model is based largely on the construct "image" which represents perceived service quality which in turn represents the 'gap' between 'expected services' and 'perceived services'. He explores the use of the term quality as if it were a variable itself rather than a function of a range of resources and activities. He argues that this range includes what customers are looking for, what they are evaluating, how service quality is perceived, and in what way service quality is influenced. 'Perceived quality' of service is dependent on two variables—expected service and perceived service. Service quality can have two dimensions:

(i) Technical quality

(ii) Functional quality

Technical quality lends itself to somewhat objective measurement by the consumer. It is what the consumer receives as a result of his interactions with a service firm. This could be a hotel, a room, a bed, a restaurant meal, or a doctors prescription. Functional quality on the contrary, represents the service process or the expressive performance of the service. This quality is perceived by the customer in a very subjective manner. Together, the technical quality and functional quality of the service represents a bundle of service dimensions and create an "image", a third quality dimension.

The "image" influence the consumer's expectations. In fact image is a quality dimension overriding substandard technical and functional quality delivery. It is interpreted to mean that the consumers may be satisfied in spite of some deficiency in technical and functional quality in the service. Conversely, the consumers may be satisfied inspite of their presence. It is very difficult to measure the 'image'. However, 'satisfaction of consumers' can be measured as a surrogate for 'image'. It is a reasonable assumption if there is a disparity between satisfaction and technical and functional delivery of services.

Supply Method : Thus it seems that, measuring service quality per se is not the purpose, but rather the quality in the delivery of the service is at least two and very possibly three dimensions described below. It appears at first glance to be a fine distinction but infact it is very important one because it eases the task considerably. The elusive quality now becomes a some what less elusive delivery, perhaps still intangible but less abstract.

Services in the hospitality industry are classified along three different dimensions .

(a) Person related services

(b) Product related services

(c) Information related services.

It is contended that although the hotel industry provides a number of product related services e.g. car parking, laundry etc., and information related services e.g. television and radio, more importantly it provides person-related services such as rooms and meals for individuals. Person-related services are geared towards the main objective of bringing about some change of state in the customer, or to maintain an existing state, which for one reason or other he is unable to do for himself or chooses not to maintain the existing state. Accordingly a hotel provides rest, recreation and refreshment. Consumption of persons related services generally involves four elements:

(i) direct consumption of physical goods (such as food, drinks etc.)

(ii) use of physical facilities (such as buildings and furnitures etc.)

(iii) interaction with persons providing the services.

(iv) information about the services.

The main characteristic is that the provider and consumer are inextricably involved in the process of delivering the services. Indeed the process is frequently as much a part of the service as its outcome.

There is a similar way of defining the quality of services. There are two meanings of the term "quality". The first relates to the particular attributes, which serve to define the nature of the service. The second usage refers to a qualifier in measuring such an attribute. The two meanings combined together gives a particular value or level of service characteristic. As an illustration it means that the menu is an attribute of a restaurant meal but the choice of menu is a qualifier, wider choice of menu is a service characteristic.

So service quality per se is so confounded in many cases that it is extremely difficult if not impossible to measure. The consumer of a particular service seeks to satisfy a somewhat hierarchical set of needs and wants partly related to the essential service and partly to subsidiary attributes. An essential purpose might be an overnight stay in a hotel. Subsidiary attributes may include accessibility, convenience of location, availability, timing and flexibility as well as interaction with those providing these service and with other customers. Customers always have the expectations as to now all these needs be met, which are in themselves rather hazy and imprecise.

When presented with the actual offering of these multiple variables, the consumers from an impression which is almost immediately compared with expectations and the resultant level of satisfaction is determined. Each customer regards various service attributes as more or less important and various service characteristics as more or less desirable. All together the consumer obtains a service experienced comprised of multitude of service transactions which he selects from an offering. Each transaction contributes to the service experience and has characteristics relating to the whole set of transactions which is more than the sum of the individual elements, which creates an 'overall feeling' or 'image' about the firm.

There exists a considerable amount of difference in perceptions between customers and providers, usually which comes as a surprise to the management of the hotel concerned. There are various evidences that management perception of quality of service frequently differs from the perception of customers, colleagues and hotel staff even. This difference in perception is termed as 'service gap'. Here an attempt has been made to undertake an exploratory qualitative study investigate the concept of service quality. Four different categories are investigated to gain an insight into:

(i) What managers perceive to be the key attribute of service quality?

(ii) What customers perceive to be the key attributes?

(iii) Whether discrepancies exist between these two perception?

(iv) Whether these results can be utilised to establish a general model to more efficiently explain service quality from consumers' stand point?

The upper managerial personnel of 18 hoteliering firms, six hotels each from the High spending hotels, medium spending hotel and low spending hotels existing in the cities of Orissa are surveyed as to what they believe their customers expectations in selecting a hotel, their perception of their own hotels service delivery, what customers particularly like and dislike about their hotel and the overall fulfilments of expectations and satisfaction with their hotel in the view of customers who had spent nights there. The same questions are asked at 200 randomly selected customers staying in those hotels over a period of two weeks, during the month of January 1990. Out of 200 customers 93 were foreign tourists.

Both management and customers are asked to evaluate sixteen attributes on a 1-5 scale where 5 represents the highest rating. T - tests are used between each pair of attributes that represented a potential for service quality gaps. Mean score and significance levels are represented in data.

Four types of gaps are found as shown in the data. I_1 (= a_1a_4) represents the gap between management's perception of consumers expectations (a_1) and consumers' expectations (a_4). I_2 (= a_3a_4) represents the gap between consumer's perceived service (a_3) and consumer's expectation (a_4). I_3(= a_2 a_4) represents gap between management's perception of hotel service delivery (a_2) and consumer's perceived service (a_3).I_4 (= a_2a_4) represents management's perception of hotel service delivery (a_2) and consumer's expectations (a_4). Lastly I_5 (a_1a_2) represents the gap between management's perception of consumer's expectation (a_1) and management's perception of its service delivery (a_2). A service quality model has been developed here. The gaps leveled in these five propositions have definite impact on the consumers rating of service quality.

It is the gap between management perceptions of guest expectations and the expectation of the guests to determine if management actually knows what its guests expect. The survey reveals that for the most part management believes that guests expect more than the guests themselves expect. In the 10 cases where the gap is significant at < 0.10, guest expectations are higher than that of management only in 5 cases. Three of these five cases, however is considered extremely critical ones where management does not realise their importance: size of room (< 0.01), eating/drinking options (< 0.01) and shops in hotel (< 0.05). It is to be noted that all the five critical areas are clearly intangible functional qualities. These five areas also show up repeatedly in the survey as high in the list of features that travellers, particularly the foreign tourists look for in a hotel which encourage them to return. It should also be noted that many of the attributes which management perceives as eliciting higher consumer expectations are tangible technical qualities in character.

It is the gap between consumer expectations and their perceptions of services received effectually, i.e. what they actually get. In this case the respondents expectations exceed on 5 out of 9 attributes at a significance level <0.10. They are not exceeded, however on attribute 5, 8, and 14, all at < 0.05 significance. All these are critical attributes which primarily constitute the intangible functional qualities.

It measures the difference between consumers perception of delivery and what management believes they deliver i.e. managements success in carrying out what they perceive to be customer's expectation. It is not too surprising to learn that management perceives their service delivery as being more successful than customers perceive it to be in all cases, 9 out of 16 attributes at < 0.10 significance level. It implies therefore that the management of the high spending group and medium spending group hotels are very self-assured and complacent and very oblivious of their failings.

A subjective assessment of gap (X_3) is also done. Respondents of both the samples are asked open ended questions such as what do you (people) find particularly satisfying and dissatisfying about the hotel, where they stay. As multiple responses are permitted there is no significance test. However the most frequent responses and their percentages of total responses are shown in data. These findings show that the intangible are not as outstanding at the high spending group hotels as the management believes them to be. They also show that it is the intangibles at the HSG hotels which upset customers more and not the technical qualities which the management believes are upsetting.

It reflects a comparison of managements delivery to consumers expectations. The service gap pattern of A_3 prevails here. Management perceives their services delivery as lower than customers expectation in only three cases. In only two of these, cleanliness and food quality are the difference is significant at < 0.01 level. This clearly indicates a very high expectation of guests in these areas.

It measures an internal situation: Does management believe they deliver as much as they believe customers expect? In this case they clearly do believe it, with no significant exceptions.

The respondents of both the sample are asked to indicate on a 1-5 scale, whether the hotel experience is satisfying to them. Whether it meets their expectations. Customers, are asked to rate the hotel in terms of its overall 'image' or quality. The data shows that management once again believes that it is doing a better job of meeting customers expectations and satisfaction than the customers actually feel. It clearly indicates a major gap in service quality of sample hotels. The quality rating by the customers is good in case of H.S.G. hotels but in case of M.S.G. Hotels it is worse and it does indicate a real Jack of service quality. There is no reason for complacency from the management's point of view. The customers of HSG hotels are not really dissatisfied with its services they are less vulnerable to competition in the hotel industry of the state especially in the event of new constructions in a nearby location of the same city. On the contrary the customers are not really satisfied with the service quality of both MSG Hotels, LSG and which are highly susceptible to competitive threats of rival firms, operating in the same locality or cluster.

Quality of services itself largely depends upon the good and effective management. Management should not be centralised or departmentalised in the same way as other tertiary activities. It is supposed to be variable and flexible. It should relate to all activities and be undertaken at all levels of the organisation. It is essentially an integrating process. And hotel industry is very much a people-industry with humane elements. Many customers need to have direct access and interaction with the working staff. Their behaviour and attitude are an essential ingredient of the hospitality functions. They are the part of the finished product that the customer is paying for. An understanding of the pervasive influences, determining the attitude of workers within the establishment, which ultimately determines the quality of services, should therefore, form a central focus of the management. Customers satisfaction which affects the economic return of the hoteliering firm, is likely to be affected as much by the attitudes and behaviour of the staff as by the standard of accommodation and quality of food and other services.

The essential element in any hoteliering organisation's survival and growth is its ability to generate facilities and opportunities. With increased competition, evolving technologies and changing market needs, food service and lodging concepts are becoming gradually outdated or obsolete than ever before. Attempts to adapt to these changes have resulted in a wide variety of trends: menu diversification, fast food service, computerising the front desk, audio-visual entertainments, specialised conference halls, and ceremonial lounges. Unless the firm keeps abreast of the changes in the market place and manages to generate appropriate opportunities that satisfy consumer needs and anticipate their wants, it risks losing any competitive advantage it might have enjoyed or could attain.

There are many reasons why every department of a hotel should implement GO (generating opportunities) system. The reasons why the marketing function could benefit from a GO system are outlined here:

(a) The industry is fiercely competitive. The business that is constantly identifying, assessing and choosing appropriate market opportunities is likely to become a market leader. By GO system it is able to develop a unique selling proposition which results in a competitive advantage.

(b) The markets for hotel services are highly vulnerable to many factors. The firm has no special protection from competition, moreover shifts in technology, taste, fashion, travel, life-styles and even substitutes products or services can seriously erode a firms' market share.

(c) There is a constant need for novelty and excitement among many customers today. Those that succeed and grow in this business are those that identify what this need means and are able to generate viable opportunities that attracts clienteles.

(d) Market opportunities need not always focus on the new and different but on refinement and improvement of the critical factors. Constant attention on the aspects that ensures improved quality, reliability and care, helps make every guest feel important, welcome, comfortable, secure and safe.

(e) These establishments suffer from irregularities of demand which are difficult to control. By creating new products or services the level of demand of new segment of customers can be brought into a better balance. It raises the frequency of visits of a customer, amount spent per visit and length of his stay.

(f) All products and services offered by a firm, regardless of how novel or unique they once were become obsolete. So there is need to update or replace the concept and facilities when or before their popularity declines and sales fall off.

(g) An attempt to revive a moribund concept, menu or facility through revision, renovation or refurbishment and so forth can help to recycle the demand. It can endure, thrive or grow only if a stream of new products or services replaces those that have been saturated in the market or are of declining importance.

Thus in hotel operations it is necessary to combine the 'production' element of the speedy and efficient provision of accommodation and food and beverage with the people element of a high standard of service and an appropriate attitude and behaviour from its staff. This suggests the need for consultation and team work and for a participative style of managerial behaviour based on the effective integration of a high concern for production balanced with a high concern for customers. In order to realise the aims of the hoteliering firm, the well-trained manager is an essential asset: the professional who combines an understanding of the interlinking roles of marketing, finance and technology with a finely-tuned creative mind and service attitude. Creativity comes into play with the need for introducing services, which without increasing costs encourage guests to spend more within the hotel.

The managers would discuss problems directly with the staff, allow them freedom of action within accepted terms of reference and handle difficulties in working relationships by attempting to find solutions agreed with them. A balance needs to be struck between the more easily identified financial costs and profitability and less obvious but equally important long term benefits which makes a positive contribution to the organisational effectiveness and the achievement of objectives.

3

The Organisation

Among the important inputs which flow into the tourist system is tourist accommodation. Accommodation facilities constitute a vital and fundamental part of tourist supply and an important feature of the total tourist image of a country. Many countries have recognised the vital importance of accommodation industry in relation to tourism and their governments have coordinated their activities with the industry by way of providing attractive incentives and concessions to suppliers of tourist accommodation, which have resulted in the building up of various types of accommodation. For instance, availability of sites for tourist accommodation on liberal payment terms, special concessions in the form of long-term loans, liberal import licences and tax relief, cash grants for construction and renovation of buildings, and other similar concessions are provided to the accommodation industry.

The United Nations Conference on International Travel and Tourism held in Rome in 1963 considered, in particular, problems relating to means of accommodation. The Conference acknowledged the importance of means of accommodation, both traditional (hotels, motels) and supplementary (camps, youth hostels, etc..) as incentives to international tourism. The Conference recommended that governments should consider the possibility of including tourism projects, and particularly those relating to accommodation on the list of projects eligible for loans from their industrial or other corporations, and that, where required, they should establish special financial corporations for tourism. It also recommended that governments should give sympathetic consideration to the possibility of granting special facilities and incentives for accommodation projects. An adequate supply of accommodation suitably tailored to the requirements of the tourist market is one of the basic conditions of tourism development. The provision of accommodation facilities and their growth should, at the same time, be regarded in a much broader context as they make an important contribution to the economy as a whole, by stimulating economic development, social contacts and commercial activities.

In the promotion of tourism, of all the constituents of the tourist industry, the accommodation sector thus constitutes the most important segment. Tourism is, to a great extent, dependent on the type and quantity of accommodation available. Accommodation is a very important part of the tourism infrastructure and the expansion of tourism inevitably brings about the development of accommodation. It is rather the core of the tourist industry. Accommodation is, in other words, the matrix of tourism, and is thus the obvious choice to play a distinctive role in the development of this expanding industry.

According to the World Tourism Organisation, WTO Report on 'The Development of the Accommodation Sector, tourist accommodation is used to denote the facilities operated for short term accommodation of guests, either with or without service, against payment and according to fixed rates. For the purposes of classification, all tourist accommodation has been divided into the following groups: (i) hotels and similar establishments (the hotel industry proper) and, (ii) supplementary means of accommodation.

The first group usually includes hotels, motels, boarding houses and inns, while the second includes registered private accommodation (rented rooms; apartments, houses), camping and caravan sites, youth hostels, recreation centres for children, mountain huts and shelters as well as health establishments, that is, sanatoria and convalescent homes.

Origin and Growth

The early history of accommodation for travellers can be said to have its origin in the Greek Word 'Xenia'. By this word ancient Greeks meant not only hospitality but also all forms of protection given to a visiting stranger. In ancient Greece, hospitality was a sort of divine order. The city or a town itself was bound to offer hospitality to a visitor and protect him from any discomfort. This was a custom. In the city of Sparta, whose extremely rigorous customs did not attract many visitors, it was the goddess Athena who was considered as protector of strangers, and hence her name 'Xenia Athena'.

Travelling during this period was not an easy affair. Travellers were mainly diplomats, philosophers, intellectuals and researchers. There were no lodgings specially designed to receive visitors. Guests were invited to stay in the dwellings of noblemen. This was rather a gift comprising a place to stay, food, care and bath. This explains the presence of baths in most archaeological finds. In ancient Olympia one can find one of the first buildings constructed with the aim of accommodating strangers, called the "Leonidio", built in 4th century B.C.

As travelling became more frequent, accommodation for travellers was viewed in two ways. The traveller who left his home required accommodation at his destination and, during journeys which could be completed in a single day, he needed overnight accommodation. The institution of 'inns' came into being. Inns can perhaps be considered to be the first of such accommodation units which catered to the needs of travellers in early times. During the Roman Empire many such inns were established which provided food, drink and also entertainment to weary travellers. However, with the decline of the Roman Empire by about A.D. 500, the institution of inn-keeping lost its importance and for many years there was not much development since people travelled very infrequently and there being not much trading activity, there was not much need felt for inn-keeping.

Later, when travelling began to be undertaken in coaches, travellers were lodged in 'Hostelries' situated at the relay stations where both the traveller and their horses found rest and food. From this time onwards, hospitality was not always offered free. Payment for accommodation used was being resorted to.

After the advent of Christianity, it was the Church which came to the rescue of the travellers. Travel grew again for religious pilgrimage purposes. Travellers in thousands visited religious centres. Monasteries took over the role of providing lodgings and facilities to travellers who were mainly pilgrims. These welcomed the travellers and made their stay a comfortable experience. Every large monastery had a person responsible for reception of visitors and their well-being. The accommodation and the hospitality provided were free.

By the 15th century, the institution of the 'inn' once again developed in several countries in Europe, specially in England and France. During the seventeenth and eighteenth centuries, the facilities provided in the inns were expanded. Some of the inns had as many as 30 or more rooms. The English Common Law declared the inn to be a public house and imposed social responsibility in the innkeeper for the well-being of the traveller. Even today over one hundred odd inns are still operating in England as hotels as part of Trust House Limited. Some of these were built about four hundred years ago.

In the United States of America another type of accommodation unit, known as the 'tavern', was opened in the year 1634 by a man called Samuel Coles who had come by ship to the New World in search of a fortune in the year 1630. By 1780, taverns were popular meeting places where people used to come for eating, drinking and entertainment. Many important events were associated with taverns. In the year 1783, General George Washington bid farewell to his top ranking officers at the Frances Tavern in New York city. The famous Boston Tea Party was planned in a tavern called Green Dragon.

In India the concept of shelter for travellers is not new. In fact, it is as old as its recorded history. The historical records are replete with the mention/references of *viharas, dharamshalas, sarais, musafirkhanas,* etc. These establishments provided a home to all wayfarers, be they pilgrims, scholars, adventurers or merchants. The shelter under various names has always been a part of India's culture as a valuable institution, providing a vital service. The ancient Buddhist monks were probably the first to institutionalise the concept of a shelter in India. The cave temples scattered all over the south-western region of India have both a *chaitya* (sanctuary) for worship and prayer and a *vihara* (monastery). These monks, although living in their quiet retreats, away from towns and villages, were nevertheless mindful of the needs of travellers and pilgrims who found shelter and food at these monasteries. It is interesting to note that these monasteries were located on the ancient trade routes between important centres of pilgrimage of the region. It is gathered from some inscriptions that merchants gave liberal donations for the construction and maintenance of these establishments. Mere charity was obviously not the motivation in these displays of generosity. The trader travelled with their merchandise and money on these routes and the *viharas* were their 'hotels'.

In the medieval period this ancient institution gradually assumed a more secular character. Although religious centres invariably had *dharamshalas* and *musafirkhanas* attached to them, the caravan *sarai* appeared as an exclusive traveller's lodge with a *Nanbai* or the cook attached with it. Sher Shah Suri, the Great Afghan Emperor and the builder of the Grand Trunk Road, is credited with having built caravan sarais at regular intervals all along this highway creating favourable conditions for commerce and travel. However, he was not alone in this venture. The Mughals built such facilities all over their empire. Later kings, rajas, nawabs, rich businessmen and philanthropists built *sarais* making travel less arduous.

At approximately the same point in time, the inn was the western counterpart of India's *sarais.* With the expansion of commerce, travelling became profitable and with it emerged the business of providing comfortable shelter and good food to the growing number of travellers. The *sarais* in India, like the inns in Europe, or the stage coach stations in the USA of the 18th and 19th centuries, stood all along the well-travelled routes. They provided food and shelter to the travellers and fodder to their horses. The amenities these early hotels offered would seem to us to be primitive but they conformed to the life-style of that age. However, with the passage of time, the age-old institution of the *sarai* or the inn adapted itself to the ever changing and constantly growing requirements of the market.

Meaning and Definition : The institution of hotel had its beginning in the early fourteenth century. The first hotel in the classical sense, the forerunner of the present day existing complex unit, is said to have been created in Paris, in the year 1312. Other similar hotels were soon established in France, Holland, Italy, Germany and many other countries.

With the growth of travel in the eighteenth century, there appeared in London the prototype of the modern hotel with the opening by one David Low in 1774. The next fifty years saw a gradual increase in the hotels and resorts in many countries of Europe. In the United States of America, hotels emerged from institutions known as 'Tavern' by the simple expedient of a change of name. By about the beginning of the nineteenth century, the terms tavern and hotel were used to describe the same thing. By the year 1820, 'hotel' became the accepted term to describe a place where people stayed for the night and took their meals on payment. In the 1820s the first tourist hotel appeared in Switzerland. The period preceding World War I also saw many hotels coming up in Europe especially in resorts of France, Italy, Switzerland and Germany. The hotels in fashionable resorts such as Vichy and Evian in France, Montecatine in Italy, Baden-Baden in Germany became very popular with tourists. In the same way hotels also came up in summer resorts along the French and Italian Riviera.

From the age of carriage and horses through the age of railroad into the era of jumbo jet, the hotel industry developed with the simultaneous development of transportation systems. In the field of mass passenger transport, railways could perhaps be credited with being the pioneers. The evolution of the railway system in the eighteenth century greatly affected the quality and the quantity of accommodation used in conjunction with travel. The growth of the railways also brought in a speedy network of stage coach services. By the mid-nineteenth century the use of the stage coach as a means of travel had almost ceased. The industrialisation in its wake brought increased urbanisation. The great number of people who flocked to various urban towns in search of employment and also entertainment needed some kind of accommodation.

This need for accommodation enabled promising and enterprising people to build hotels and inns in many such urban towns to cater to an increasingly local market and also to serve the large number of travellers carried by the railways. Until about the middle of the nineteenth century, the bulk of the journeys were undertaken for business and vocational reasons, by road and within the boundaries of individual countries. The volume of travel was relatively small and was confined to a fraction of the rich segment of the population in any country. Inns and similar establishments along the main highways and in the principal towns grew to become the hallmark of the accommodation for the travellers. The traveller could reasonably expect, at most inns, a clean and comfortable stay when he wished to eat or spend the night. It provided the bulk of accommodation *en route*. This trend continued until the end of the nineteenth century, as most people travelled by coach.

Although the earliest hotels date back to the eighteenth century, their growth on any scale occurred only in the following century when the railways created sufficiently large markets to make large hotels possible. During this period a large number of hotels grew up at important destinations. The hotels were developed along the main railway and highway routes in major towns. Substantial development of the hotels thus awaited the volume and the type of traffic only the railways could bring. With the development of railway systems in many other countries within and outside Europe, the number of hotels also increased. These hotels catered to the increasing volume of traffic. The 1860s also saw the introduction of Thomas Cook's railway and hotel coupons. Starting in 1868 Cook arranged regular circular tours of Switzerland and Northern Italy from England. By the 1890s, l200 hotels throughout the world accepted hotel coupons. Thus we find that railways greatly influenced the development of hotels during the early twentieth century.

The demand for accommodation of tourists was thus met by a variety of facilities ranging from inns, taverns, private houses to hotels. The main changes in the demand for tourist accommodation have come about from changes in tourist transportation and in the popularity of different forms of holidays. After the introduction of the motor car and the aircraft, a large number of hotels sprang up at various tourist areas and destinations. The growth of hotels continued until the 1950s. Hotels as a unit of accommodation dominated the scene all over the world.

Hotels provide accommodation, meals and refreshments for irregular periods of time for those who may reserve their accommodation either in advance or on the premises. In broad terms, hotels provide facilities to meet the needs of the modern traveller. The dictionaries define hotel in several ways: 'a place which supplies board and lodging', 'a place for the entertainment of the travellers', 'large city house of distinction', and 'a public building.'

The common law states that a hotel is "A place where all who conduct themselves properly, and who, being able and ready to pay for their entertainment, are received, if there be accommodation for them, and who without any stipulated engagement as to the duration of their stay or as to the rate of compensation, are, while there, supplied at a reasonable cost with their meals, lodging, and such services and attention as are necessarily incident to the use of the house as a temporary home."

A definition of the hotel as a business entity worthy of study was presented by hotel operators during the consideration of the hotel business to authorities of the National Recovery Administration, in Washington in 1933. This definition, as formulated by Stuart McNamara, was:

> "Primarily and fundamentally a hotel is an establishment which provides board and lodging, not engaged in interstate commerce, competitive with or affecting interstate commerce (or so related thereto that the regulation of the one involves the control of the other), but is a quasi-domestic institution retaining from its ancient origin certain traditional, and acquiring, in its

> modern development, certain statutory rights and obligations to the public, where all persons, not disqualified by condition or conduct, prepared to pay for their accommodation, are to be received and furnished with a room or place to sleep or occupy if such accommodations are available, and with such services and attention as are incident to their use of the hotel as a home, and/or with food, at stipulated prices, and with or without contract as to duration of visit, and which conducts, within the confines of its physical locations, this business of supplying personal services of individuals for profit. Incidental to such fundamental and principal business, the hotel may furnish quarters and facilities for the assemblage of people for social, business or entertainment purposes, and may engage in renting portions of its premises for shops and business whose contiguity is deemed appropriate to an hotel".

Accommodation can be categorized in different ways. These could be categorized by location, price, by type of visitors and by type of facilities they offer. Luxury hotels are at one end of the scale while budget or economy hotels are at the other end. Some are within the city limits or in city centre while others may be in suburban areas. Some properties may cater to business travellers while others may cater to families on holiday. Yet another way to categorise them is on the basis of whether they are fully serviced, partially serviced or non-serviced. It is however, difficult to place international lodging accommodation into strict, exclusive categories.

According to the organisation for Economic Cooperation and Development (OECD) there are eleven different types of accommodation plus two 'other' categories. The 'other' categories refer to other "hotels and similar establishments" and "supplementary means of accommodation". Following are the main categories of accommodation:

Hotels

(i) International Hotels

(ii) Commercial Hotels

(iii) Residential Hotels
(iv) Resort Hotels
(v) Floating Hotels
(vi) Capsule Hotels
(vii) Airport Hotels

Standard in the World

International hotels are the modern western-style hotels located in almost all metropolitan and other large cities as well as principal tourist centres. These hotels are luxury hotels and reclassified on the basis of an internationally accepted system of classification. The hotels are placed in various star categories. There are five such categories ranging from five star to one star, depending upon the facilities and services provided. These hotels provide, in addition to accommodation, all the other facilities which make the stay a very comfortable and interesting experience. These facilities include well-appointed reception and information counter, banquet halls, conference facilities, etc. There are also a number of shops, travel agency, money changing and safe deposit facilities. Restaurant facilities, bars and banqueting are an integral part of the business of a hotel. The various services provided in these hotels include international and local cuisine, food and beverage service and speciality restaurant service. These hotels also provide entertainment for the guests in the form of various dance and music programmes, sports and games.

A number of these hotels belong to the luxury category. There are some international chains which own a large number of such luxury hotels. Hotels belonging to international chains are mostly owned by public companies and controlled by a Board of Directors. These hotels have various departments which are managed by persons qualified and experienced in the field of hoteliering. The chief of the hotel designated as General Manager is responsible for the overall management and operation of the hotel through his departmental heads. International hotels are suitable for metropolitan cities and for other large business and commercial towns and principal tourist centres. The potential of these hotels is therefore limited to these areas. A number of this type of hotels have conference/convention facilities and are suitable for holding meetings, conventions and conferences.

Resort hotels cater to the needs of the holiday-maker, the tourist and those, who by reasons of health, desire a change of atmosphere. Resort hotels are located near the sea, mountain and other areas abounding in natural beauty. Rest, relaxation and entertainment are the key factors around which resorts are built. The primary motive of a person visiting them is rest and relaxation which he is looking for, away from his routine, busy work life. The resort hotels, in order to provide special services to the visitors, are built to give a visitor special welcome and an atmosphere of informality. The type of services and amenities located in resort property include recreation facilities such as swimming pool, golf course, tennis courts, skiing, boating, surf-riding and various indoor sports. Other important amenities include coffee shops, restaurants, conference rooms, lounge, shopping arcade and entertainment. Emphasis in resort hotels, however, is on recreational facilities. The clientele of resort hotels is mostly persons with considerable income looking for relaxation and recreation. Resort hotels rarely attract commercial patronage.

Resorts can be of various types and can be classified on the basis of climate and topography. Broadly they fall in the following categories: (i) Summer resorts, (ii) Winter resorts (iii) Hill resorts, (iv) All season resorts, and (v) Health resorts.

A majority of the resort hotels are seasonal establishments which work to capacity during the high tourist season. Generally the high tourist season is the period when there are holidays at educational institutions. However, in recent years many of the resort hotels, with a view to extend the season, provide certain special facilities and various other concessions to the guests. The concessions provided include reduced tariffs, free entertainment, sight-seeing, gifts, etc.

The commercial hotels direct their appeal primarily to the individual traveller as compared to international or resort hotel where the focus is on group travel. Most of the commercial hotels receive guests who are on business although some have permanent guests. As the hotel caters primarily to people who are visiting a place for commerce or business, these are located in important commercial and industrial centres of large towns and cities. These hotels are generally run by the owners and their success depends on their efficient running and the comfort and facilities they provide. In some of the large industrial towns, fully licensed commercial hotels exist complete with restaurants, grill room, functional accommodation and a garage for those travelling by automobile.

These hotels can be described as apartment houses complete with hotel services. These are often referred to as apartment hotels. The tariff of rooms in these hotels is charged on monthly, half-yearly or yearly basis and is charged for either furnished or unfurnished accommodation. These hotels, which are located mostly in big cities, operate exclusively under the European plan where no meals are provided to the guests. These hotels were developed in the United States of America where people discovered that permanent living in hotels offers many advantages. Services and amenities provided in these hotels are comparable to those of an average well-regulated home. These are very popular in the United States and western Europe where these are also popularly known as Pension.

As the name suggests, these hotels are located on the surface of the water. It may be on the sea or on a lake. All the facilities and services of a hotel are provided here and these are very popular in many countries. In some countries old luxury ships have been converted into floating hotels and are very popular among tourists. The atmosphere they provide is exclusive and exotic. In India, floating hotels in the form of houseboats are very popular with tourists.

Capsule hotel is the newest innovation in the budget hotel market. The first of its kind was opened in Osaka in Japan in the year 1979, as a spin-off of the 1970s fashion in Japanese architecture for capsules. These have now sprung up in increasing numbers in big cities of Japan.

The capsule is a box made of glass-reinforced plastic or cement, open either at one side or one end, in which are concentrated some of the functions of a traditional hotel room — bed, a clock, radio, TV, flexible lighting, a box for valuables and a miniature table for writing. Rooms in a capsule hotel generally are lined up in double-decker fashion along a central aisle as in a sleeping compartment of a train. Toilets and washrooms, vending machine room, and lounge are close by on each floor, of the hotel. The functions of each capsule are controlled and monitored by a central computer system and the security is controlled by close circuit TV cameras. The hotels cater mainly to business travellers. The low tariff and vintage locations are the major factors for their popularity. The hotels are well located near major transportation centres in Japan's largest cities.

Airport hotels, as the name suggests, are located near the airports primarily to cater to the needs of transit passengers, airport crew as also passengers of delayed or cancelled flights. The various facilities provided in these hotels are designed to offer comfort and convenience to the air travellers. The various services may include parking and shuttle service to and from the airport terminal. The hotels may also provide services for business travellers for organising meetings, conferences and conventions etc.

Space tourism is probably just another decade or so away. A brand new phenomenon in the hotel stay to be available in space travel would be called 'Skotel'. It would perhaps be the world's first airborne hotel. In the initial stages, space travel may start off as suborbital flights which would mean taking off in a shuttle and staying put in space for a few days. It may limit to flying off from an airport orbiting the earth once and then landing back on it. According to the International Institute of Tourism Studies, space tourism is broadly applied to the concept of paying customers travelling beyond earth's atmosphere. It can include parabolic flight, vertical suborbital flights, orbital flights lasting upto three days or week-long stays at a floating space hotel, including participatory educational, research and entertainment experiences as well as space sports competitions.

Many experts have conceived different designs and ideas regarding the structure of space hotels. Some experts feel that space hotels wouldn't be anything more than clusters of pre-fabricated cylindrical modules. Inside these cylinders there could be lots of fun. Since there would be zero gravity one may find the bar of the hotel merrily perched on the ceiling, while the other guests laze on the ground below. Studies are, however, going ahead on Space Hotel concepts. Some of these concept hotels including one called space Hotel Europe can room around 50 guests. Most travel specialists would advertise them as elevated or uplifted establishments, since space hotels would be above earth hotels simply because of the physical reality of being airborne or floating in space.

Supplementary accommodation may be of various types other than the conventional hotel type. Although hotels have been and still are the principal form of accommodation, there has been a growth and development of some other forms in various parts at the world. Supplementary accommodation can be classified on the basis of its location, type of construction, type of management, etc. A study of these indicates that their diversity is a reflection of the specific nature of each one and their names simply indicate various ways in which one and the same function can be fulfilled or a need can be satisfied.

Supplementary accommodation may be described as the premises which offer accommodation, but not the services, of a hotel. Services provided here is minimal and not comprehensive as in the case of hotel establishments.

All establishments under the heading of supplementary accommodation are designed to offer the possibility of stay overnight and meals in return for cash payment per day and on the basis of services provided. The standard of comforts is modest compared to that of a hotel. On the other hand, however, there are certain inherent advantages in this type of accommodation. The biggest advantage is that of price. It is moderately priced. In addition, the atmosphere is informal and there is more freedom with regard to dress, etc. There is also more emphasis on entertainment and sports resulting in increased social contact among the guests.

Supplementary accommodation plays a very important role in the total available tourist accommodation in a country and can cater to both international as well as domestic tourist traffic. In fact, in some countries more tourists utilise this type of accommodation than hotels. In France and Italy as also in some other countries in Europe and elsewhere there are more campers than there are hotel clients. The following are some of the principal forms of supplemental accommodation:

(i) Motel

(ii) Youth Hostel

(iii) Camping Sites

(iv) Pension

(v) Bed and Breakfast Establishments and

(vi) Tourist Holiday Villages.

The concept of motel and motel-hotel originated in the United States of America. Motel was meant for local motorists and foreign tourists travelling by road. Primarily designed to serve the needs of motorists, motels almost exclusively meet the demand for transit accommodation. They serve the function of a transit hotel except that they are geared to accommodate motor travelling guests for overnight stay. The important services provided by motels include parking, garage facilities, accommodation, restaurant facilities, public catering and recreational facilities. Hence all motels are equipped with filling stations, repair services, accessories, garages, parking space, "elevator service to the automobile, restaurants, etc. There are also equipment and tools available which the guest can use himself if he wishes to repair his vehicle. The price charged for accommodation and meals/refreshments is much cheaper as compared to that in hotels.

Motels are mostly located outside the city limits in the countryside along the main highway and preferably at an important road junction. Since these establishments cater mainly for persons travelling by road, their development is linked with the development of new motorways along which these are necessarily located. Motels are of different types. Some provide just the minimum services while others are well-furnished, with comfortable accommodation and excellent facilities. The accommodation provided is of a chalet type, which is furnished, having a dining hall and a fixed menu. Shopping facilities for travelling public are also provided.

In many countries, especially the United States of America,

motel accommodation is ranked with hotel accommodation and subject to general standards applicable to the hotel industry. In countries like Norway, France, Ireland, Turkey, etc., specific legislation has been introduced for motels. This includes requirements for the approval of plans, easy access of cars, minimum capacity, provision of restaurant where necessary, minimum standards for facilities and provision of petrol pump or service station where they exist and model classification standards similar to those for hotels. For instance, in France, there are three categories designated by stars, the classification being based on location, sanitary fittings and collective amenities. An increasingly important segment of the accommodation industry, motels are looked upon as a distinct asset, as these have enabled the industry to meet the changes in travel patterns and personal preferences of the modern day traveller.

Youth hostels made their first appearance in Germany in the form of a movement in about the year 1900. The movement which spread rapidly all over the world was based on the need of city youth to travel throughout the country. In order to provide some sort of accommodation and services the dormitories in the inns were equipped with cots, mattresses, sheets and blankets. Large rooms in inns were used as dining and living places providing full board at low cost to the guests. There was also provision of additional kitchen where travellers could prepare their own meals. Since the movement was started with a view to encouraging youth to travel - in order to learn and know more about the country and also to socialise, it had an educational value. As such, no service was provided in the inn. The persons staying in the inn were themselves required to look after the inn. Subsequently, exclusive youth hostel buildings were constructed to accommodate young travellers.

A Youth hostel can be defined as a building which offers clean, moderate and inexpensive shelter to young people exploring their own country or other countries and travelling independently or in groups on holiday or for educational purposes. It is a place where young people of different social backgrounds and nationalities meet and come to know each other. The objective of youth hostels, therefore, is not merely to provide accommodation and board, but also to serve as centres which offer an opportunity to young people coming from different parts of the country, as also young travellers from abroad, to know and understand each other. It is a place of friendship, recreation and out-of-school and college education.

The youth hostels are equipped to accommodate young men and women who travel on foot, by bicycle or other means of locomotion and who, at very little cost, are provided with a place to sleep, eat or to make their own meal. The services provided include accommodation, meals and also recreation. The charges for these services are very modest. The hostels are also equipped to enable the users to prepare their own meals if they so desire. The accommodation provided in the hostels is for a limited number of days.

In most countries, youth hostels are developed and managed by non-commercial organisations whose main aim is the development of youth tourism. Since World War II, the number of such hostels has increased greatly. These hostels are now planned to provide comfortable accommodation as also such other services and facilities which are required by youth. Also the number of those using these hostels has grown tremendously. Many hostels receive an increasing number of groups and organise stays for winter sports or sailing.

The construction of youth hostels is based on certain norms laid down from time to time all over the world. International requirements for these include provision of separate dormitories for men and women, appropriate and clean toilets, washrooms for both men and women, a kitchen where hostelers can prepare their own meals, common rooms, living accommodation for warden and a left-luggage room. There is also a provision of a kitchen where warden and staff can prepare meals to supply to hostelers, separate small room for instructors, a dining room and classroom for school parties and a warden's office. Some youth hostels have playgrounds attached for the use of hostelers.

The International Youth Hostel Federation has laid down certain minimum requirements for accommodation in the youth hostels. These include:

(i) Separate dormitories for men and women with separate entrances;

(ii) Separate toilets and washrooms for men and women with separate entrances;

(iii) A members' kitchen where hostelers can prepare their own meals;

(iv) A common room, separate from members' kitchen, wherever possible;

(v) Living accommodation for warden(s), on the premises wherever possible.

Caravan and camping sites constitute a significant accommodation category in many holiday areas. These are very popular in some European countries as in the United States of America. These are also known as open-air hostels, tourist camps or camping grounds. Camping, originally practised by hikers on foot, is increasingly giving way to car camping. The sites are usually located within the large cities in open spaces. Equipped to receive mobile accommodation in the form of caravans, the camping sites provide facilities for parking, tent pitching, water, electricity, toilet, etc. Though the services provided generally include restaurants, recreational rooms, toilets and at certain places a grocers shop, the type of services often vary from place to place. Some countries have enacted legislation establishing the minimum facilities that must be provided and these include health and sanitation standards, prices to be charged for parking and use of various services and facilities.

This type of accommodation is very popular in certain European countries. Particularly in Italy, Austria, Germany and Switzerland these establishments are used extensively by the tourists. Pension is also described as a private hotel, a guest house or a boarding house. Catering facilities are optional and are usually restricted to the residents. Many of them stay for longer and definite periods such as a week or a fortnight. The reservation of accommodation is made in advance. Mostly managed by a family, a pension is much cheaper than a hotel.

Also known in some countries as apartment hotels and hotel

garnis, they represent a growing form of accommodation units catering for holiday as well as business travellers. These establishments provide only accommodation and breakfast but not the principal meals. These are usually located in large towns and cities, along commercial and holiday routes and also resort areas and are used by en route travellers. Some of these are very popular with holiday-makers.

Tourist villages were established in some European countries after World War II. These are situated at warm seasides and in the regions which offer certain facilities for tourists. In Italy and Spain, tourist villages are located in the regions not economically developed, thereby helping the region economically. The villages are mostly promoted by important clubs, social and tourist organisations.

The village complex is a centre of accommodation providing extensive sports and recreation facilities, riding, swimming, tennis, volleyball, football, sauna, mini-golf, badminton, table tennis and yoga. These provide both board and lodging. The atmosphere in these villages is kept as informal as possible. Telephones, radios, newspapers and TV are banned unless there is an emergency. Wallets and other valuables are locked away at the beginning of one's stay. The staff are chiefly educated young people who live on an equal basis with the holiday-makers. The accommodation provided is usually in multiple units and many provide for self-catering. The furnishing provided in the rooms is minimal. The easy mixing of guests is encouraged by the banning of advance booking of tables in the village restaurants. One rarely finds oneself sitting with the same group twice.

The holiday villages are usually based on family units, each providing a convertible living room, bath/shower and sometimes a kitchen. The villages are self-sufficient, providing almost all necessities required by the residents. There is also a small shopping complex where one can buy articles of daily need. The services of a doctor are available. The accommodation is sold for a week or a fortnight at an all-inclusive price. In Spain and Italy, these are classified into three categories according to the services and amenities provided.

Through time-share and condominium concepts a tourist has a unique range of options for resort holiday and lodging. In the case of condominiums, a tourist owns a room or a suite within a condominium or hotel complex and uses the same as required by him or it can be rented to other tourists. The owned condominiums usually are within the complex of rooms or suites that are rented as regular hotel or resort rooms. It is difficult of tell the difference between an owned and a rented room.

Time-share on the other hand is a modification of condominium ownership. The units are owned partially. The time-share owner may own one-fifth of a unit thereby sharing the unit's use and costs. In some cases the owner may only purchase a certain set of weeks to use the unit. In other cases, a group of investors may jointly own a property through actual deeds. The time-share title implies that the unit is shared with others throughout the year.

Time-share began in the French Alps during the mid sixties. However, it was in USA that the concept began to take a proper shape. It is said that Time-share was born when distressed real estate developers of United States in the Florida region, could not sell their second homes in the mid-seventies and decided to sell one apartment fifty times over for each week of the year. Holiday time-share brings a number of benefits not only to the buyer and developer but also to the holiday resort areas and the traditional suppliers of services to the holiday industry.

Today, time-share owners have the choice of trading the use of their units with others. This provides the owners a unique opportunity to vacation at comparable prices at destinations throughout the world. May time-share companies are available to help time-share owners locate others interested in exchanging units.

Time-share today has become quite popular with holiday-makers especially with families. It offers high quality accommodation and associated amenities ideal for repeat visitors. It also offers better price and value than a hotel room for extended stays and is a hedge against room rate inflation. Time-share offers flexibility of use and a variety of experiences through exchange options as also peripheral benefits offered through an exchange company.

Tourist accommodation is an important component of a tourist plant. As an individual product it is intangible, often bought in advance of its use. The tourist at the time of making purchases thus cannot inspect or accept or reject. Accommodation as such, raises some issues in its development and in its marketing, both as an individual product and as a part of a package. It creates a need for reliable and accurate information for both the tourists and the travel agents, and therefore, may require supervision and control. An individual operator needs to bring information about his accommodation to the tourist before he sets off on his journey and also when he reaches his destination. Similarly the tourist on the other hand, needs to know in detail what accommodation is available at what price in a particular destination from which he can make a choice about where to stay. Schemes of classification, registration and grading of the tourist accommodation are intended to meet these requirements.

The United Nations Conference on International Travel and Tourism held in Rome in the year 1963 also emphasised the need for some sort of regulation of accommodation with a view to safeguard the interests of the users. Considering that special attention should be given to relations between the public authorities and the operators of tourist accommodation facilities, the conference advocated the adoption of a hotel trade charter codifying the regulations applicable to the hotel industry and, in particular, giving official tourist organisations powers enabling them to perform the activities devolving on the state in that field. The conference observed that many states classify tourist hotels or are considering doing so. Acting upon the recommendations put forward by the International Chamber of Commerce, the conference advocated the standardisation of methods of classification and in particular the subdivision of hotels into five categories, each identified by a conventional sign (stars) in conformity with the sets of standards appropriate to different climatic conditions. The conference also considered the question of classifying supplementary means of accommodation such as tourist bungalows and camps.

The aim of registration is to provide a complete list or register of tourist accommodation within a particular definition. A registration scheme results in an inventory of accommodation which can be kept up-to-date. In order to be comprehensive, it normally has to have statutory legal authority and is administered by a government authority or a statutory body. Because of the wider range of accommodation used by the tourists, a scheme of registration should normally cover all forms of accommodation used by them.

Grading separates accommodation into different categories or grades, on the basis of judgements such as standards of amenities and service. A grading scheme provides qualitative judgements on the amenities and facilities of a particular accommodation unit in a form which enables the user to choose the quality of accommodation he requires. This may refer to the physical facilities, food and other services of the establishment, various amenities provided, etc. The establishments are graded individually or collectively by way of giving them numbers, letters or symbols.

The chief aim of classification is to maintain standardisation of services and security for tourists. By establishing uniform standards of classification, it is easier for all concerned with tourism (tour operators, travel agents, tourist enterprise and tourists themselves) to know exactly what standard of services is offered by each hotel (according to the number of stars) thus leading to more effective uniformity both in statistics and in regulatory and control standards. The adopted scheme envisages that hotel establishments are to be divided into five categories, symbolised by stars, and based on objective standards. The categories are assigned on the basis of two types of requirements:

(i) minimum requirements common to all categories, as stated in the classification scheme, concerning health, sanitary, material and staff standards;

(ii) minimum requirements for each category, expressed as specific conditions for the hotel (as a building), the rooms, additional accommodation, facilities and guest service. The classification scheme is intended as a guide for National Tourism Administrations in their efforts to perfect a classifications system in collaboration with the hotel sector, on the basis of the principles set forth in the scheme. The classification system is to be adopted in a flexible manner so that any establishment failing to comply with a particular, though not fundamental requirement, would not be downgraded provided it complied with all other requirements.

Founded on 18th March, 1946 in London on the initiative of Societe Suisse des Hoteliers, the International Hotel Association (IHA) replaced the International Hotel Mens Association set up in June 1869 and International Hotel Alliance set up in April 1925. The main aim of the new association was to bring together members who could be of mutual benefit to each other. The IHA was registered by a French Ministerial Decree of 23 September 1949 having its headquarters in Paris.

The priority objectives of IHA include the protection and coordination of hotel interests in their relations with travel agencies who often play an important intermediary role between hotels and clients. Through the IHA/UFTAA Convention, there is a formal codification and confirmation of international practice governing relations between hoteliers and travel agencies. It informs hoteliers on their rights concerning payment, commission, cancellation, late arrival or no-show and relevant compensations.

IHA has a membership spanning 160 countries, comprising hotels and restaurants whether chains, both national or international, or individual establishments, who wish to participate directly in the Associations activities, even whilst being represented by their National Associations.

In addition, there are hotels and tourist personalities as individual members. Affiliates like hotel schools, training centres, tourist organisations, suppliers and services companies etc. also participate in IHA activities. The Association today represents more than 700,000 hotels and restaurants throughout 160 countries and more than seven million hotel industry wage earners.

There are over 90 National Hotel Association members of the IHA. Each Association has the right to send delegates to vote their numbers being determined by the number of hotels who are members of the Association in the respective country. Independent hotels, which constitute about 80 per cent of IHA membership, are entitled to the numerous services offered to IHA. All members receive a personalised membership card which entities them to 25 per cent discount on accommodation in IHA member hotels.

The aims of IHA include the following:

(i) to federate National Hotel Association of all countries;

(ii) to study problems affecting the international hotel industry and international tourist traffic including re-establishment of free traffic, economic policy for hotels and restaurants, hotel guides, international currency exchange, hotel insurance and conditions of work and personnel;

(iii) to create an international employment service for qualified hotel personnel and for the exchange of apprentices;

(iv) to inform members of international problems concerning hotels; and

(v) to give commercial information concerning travel agencies.

The association has a General Congress which meets at least every two years, an Executive Committee consisting of 30 members and a Council having 180 members. The Association is headed by the President and assisted by a Deputy President and five Vice Presidents. There is a General Secretariat responsible for looking after administrative and personnel matters. Planning and Finance Committee looks after all matters pertaining to finances including membership. Publications Committee is responsible for various publications of the association and their distribution. In addition, the following Functional Committees look after various subjects of the Association:

(a) Industry Economic Committee

(b) Sub-Committee on Computerisation

(c) Travel Agencies and Commercial Relations Committee

(d) Seasonal and Resort Hotels Sub-Committee

(e) Legal Committee; and

(f) Labour Relations and Training Committee.

One of the most important activities of IHA is, however, the provision of a wide range of practical services for hoteliers interested in attracting business from all over the world. The services include the following:

> Annual IHA international meetings are held where the most pressing issues confronting the large hotel chains", individual hotel owners, and service and supply companies are addressed. These meetings provide an ideal environment in which members can exchange valuable ideas, promote individual properties, and discuss specific problems and concerns of the industry.

An annual listing of all IHA members is provided to members free of charge. The guide is an automatic sales tool: used by travel agents, hoteliers, airlines, international corporations and business and professional offices worldwide promoting all the properties and services listed. *Hotels & Restaurants International,* a bimonthly magazine published in the US, with a special IHA section in every issue. This magazine keeps the industry well informed of all the activities of the IHA, its members and councils.

A publication listing books in western languages concerning hotel-related information, administration, proper management, hotel catering, etc. available to members upon request.

The World Directory of Travel Agents, a valuable reference book for hoteliers, listing 6,000 reliable travel agencies approved by the IHA. All listed agencies must belong to their national association, and must be in business for at least one year.

Debt Recovery Service is available to members upon request. The IHA intervenes and assists member hotels to claim payments overdue from foreign travel agencies.

Statistical Service on Payment Incidents, is a subscription service offered to members. Monthly lists are provided of at least 100 slow-paying travel agencies worldwide. Confidential information concerning travel agents is available upon request.

The IHA brings together hoteliers and distinguished specialists in hotel education. The IHA offers a hotel trainee network that facilitates the mobility and coordination of hotel training worldwide. The network also organises introductions for the placing of upper management.

The IHA provides members with a wide and varied range of information on the hotel and tourism industries. For example, the

IHA member may obtain lists of hotel publications, information on public utility charges, tariffs and all relevant hotel and industry material.

Address Labels of travel agencies worldwide are available to members for promotion and sales use at a small fee.

This card entitles the member to a 25 per cent discount on accommodations in other IHA member hotels worldwide. It encourages referral business the year round and is a valuable sales tool in low seasons.

The number of rooms that are available to the travelling public within lodging facilities varies from country to country and from region to region. Within a country most of the accommodation units will be located where the demand for these is very big. The demand will be more near the location of tourist attractions both natural or man made. Internationally the demand for accommodation will be more pressing in the regions which receive more tourists. Today Europe and America are the regions which receive maximum share of world tourists and it is here that the largest number of accommodation units are located.

According to World Tourism Organisation (WTO) estimates, or a survey conducted by them, the total capacity of hotels and similar establishments like motels, boarding houses and inns is over 20 million bed places. The largest accommodation capacity is, however, available in the continent Europe which is about 10 million bed places in the hotel industry proper. This constitutes about half of the total bed places available all over the world. The explanation for this is that the demand for both international and domestic tourists in Europe is maximum.

In several European countries, hotel development is concentrated in small and medium-sized hotel constructions. In many countries, within the framework of general expansion of the accommodation sector, the increase in hotel accommodation was outstripped by the increase in supplementary means of accommodation, such as camping and caravan sites, rented rooms, apartments, etc. This type of accommodation has become the main provider of lodging for domestic tourism and has also started to play a very-significant role in international tourism. In America the total capacity of hotels and similar establishments increased significantly in several countries of the regions.

In East Asia and the Pacific region, several countries are currently enjoying a hotel-building boom. In South Asia, the countries of the region are undertaking great efforts to develop the accommodation sector. In the Middle East, hotel construction in the region is mainly concentrated on luxury-class hotels intended chiefly to cater to business travellers. In view of the high profitability, there are many hotel projects which are under construction. In the African region, accommodation facilities are concentrated in the northern part of the continent.

Innovative Nature

The accommodation sector has undergone substantial changes in recent years. New developments in tourism and transportation, changes in the organisation of travel and technological innovations are some of the factors which are responsible for these changes. In addition, increasing consumer demand among tourists, due in turn to the improvement in living standards and economic conditions, has also changed the profile of the accommodation sector. All the above factors seem to have influenced the structure of the hotel industry as a whole. The tendency among middle-income groups to take a holiday at any time of the year has encouraged accommodation operators to offer novel kinds of arrangements which are now available in addition to traditional hotel accommodation.

New types of accommodation, particularly holiday villages suitable for family-type tourists, condominiums and apartment houses, private villas and camping facilities have proved very successful and to a certain degree are replacing traditional hotels and boarding houses. These changes reflect changes in demand with new, often younger, groups entering the international travel market and also new approaches to the problem of providing facilities in every competitive industry with a highly seasonal demand. The probable future developments in the accommodation sector were the subject of study undertaken in WTO's research programme. Some conclusions which emerge from the study are as follows:

(a) a significant growth in accommodation supply will continue to be contributed by chain operators, including airlines. This expansion will result mainly from the further development of management contracts and franchise agreements;

(b) there will be a continuing move towards the further diversification of accommodation. The development of budget accommodation, covering budget hotels, and also supplementary means of accommodation, is likely to continue as mass tourism stimulates new demands for competitively- priced accommodation;

(c) rising building and operating costs, growing environment and conservation pressures, as well as the need to keep staffing levels at a minimum, will influence design and construction of accommodation units;

(d) the standard of accommodation will continue to rise. Demand for recreational and sporting facilities will increase in both business and leisure accommodation;

(e) advances in technology will both influence the traditional construction methods, for example, more frequent use of prefabricated building techniques, as well as traditional methods of hotel operations.

In recent times, several environmental problems have come to be recognised in the accommodation sector. Several environmentalists as well as users of accommodation are demanding that environmental issues associated with accommodation industry should be addressed properly. Tourists visit different places of tourist interest and consume various products they buy. The consequences of the pressure of consumers on tourist services results in putting pressure on the environment. However, with few exceptions, industry owners are taking various steps to address the environmental issue in its proper perspective.

The various policies for the accommodation industry cover areas like environmental protection, energy conservation, waste reduction, emission reduction, recycling of waste, reduction of chemical usage and awareness and education of employees and the guests about environment. The best possible arrangement is that the commitment for environment should have full support of the top management and that it should start with them. It should be an integral part of management practice and be communicated to all personnel. Once this is agreed, corporate policies can be implemented through management techniques such as environmental audits. A proper and formal monitoring system that can be adopted to achieve the best possible results.

"Hotel" or "Inn" is defined by British law as a "place where a bonafide traveller can receive food and shelter, provided he is in a position to pay for it and is in a fit condition to be received." Hence, a Hotel *must provide* food (and beverage) and lodging to travellers on payment and has, in turn, the right to refuse if the traveller is drunk, disorderly, unkempt, or is not in a position to pay for the services.

The hotel industry is, perhaps, one of the oldest commercial endeavours in the world. The first inns go back to the sixth century B.C. and were the products of the urge to travel, spurred by the invention of the 'wheel'. The earliest inns were ventures by husband and wife teams who provided large halls for travellers to make their own beds and sleep on the floor. They also provided modest wholesome food, thirst-quenchers like wine, port, ale, etc. and stabling facilities. Entertainment and recreation were provided by the host's wife or his wench. The entire cooking service, and recreation was provided by the husband and wife team and his family.

These conditions prevailed for several hundred years. The advent of the Industrial Revolution in England, brought ideas and progress in the business of inn-keeping. The development of railways and steamships made travelling more prominent. The Industrial Revolution also changed travel from social or government travel to business travel. There was a need for quick and clean service.

The lead in hotel-keeping was taken by the emerging nations of Europe, especially Switzerland. It was in Europe that the birth of an organised hotel industry took place in the shape of chalets and small hotels which provided a variety of services and were mainly patronised by the aristocracy of the day.

In early England, public houses were normally called "inns" or "taverns". Normally, the name "inn" was reserved for the finer establishments catering to the nobility and clergy. The houses frequented by the common man were known as "taverns". In France, a similar distinction was made with the finer establishments known as "hoteleries" and the less pretentious houses called "cabarets". The word "hostel" was used after the Norman invasion derived from "host". The "hosteler" was the head of the hostel whereas the same position was called the "innkeeper" in England. The word "hotel" was used in England in about 1760 after a passage of over 80 years. In America lodging houses were called "inn" or "coffee house".

The real growth of the modern hotel industry took place in the USA beginning with the opening of City Hotel in New York in 1794. This was the first building specially erected for hotel purposes. This eventually led to great competition between different cities and resulted in frenzied hotel building activity. Some of the finest hotels of the USA were built in this era, but the real boom in hotel building came in the early twentieth century. This period also saw the beginning of chain operations under the guidance of E.M. Statler. It involved big investments, big profits and trained professionals to manage the business.

The Depression in 1930 had a disastrous effect on the hotel industry. It was felt that the hotel would never recover; but the outbreak of World War II brought a tremendous upsurge. This prosperity continued through the war years into the fifties, when two new concepts emerged:

(1) Motels

(2) International chain operations

While the growth of motels was restricted to the North American continent, international chain operations spread into all continents. Individual entrepreneurs found themselves crushed in this race for a multi-dimensional, multi-national industry. International chains could provide the expertise technology and marketing thrust that individual owners could not provide. Individual owners thus merged themselves with large international chains such as Sheratons, Hiltons, Hyatt, Holiday Inn, Ramada Inn, etc. These international chains provided the following services to individual owners:

1. Partnership—sharing equity and profits.

2. Franchise—providing "name" and "association" and marketing services in exchange for franchise and marketing fees.
3. Management—expertise in management, professional managers, technicians, manuals, systems, etc. on the basis of management fees and share of profits as "incentive" payment.
4. Marketing—active selling, chain benefits, reservation tie-ups, etc. on payment for marketing fees and incentive payment.

Today's hotel caters to all the needs and wishes of a guest and the future holds promise for a further mushrooming of modern hotels.

Different Parts : Hotels may be categorised depending upon factors such as:

1. Location
2. Number of rooms
3. Type of plan room rates that are quoted
4. Type of clientele
5. Length of guest stay
6. Facilities that it offers

It is located in the heart of the city within a short distance of the business centre, shopping areas, theatres, public buildings, etc. Rates in these hotels are normally high due to their locational advantage and also due to the fact that the rate of return on investment (ROI) computed on these capital intensive hotels is substantially high. Normally business clientele prefer such hotels.

Located in the suburbs, it has the advantage of quieter surroundings. Rates quoted are moderately low. Such hotels are ideal for limited budget travellers and also organisations who find the quiet setting ideal for conferences, seminars, educational programmes, etc.

This type of hotel is located in the hills or at beaches. It is mainly patronised by vacationers. Basic facilities are provided and the rates offered are often on American Plan, i.e. room plus all meals included.

As the name suggests, these hotels are situated at the airport and are ideal for transit passengers who have only a few hours in the city making it impossible for them to stay in a downtown hotel. Rates are on European plan, i.e. charges for room only.

This term is derived from the phrase, "motor hotels", which are located principally on highways. They provide modest boarding and lodging to highway travellers. The length of stay is usually overnight, thus rates quoted are on European plan. i.e. room only.

They are smaller in size with modest board and lodging facilities. They may be located anywhere within or outside the city. They are the forerunners of the modern motel.

The capacity of a hotel in terms of the number of rooms is a yardstick for the categorisation of the hotel by "Size". Hotels with 25 rooms and less may be termed "small"; those with 25 to 100 may be called "medium"; those with 101 to 300 are called "large". Hotels with over 300 rooms which are very common these days, may be termed "very" large.

Hotels are categorised according to the type of plan, they offer. We thus have hotels on European plan. American plan or Continental Plan for a discussion of plans. These plans are decided by the hotel on a variety of factors including type of clientele, length of stay and average customer preference.

We often hear in hotel parlance, the terms such as Group hotel, Commercial hotel, Family hotel, etc. This categorisation is based on the type of patronage. Group hotels cater to groups and thus their rates would be on American Plan. Commercial hotels cater to mostly businessmen and are on European Plan. A family hotel would again be on American plan. Such hotels are normally situated in resort cities.

This categorisation of hotels further be divided into three sub-groups: (1) Transient hotels where a guest can register for a day or even less (airport hotels could be termed thus); (2) Residential hotels where guests stay for a minimum period of one month the hotel signs a detailed lease with the customer; (3) Semi-residential hotels which incorporate the features of both the transient and residential hotels.

Facilities offered by hotels may be the most important criteria for classifying hotels. Some countries adopt the star rating system. Thus, a five star hotel which is the highest rating will provide facilities such as central air-conditioning, attached bathrooms with hot and cold water, channel music, wall-to-wall carpeting, shopping arcade, health club, swimming pool, sports facilities and a variety of restaurants and bars including a coffee shop, speciality restaurant, grill room, etc. These are just some of the criteria for star rating. Certain such facilities are denied as the star rating of the hotels goes lower and lower. They may be excluded for a variety of reasons such as cost, level of business, etc.

Hospitality Industry

Hospitality is treating people like you would want to be treated when you are travelling. In other words, it means making a tourist feel totally welcome as not only your guest, but also the guest of the complete family of the Hotel. Hospitality is genuine smiling face.

Hospitality can be termed as deliberate, planned and sustained effort to establish and maintain mutual understanding between an organization and public i.e. business of making and keeping friends, and promoting an atmosphere of better understanding.

Very frequently we hear phrases like "He is always hospitable to visitors", "We are grateful to friends for their hospitality in putting us up while we were on holiday", "She is so inhospitable that she grudges giving us any thing to eat or drink when we visit her" etc. All such statements are suggesting the positive or negative attitude of welcome towards visitors, friends or strangers. Hospitality activity covers everything i.e. providing attentive and courteous services, facilities and amenities to a traveller, meeting and greeting him at the door, providing efficient and caring service of food and beverage to him in the room i.e. providing "A Home away from Home", and making his visit a memorable and pleasant experience.

Reception, welcome and, in general, the treatment of a guest or a stranger in most friendly manner is Hospitality. In most of the countries all over the world a guest is received with a great amount of courtesy and warmth and is provided with entertainment. The basic concept of Hospitality is to make the guest feel that he has come amongst friends and that GUESTS ARE ALWAYS WELCOME. Although the basic concept of hospitality has remained the same, yet with the passage of time and development of technology and science, the needs and wants of travellers have changed greatly thus providing numerous services and facilities in terms of accommodation and other basic needs such as food and beverages. In olden days kings, lords, maharajas, landlords and sometimes the panchayats etc. used to provide food and shelter to travellers and their animals free of charges and it used to be a benevolent activity. But with the passage of time it has not only remained a benevolent activity but has become a flourishing business too.

A part of hospitality activity is being attentive, alert, and cordial with the guest without forcing yourself and your ideas on to him; at the same time being very polite and cooperative. All those working in hospitality industry have one common objective—"Creating an image of friendly reception and treatment" for guests and visitors.

As front office personnel, the hotel staff, in order to provide hospitality should make his guests feel at home and use pleasant tone of voice smilingly, offer his assistance wherever possibly can be provided. Don't ignore the guest, and don't be abrupt no matter how busy you are: anticipate his needs and wants and provide the same without his asking them.

As a hotelier, keep on checking the hospitality attitude of your organization. Make a check list and be sure that you and your staff are fulfilling each and every point of the check list. The check list may include areas such as front desk and lobby, etc. Make sure that the front desk is always kept clean, orderly and well lighted. Even the stationery used is so designed that it does not create confusion and clearly indicates how it is to be filled in, and is inviting. The lobby is kept clean and furniture kept at proper place. Lighting system is soft and appealing. The welcome spirit that the guest is looking for is there. Floor covering, pictures, furnishing etc. are appealing, attractive and aesthetically designed.

Further, the check list should include the intangibles such as training of the staff and willingness and positive attitude of the staff.

The arriving guest is always greeted with a smile and proper salutation to show interest in his trip and his well being.

Historical Aspects

Early travellers were either warriors or traders or people in search of knowledge and there were no hotels. Warriors and conquerors pitched their tents for accommodation while traders and persons travelling for knowledge placed a high value on hospitality and sometimes traded their merchandise for lodging.

Inn keeping can be said to be the first commercial enterprise and hospitality one of the first service for which money was exchanged. Inns of the Biblical times offered only a cot or a bench in the corner. Guests stayed in large communal rooms with no sanitation and privacy. The rates were, of course, reasonable. The company was rough. Travellers shared the same quarters with their horses and animals.

King James Version of Bible mentions that Mary and Joseph were turned away by a Bethlehem innkeeper, because there was "no room at the inn". According to Biblical scholars the innkeeper may have meant that the room was unsuitable for a woman about to give birth to a child. At that time, and probably for several centuries after that, men and women shared the same accommodation accompanied by their horses and livestock. The stable where Mary and Joseph spent the night was probably almost as comfortable as an inn and at the same time certainly more private than the inn itself.

In the 3rd century AD, the Roman Empire developed an extensive network of brick paved roads throughout Europe and Asia Minor, and a chain of roadside lodges was constructed along the major thoroughfare from Spain to Turkey.

Till the Industrial Revolution of the 1700s, no significant improvement was made in the inns and taverns and they were not very suitable for aristocrats. To accommodate wealthy travellers, luxurious structures were constructed with private rooms, individual sanitation and comforts of an European castle. These elegant new establishments adopted the French word for mansion—'Hotel'. Their rates were beyond the reach of an ordinary person.

In America early inns were modelled after European taverns with sleeping quarters shared by two or more guests.

Herman Melville in his novel *Moby Dick* has mentioned about a seaman who checked into a room of a nineteenth century inn and next morning woke up to find out that he was sharing the bed with a cannibal. Sharing beds was a very common practice in early American and European inns. Throughout the 1800s American innkeepers improved their services and continued to build larger and more amply equipped properties and most of these properties were located near seaport towns.

The tendency of Americans to travel more provided an inspiration to lodging operators. The nation's democratic spirit also led to the development of comfortable and sanitary lodging within the reach of an ordinary person.

Basically for all those who are away from their home, hospitality industry provides services. Hospitality industry consists of all those businesses and institutions that provide food and lodging—such as hotels, motels, lodges, inns, cruise ships and restaurants etc. To some extent it also includes the airlines industry. In a broad sense, any group engaged in tourism, entertainment, transportation and lodging are covered under hospitality.

Hospitality industry is a part of travel and tourism industry. Early travellers were mostly warriors, businessmen, scholars in search of knowledge or people in search of occupation. Mostly warriors would pitch their tents for accommodation while businessmen would look for a comfortable and safe place, and would often pay through their merchandise or cash to people providing them accommodation and food. The poor people travelling to far off places in search of job or occupation were provided the facilities of food and accommodation free of charges. As per some authentic sources, to facilitate travel throughout Western Europe a highway was constructed in 312 B.C. Travel could be done on this highway by chariots. Later in 117 AD this roadway was reconstructed and covered a distance of nearly 50,000 miles.

Hospitality business now is both profit making as well as non-profit making. For example, commercial hotels are profit making while canteens, cafeterias and religious catering outlets such as *langars* and *bhandaras* are non-profit making.

Hospitality industry provides services which are need oriented and the services vary with the needs. For example, the needs of a business executive shall be a business hotel while the needs of a student is generally a youth hostel.

Traditional ways of providing hospitality in our country varies from place to place. In Jammu and Kashmir, Kashmiri Pandits, who are very God-fearing people, consider guests as epitome of God almighty Himself and welcome the guest by a *rangoli* called *Vyog* patterned on their door-steps out of flowers and leaves. When the guests come, the host takes a glass of water and touch it on their forehead, so as to drive all evil spirits away from them. A special herb called *Isbandh* is also touched on the forehead and then burnt in the *Kangri.* The head of the Dogri family, another community of Jammu, goes to the door of the house to welcome the guest. The head female member of the family performs *aarti* of the guest and puts up a *tilak* on the forehead of the guest. Every day in the southern part of the country, ladies make *rangoli* of rice, flowers and flour etc.

It is believed that by doing so they are inviting guests and giving a message that the house is open to welcome guests. Greeting guests with folded hands, touching their feet in respect, *aarti, puja,* garlanding, applying *tilak* and ringing of bells, are numerous other ways of providing warm reception and welcome—and hence hospitality—in various parts of our country. Beating of drums, *dhols,* blowing of trumpets, exotic dances and shows such as puppetry etc. are all different ways of expressing warm hospitality in our country.

In different parts of the world, traditional style hospitality is provided. For example, ladies decorated with flowers greet the guests in Honolulu. In some countries, local people gather to welcome visitors at airports. Providing shoeshine service for every guest in the morning in a hotel in Bangkok is a part of welcome to the guests. In one of the hotels in Mauritius, after the dinner service is over the staff collects in the dining area and sings local songs in the honour of the guests. Memorizing the names of the guests and addressing them by their names is another way of providing hospitality in one of the Traditional Style Hospitality for Visitors hotels in France. Singing melodious songs at the time of departure of a guest is done in one of the resorts in Fiji.

All the above mentioned examples along with many others reflect the concept of hospitality provided by highly trained and experienced staff. Through their sincere efforts every guest feels like a VIP and a welcome syndrome is generated.

The past, present and future of the hospitality industry are linked together. Comfortable and sanitary lodging was once considered the exclusive privilege of the wealthy only, but with the rise of industry and democracy, hospitality has now become available to common men also. Hospitality has both influenced and is being influenced by cultural, social and economical changes in society. Hospitality business tends to satisfy human needs and also play an important role in the satisfaction of social needs such as belongingness, longingness, love, esteem and status.

Hospitality has a very vast market. All those who have stayed in hotels or have plans to stay in hotels or any other lodging establishment can be put under hospitality market. Hence all travellers including tourists, visitors, businessmen, leisure travellers, pilgrims and company executives etc. can be the hospitality market. Depending upon the purpose of travel people can be classified under either *commercial hospitality market* or *leisure hospitality market.*

Common Law states that a "Hotel is a place where all who conduct themselves properly, and who being able to pay and ready to pay for their entertainment, are received, if there be accommodation for them, and who without any stipulated engagement as to the duration of their stay or as to the rate of compensation, are while there, supplied at a reasonable cost with their meals, lodging and other services and attention as are necessarily incident to the use as a temporary home."

A hotel may be called as an establishment where primary business is to provide to the general public lodging facilities and which may also furnish one or more of the various services such as food, beverage, laundry, uniformed services etc. Hence, hotel can also be called as home multiplied by commercial activities.

As per the *Reader's Digest Dictionary* the term 'Hotel' refers to 'a house of entertainment of travellers'.

According to the *Encyclopaedia Britannica* the word 'Hotel' is of ancient origin, but its use in English for a house offering lodging and food for travellers is recent. The Hostlers of London took the name of Inn-keeping in 1473. The word 'Hostler' or 'Ostler' having come to mean an inn servant.

The term 'Hotel' was used in England in about 1760. Hotel or inn is defined by British law as a "place where a bonafide traveller can receive food and shelter, provided he is in a position to pay for and is in a fit condition to be received".

In legal terminology a hotel is an inn and is required under common law to offer to its visitors lodging, food and protection to their baggage. Hotel service is generally based on these three fundamental necessity of life. In addition to these a modern hotel provides its visitors many luxuries of modern urban city living, all under one roof.

Inns : Public houses in early times in England were called inns. Normally the term 'Inn' was meant for the finer establishments catering to nobilities and clergy. In France these were called 'Hoteleries'.

Taverns : The house frequented by common man were known as taverns. The less important establishments in France were called 'CABARETS'.

Hostel : Derived from the word 'Host' and was used very late. The head of the hostel was called 'HOSTELER' in French, while in England he was called 'Inn Keeper'.

Evolution and Development

Early history of accommodation for travellers can be traced back to the Greek word 'Xenia', which not only meant hospitality but also the protection given to a traveller from discomforts. The city was bound to offer hospitality. In Sparta city, although due to rigorous customs visitors were not encouraged, yet goddess Athena was considered as protector of strangers and hence her name was 'Xenia Athena'.

In this period travellers were mainly diplomats, philosophers, intellectuals and researchers. Guests were invited to stay with noblemen. In ancient Olympia, buildings constructed with the aim to accommodate strangers can be seen. They were called 'Leonidio' and were built in 4th century B.C. The concept of hospitality can also be drawn back to ancient times. Mention of it is found in 'Iliad' and 'The Odyssey' by Homer.

Hotel-keeping can also be traced back to many centuries and its evolution through the ages has been brought about by Britain's economical and industrial changes and developments.

During the seventh and eighth centuries, it was the monasteries that supplied hospitality to strangers and, as no charge was made for the accommodation, all travellers were expected to contribute according to their means to the Abbey funds. As more people began to travel they grouped themselves together, not only for company, but for mutual protection from highwaymen and robbers. Consequently, travellers arrived in groups at a monastery and it was often difficult to accommodate them all. To overcome this, separate lodging houses called 'Inns' (a Saxon word) were built. The word 'Inn' came to mean a 'Lodging House' and until the passing of the Hotel Proprietors Act in 1956, it was the legal term for 'Hotel' and hotel proprietors were legally referred to as 'Common Innkeepers'. 'Common' in this sense referred to Common Law.

In the thirteenth and fourteenth centuries, manor houses, being hospitable places, willingly gave accommodation to travellers. As no payment was expected, travellers tipped the servants as a 'thank you' for the generous hospitality received—thus the practice of tipping was born.

When high taxes crippled the generosity and hospitality of the owners of the manor houses, many became commercial inns. During Elizabeth the First's reign, posting houses were established and travellers, in addition to getting refreshment were able to change horses before continuing their journey.

The turn of the century saw an era that was called the 'Belle Epoch' when the grand and luxurious hotels flourished. A few hotels are still operating today. In London and some other cities attempts have been made to recapture some of the grandeur of the past era in the making of modern hotels, and bring back the memories the grand hotels of olden days.

The next stage in the cycle of evolution of the hotel industry was the coming of the motor car. It enabled people to visit those parts of the country not reached by railways. This gave birth to inland resorts and the hotel industry began to flourish.

International air travel has helped create the modern 'stop-over' hotel. With the increase in this form of travel, the number of hotels built close to airports has multiplied.

Another trend in Hotel-keeping is the motel which is the twentieth-century version of the old 'Coach Inn'. People travelling the country by car, stopping overnight here and there, require not only refreshment for themselves, but also safe parking for their cars. Post Houses, developed by the Trust Houses Forte Group are in fact the modern version of the old coaching inns.

Hotel industry has followed the path of the traveller

- Travel by foot
- Travel by animal
- Rest for both (rest houses, monasteries and inns)

Inn-keeping

- An outgrowth of man's urge to travel. Roads used by merchants and couriers.
- Believed started 12,000 years ago.
- Concept of hospitality mentioned in writings dating back to Greece, ancient Rome and Biblical times.
- 6th century B.C. (Establishment of money)
- Rest stops were made near or accessible to water.

Rest Houses

- All along 'Roman Highway' (for troops, civilians and merchants).

- Later 'Coach Inns' were brought by stage coaches and travellers were put in 'Hostelries.'

In Florence (Italy) 1282

- It is believed a rest house was build here.

Paris (1312)

- It is believed a hotel in true classical sense was built in this year.

Early Inns

- Fairly clean.
- Self service unit (guest making their own bed).
- Small part of a self dwelling unit.
- Run by unreputed and unprogressive persons.
- Unheated rooms, straw beds for nobilities and stone beds for servants.
- Protection from robbers and pirates.

Pascal (1650)

- Cafe and coffee house were opened by him in Paris and London respectively.

Industrial Revolution (1750-1820)

- English inns—finest in the world.
- Development centered in and around London.

David Low (English Inn)

- English inn—was opened in London.

Hotel de Henri IV

- Built in Nantes in 1788 for a sum of £7500 (one of the first European hotels). It had 60 rooms.

Francis Tavern (1783)

- General George Washington gave farewell party to his top ranking officers here.

Colonial Inns

- Early inns were located at seaports and were established in their mother country style.

- Sleeping on floor, feet towards fire and head on rolled coat with a dozen or more people of both sexes sleeping together.
- Quick cold water bath in an outside basin.
- Use of communal towel.

Charlemagne Laws

- Free accommodation for travellers and free food bonus to travellers for 3 nights at one place in a continuous time period.

European Inns

- Formal atmosphere and patronized by aristocrats.
- Out of reach of common public.
- Mainly for aristocrats only.

American Inns

- U.S. assumed leadership after 1850. More progressive inns were used for gatherings, court of law, schools and town meetings etc. and the Massachusettes passed a law -"Penalty on towns that did not provide these facilities".
- Inns based on equalitarian enjoyment concept with 'informal' atmosphere.
- Informal atmosphere.
- Accommodation for all who could pay.
- Developed faster because of the
  - (i) Free and informal nature of Americans
  - (ii) Their Pioneering spirit and
  - (iii) Their Love of travelling

Growth of Organised Hotel Industry

- Switzerland and other emerging nations of Europe helped in more organized growth of hotel industry.
- Concept of small hotels and chalets started from Switzerland.
- Family hotels i.e. run by the family members and were called "Mom & Pop" in England.

Invention of Railways

- By the middle of 19th century brought in railway refreshment rooms.

Just before World War I

- Many fine hotels were made at resorts of France (Vichy and Evian), Germany (Baden-Baden) and Italy (Monte Catine) etc. and summer resorts of French and Italian Riviera. U.S. Became the leader in hotel industry.

First Building Created Specially for Hotel

- With 'City Hotel' (73 rooms) at 115 Broadway, New York in 1794 the U.S. became the leader in hotel industry.
- The hotel became obsolete within 15 years and was converted into an office.
- Later, hotels were made in Boston, Baltimore and Philadelphia.

Boston Tea Party

- The famous Boston Tea Party was planned in Green Dragon Tavern.

Tremont House

- A first class hotel was made in Boston in 1829.
- Provided private guest rooms. Doors with lock. A wash bowl with water pitcher. Free soap. Bell boy service.
- Closed after 20 years for renovations.

Thomas Cook (1860)

- Started railway coupons.

By the end of 19th Century

- Many elegant hotels such as 'Waldorf Astoria' in New York, Denvels Brown Palace, San Francisco Palace, Palmers House in Chicago, Planters House in St. Louis, etc. were made.

Cesar Ritz (1889)

- Introduced luxury hotels such as Savoy, Carlton and Hyde Park hotels in England.
- Started Gordon Hotels in London.

Sir George Reeves Smith

- Took over Savoy from Ritz and named it Savoy London.
- Also managed Metropole, London.

Berkley and Claridges

- Two famous chains emerged in England.

Sir Isador Salmon

- Chairman, J. Lyons & Company, started Cumberland, Strand and Regent Palace under Popular Hotel Company, London.

Fredrick Gordon (Former Solicitor)

- Built Holborn Restaurant

Sir Blundel Maple (Furniture Manufacturer)

- Fredrick Gordon and Sir Blundel Maple became partners and launched two companies.
- Gordon Hotels, 1890 and Fredrick Hotels Ltd., 1899.

Ellsworth, M. Statler

- Started a new chain and made his first hotel Buffalo Statler on 18th Jan. 1908.
- Gave the slogan, "Room and a bath for a dollar and a half. Free newspaper, circulating ice water and full length mirror were provided.

Conrad N. Hilton (Born in St. Antorio, Mexico)

- Purchased a hotel called Mobley in Cisco (Texas) somewhere around 1920.
- Opened a company Hilton Hotels Corp. in 1946.
- Purchased Statler chain in 1954.

_1910-1920_

- Period of relative inactivity.
- Then came N.Y. Pennsylvania (Largest hotel of that time).

_1927_

- Stevens Hotel (3000 Rooms). Now named Chicago Hilton, was made.

- Then came Pierre Hotel, N.Y., a very famous hotel of its time.

1930

- U.S. Depression. Affected hotel industry in particular and occupancy fell down to nearly 50%, and 85% hotels went into liquidation. This period was useful to hotel chains such as Hilton and Sheraton etc. who acquired properties from out of business hoteliers.

1940

- Situation improved and outbreak of World War II.

1950

- New concepts such as motels, boatels, floatels, rotels and loatels etc. developed.

Second World War

- Many trained staff joined army hence standards of service lowered. However occupancy improved with mass movement to approximately 90%.

1952

- Kemmons Wilson formed 'Holiday Inn' chain and first Holiday Inn was made in 1952 at Memphis-Tennesse.

1. *Motels:* Motels or motor hotels were born during this period. More and more American families travelled by their own automobiles. Moreover, habits, tastes and desires underwent a considerable change. A new mode of informality had come into the American way of life. Suddenly there was a way out to eliminate formal dress, tipping and parking problems. The rooms were well furnished in a modern way, wall-to-wall carpeting was provided, and T.V., a swimming pool and the convenience of one's own transportation was an added attraction.
2. *Boatels:* These are hotels on boats, sometimes named as houseboats.
3. *Floatels:* Hotels on ships giving the facilities and conveniences of a luxury hotel.

4. *Roatels:* These are hotels on wheels. A limited number of rooms or cabins are there for couples. All conveniences of guests are looked into.
5. *Loatels:* Refers to 5-star deluxe properties with the facility of helicopter landing on the terrace.

1960

- Development of Atrium Hotels of Hyatt.
- Many individual owners merged themselves with large chains such as Sheratons, Hiltons, Hyatt, Holiday Inns, Ramada Inns, etc. for franchise by paying a fee and then they could use the name, logo, reservation systems, national and international advertisement and operation manuals.
- Budget Hotel/Motels: In the later part of 1960s hostelries offered accommodation at prices significantly lower than the prevailing rates of first class motor-hotels by incorporating three important factors as follows.

Lower Initial Investment Cost (due to the following)

(i) *Smaller Guest Room :* 250 sq ft. as against 335 sq. ft. Less expenses on land (1.6 acre of land as compared to 2.5 acre for a 100 room hotel), decoration etc.

(ii) *Minimum Public Space:* Cutting down on large executive offices, large lobbies etc.

(iii) Simple and no frills designs.

Operating Efficiency

(i) *Compact Facilities :* Less time required to clean and maintain and less power consumed for heating and lighting.

(ii) *Fewer Guest Services :* Elimination of valet services etc.

High Volume

(i) *Price Location:* Reduction in price increases the business volume. Many budget hotels are situated next or adjacent to higher price hotels to attract price conscious travellers.

(ii) *Value:* The budget hotel provides clean, good quality guest room, comfortable bed, full baths, colour T.V., carpeting, standard furniture and fixtures, wall covering, bedspreads and cheerful drapes etc.

Reminiscent of the 1920s boom, the hotel industry experienced the start of construction boom in the 1970s. Hilton, Sheraton and Westin Corp. opened convention oriented hotels. Airport hotels location also appeared in 1970s and also the Marriott location of major properties outside of central city area in the same year. Large amount of finances were made available by money lenders particularly by REIT (Real Estate Investment Trust).

Readily available franchise resulted in over building many poorly located and undercapitalized properties with inexperienced owners.

(i) Later there was energy crisis that curtailed travel.

(ii) Inflation caused construction cost and interest rate go very high.

(iii) Recession curtailed the business trips, conferences and conventions.

(iv) Marginal properties could not pay the mortgage amount and the lenders became owners. They either hired experienced hoteliers or contracted professional management companies to assume operational responsibilities. Since then a lot of changes in technological and management approach have taken place and today's hotel industry is progressing day by day. International business is rapidly developing and with this a lot of business executives are travelling out. Modern hotels are developing as per the needs and wants of the tourist and business class guests. Many international hotel chains such as Inter Continental, Sheraton, Park Royal, Hilton, Trust House Forte, Holiday Inn, Ramada Inns, Meridien, Sofitel, SRS Hotels, Utell International, Howard Jonsons, Wolfe International, Hyatt, Golden Tulip, Marriott, American International Hotel & Travelodge, Quality Inns, Accor, Imperial, Motel 6, CEDOK, Club Mediterranean, Red Roof Inns, Friendship Inn, Red Carpet Inn, Western International Hotel, United Inn, Super 8 Motels & Topeka Inns and a lot more have emerged from time to time.

(Some of the important developments in U.S. Hotel Industry)

1846: Central heating

1859: Elevator

1881: Electric lights (2 years after patent)

1907: In-room telephones (31 years after invention)

1910: American Hotel Association (Now AHMA) began

1927: Radio in room (21 years after invention)

1940: Air cooling (Mostly in public areas)

1950: Electric elevator

1958: Free television

1964: Holiday Inn reservation system with centralized computer

1965: Message light on telephone

1965: Initial F.O. systems followed by room status

1970: Colour T.V. (Invented in 1954)

1970 (Early) : E.C.R. (Electronic Cash Register)

1970 (Mid) : POS. system and key less locks

1973 : Free in-room movies (Sheraton)

1983 : In-room personal computers

Landmarks in the Growth of Hotel Industry

1650 : Pascal opened a cafe in Paris and Coffee House in London.

1794 : City Hotel (73 rooms) at 115 Broadway, New York. First building specially made for a hotel.

1829 : Tremont House. Adam and Eve of modern hotel industry was opened at Boston (170 Rooms)

1889 : Cesar Ritz introduced luxury hotels such as Savoy, Carlton and Hyde Park hotels in England.

1890-1899 : Fredrick Gordon and Sir Blundel Maple launched Gordon Hotels and Fredrick Hotels Ltd.

Late 19th Century : Famous Waldorf Astoria in New York

18.1.1908 : Buffalo Statler by Ellsworth Statler in U.S. Considered to be the birth of commercial hotels.

1927 : Stevens Hotel in Chicago, later renamed as Hilton Hotel (3000 rooms) :

1950 : 2 new concepts (a) Motels and (b) International chain operations :

Hotel Rossia or : Moscow (Remained largest hotel of world for quite sometime) : Rossiya

West Inn Stanford : Singapore (Remained tallest building for quite sometime) :

1930 depression in : Decline in hotel industry world economy :

World War Period : Upsurge in hotels :

An example of Hotel Advertisement and Tariff Card in 19th Century England is given on the next page.

Indian Scenario

In India too the development of hotel industry is closely linked to travel. In India travel was mainly on animals (mule, horse and camel) and for rest during their travel at strategic points *Dharmashalas, Sarais, Chaupals* of *Panchayats, Chowltry* (in South India) and temples and religious places were provided by rich people such as Rajas, Kings, Zamindars etc. Usually free accommodation and food for travellers was given. During medieval period it was mandatory for the state authorities to provide food and shelter to the wayside traveller.

These developed during the Muslim period. Many famous and well known *musafir khanas* and *sarais* were made in the Sindh province during the Arab invasion, and also at Peshawar and Lahore. Muhammad Tughlak and Feroz Shah Tughlak made inns in the northern part of India. Later, Sher Shah Suri, Akbar, Jahangir and Shah Jahan made inns in different parts of India. Jahan Ara

Begum built a very beautiful *sarai* at Sahibabad (Begamabad) and its beautiful garden is still there and is called Queens Garden or Azad Park. The fountain in the upper garden has the inscription *"Gar Firdaus Bar Rui Zaminast-Haminhastu, Haminhastu, Haminhastu"* .

Delhi has always been traditionally hospitable, and we find overwhelming evidence of this in the innumerable *sarais* and rest houses of this ancient city. Delhi has been built seven times in the area spanning from Mehrauli to Shahjahanabad. Delhi is believed to be the oldest living capital of the world. During their reigns rulers of Delhi built *sarais* throughout their kingdom for the comforts of travellers. The *sarais* afforded a *baoli* or a *talab* (a bathing tank), a stable, a *dargah* for prayer and sometimes a *bimarkhana*—a place for sick and ill travellers. A sufi or saint also lived often in the *sarai.* Many rulers such as Allauddin Khilji banned the selling, consumption and drinking of spirits in *sarais.* Most of the *sarais* in Delhi belong to the Slave Period. As per Shiab-ud-din Alumrai there were 2000 *Khanqahs* and *sarais* in Delhi and its suburbs. Most of these have not survived. Some of the famous *sarais* are mentioned below:

1. *Qutub Sarai:* At the entrance of the tomb of Kamali Jamali, it had a 50 feet deep *baoli* in its courtyard.
2. *Ladha Sarai:* Also called as Baghi-Nazir, it is 300 yards south of the tomb of Jamali. It was built in 1748.
3. *Lado Sarai:* Also in the same vicinity, it was originally a caravan *sarai.*
4. *Sarban Sarai:* It is in Kamlapati Garden, very close to Delhi-Qutub Road.
5. *Daud Sarai:* It is situated about 500 yards south of the tomb of Maulana Qutub Quli Khan in Qutub area.
6. *Kallu Sarai:* Built during Tughlaq period, it is in the vicinity of Sarvpriya Vihar area. Its main feature, a rubble masonry building, is called as Bijay Mandal.
7. *Arab ki Sarai:* It was built in 1560-61 by Hamida Banu Begam, wife of Humayun, as a settlement of 300 Arabs (whom she had brought with her while returning from a pilgrimage to Mecca)

8. *Sheikh Sarai:* It was named after a popular saint Sheikh Allauddin who lived there and had his tomb during his own lifetime.

Some more popular *sarais* of Delhi are *Sarai Shahji* built in Mughal period, *Gur Ki Sarai* on the eastern side of Karnal Road with its mosque of Hyrewali, *Sarai Bangash* near Fatehpuri mosque, *Sarai Topkhana,* the *Darghah Shah Sabi Baksh* with its *musafir khana* on Faiz Bazar road, *Jai Sarai* on southeast of Hauzkhas village, *Katwaria Sarai* in the centre of the village, *Phus ki Sarai, Ghatu Sarai, Nepa Sarai* and the famous *Yusuf Sarai,* etc.

Journeys undertaken by some famous thinkers and philosophers in olden days in India: Fa Hien (Visited India in 402 A.D.), Hieun Tsang (626-643 A.D.), Marco Polo (1273).

These people have also mentioned of shelters for travellers in their accounts on India.

- *Sarais* started developing into inns and western style hotels with the coming of Britishers in important cities like Calcutta and Bombay.
- During this period boats were kept ready at ports. Agents took care of travellers and their luggage. Private carriage would take them to hotel on their arrival at the shore.
- As early as 18th century there were excellent inns (taverns) in India. Some famous inns were: Portuguese Georges, Parsee Georges and Paddy Georges.
- Some famous hotels of that time: Albion Hotel, Victory Hotel, Hope Hall (Rs.6 per day for room and meals).

Records are available showing that Philip Stanhope (1778), a traveller, stayed in a luxurious and excellent tavern in Bombay. David Prince, who visited India, stayed at Mac Farlanes Hotel.

A dinner to commemorate the capture of Shrirangapatnam was served at Maclean's Hotel in 1800 at Bombay. The same remained a resort for many years of Sans Souci Club which entertained Duke of Wellington, Lord Nelson and Sir Arthur Wellesley.

- Pallanjee Pestonjee (1840) started the first luxurious hotel in Bombay. It was famous for its excellent cuisine, beers and wines and its excellent management.

Later he opened another hotel at Fort in Bombay.

- Auckland Hotel (1843) was established in Calcutta.

  Later it was renamed as Great Eastern Hotel in 1858 and later renovated for a sum of Rs. 10 lacs.
- Esplanade Hotel (1871) was built in Calcutta by John Wakson (Britisher), a silk drapery merchant (also believed to be an architect and builder). The hotel had 130 rooms.
- Later, some Swiss and other families also owned hotels in India. One such example was Hotel Fonseca in New Delhi which was later demolished and Hotel Taj Mahal at Mansingh Road was built, there.
- In 1903, JRD Tata constructed the Taj Mahal Hotel in Bombay. It was the first hotel of international standards and repute, built by an Indian for Indians.
- The Government realized the importance of tourism in 1962 when there was a drop in tourist arrivals from 1,39,804 to 1,34,360.
- Incentives were offered by the Department of Tourism (DOT).
- Hotel Corporation and Tourism Corporations were established.
- Ashoka Hotel Ltd. and Vigyan Bhawan were made in 1956 in a record time of one year.
- Later, the Union Ministry of Housing and Welfare constructed 3 hotels: Lodhi Hotel, Hotel Janpath and Ranjit Hotel.
- In 1963 an ad-hoc committee (Jha Committee) was set up by the Government of India to give recommendations about the development of Hotel & Tourism Industry and one of its major recommendations was that 'if adequate hotel accommodation of the right type for the kind of growth of tourism is to be provided, public sector will have to play a major role in this field'.

- Later, the Dewan Chaman Lal Committee was set up by the Government of India (Hotel Standard and Rate Structure Committee) to:

1. Lay down criteria for classification of hotels in view of international standard.
2. Suggest guidelines for the promotion of tourism to India and within India.
3. Suggest improvements on the existing arrangements and availability of sources for the promotion of national and international tourism.
4. Suggest a rate structure keeping in view the existing price structure in hotel industry. Till 1963 hotels were mainly run by private operators and only rest houses and tourist bungalows were run by the Department of Tourism. Hotels at Puri, Aurangabad and Ranchi were traditionally run by the Railways and State governments. Hotels at Brindaban-Mysore were also run by the State government.

- Formation of three corporations and ITDC

In 1964 three corporation were set up by Government of India, viz.

1. India Tourism & Hotel Corporation,
2. India Tourism Corporation Ltd., and
3. India Tourism & Transport Corporation.

On 24th September 1966, the Government of India decided to merge these corporations and issued "India Tourism Corporation Amalgamation Order 1966" and formed a new corporation—India Tourism Development Corporation (ITDC) with an authorized capital of Rs. 5 crores. Soon ITDC took over tourist bungalows at:

(i) Mahabalipuram, Tanjavur, Madurai and Tiruchirapalli (Tamil Nadu)
(ii) Bijapur and Hassan (Karnataka)
(iii) Khajuraho, Sanchi and Mandu (Madhya Pradesh)
(iv) Kullu and Manali (Himachal Pradesh)
(v) Bodhgaya (Bihar)

(vi) Bhubaneshwar (Orissa)

(vii) Kashi Nagar (Uttar Pradesh)

(viii) Ghana (Rajasthan)

Many small and big Indian hotel groups are operating in various parts of India. Some of them are given below. Apart from Indian, some international hotel chains such as Sheraton, Hilton, Ramada, Sofitel, Meridien, Hyatt and Mariott are either operating or planning to operate in India on franchise basis.

It is the hotel division of I.T.C. Ltd. ITC entered into hotel business in 1975 with the opening of Hotel Chola Madras.

The logo represents a traditional Indian welcome in the form of 'Namaste' in an open doorway with the slogan "Nobody gives you India like we do". The motto of Welcome Group is "We enjoy people".

Welcome Group has hotels in various cities in India such as Agra, Delhi, Aurangabad, Jaipur, Goa, Gwalior etc.

Rai Bahadur M.S. Oberoi started his hotel career as a clerk in 1922 at Faletti's Cecil Hotel in Simla. Later Mr. Ernest Clarke sold his share to Mr. M.S. Oberoi, who under the deed of dissolution dated August 14, 1934, became the sole, absolute, and exclusive owner of Clarke's Hotel, Simla and Delhi. Mr. Oberoi later took over the Grand Hotel at Calcutta on lease and by the end of World War II, the Grand Hotel became a byword for good service and elegant comfort in hotels. He established Oberoi Hotel Pvt. Ltd. in 1946 and later, on 26th May 1949, established East India Hotel Ltd. (EIHL) at Calcutta. Many hotels were added to EIHL during the period. Later two very important hotels were added—Oberoi Intercontinental in August 1965 in New Delhi and Oberoi Sheraton in 1973 in Bombay. EIHL is now one of the largest and one of the most reputed hotel chains of India with hotels not only in India but also abroad. Oberoi has a hotel training institute at Delhi and future plans of expansion.

One of the flagship hotels belonging to Lala Ram Parshad who is considered as one of the pioneers of the Hotel Industry in India (now managed by Taj Hotel in Delhi). In 1946, he purchased two hotels in Mussoorie, U.P. and operated one hotel in Bokaro. Lala

Ram Parshad was appointed Technical Director of Hotel Ashok, New Delhi during its construction stage and was the first Asian to be elected as an executive member of International Hotel Association (I.H.A) in 1969. He was amongst the first few hoteliers to realize the importance of trained manpower in hotel industry and was associated with various Hotel Management Institutes and Food Craft Institute in India.

Famous as Clarke's Group of Hotels, it was established on 13th February, 1961. It started with its flagship hotel Clarke Shiraz Agra. Later hotels—Clarke's Awadh, Clarke's Amer, and Clarke's Varanasi at Lucknow, Jaipur and Varanasi, respectively, were added to this chain.

A chain belonging to R.N. Kapoor family with hotels at Mumbai, Hyderabad, Kolkata and Coonoor (in South India). Specialised in Italian cuisine.

Started hotel business in 1912 in Calcutta. Purchased Connamera Hotel in Madras and opened West End in Bangalore, Malabar at Cochin and Trivandrum, Blue Mountains at Kotagiri in 1942 and Savoy in Ooty in 1943. Vegetarian hotels in Madras (Geetha, Ashoka and Ajanta) and Hotel Arakua in Bangalore.

A chain of hotels operating in eastern part of the country with hotels at Darjeeling and Takdah.

A corporation set up in 1971. It started with its first hotel at Bombay in 1974. Later hotels in Delhi, Srinagar, Rajgir etc. were added to this group.

It has hotels at Mumbai and Goa.

The group has tied up with Hyatt chain and has two hotels in Delhi. It plans to have property in Jaipur and Agra.

(Park Hotel): It started with its first hotel Park Calcutta in 1967. Later a large hotel was added in Delhi and Resort hotel at Visakhapatnam was added to the group.

The group has hotels in Delhi, Agra and Mussoorie.

Palace Hotels

1. Maharaja Hari Singh Palace was the first to be converted into Oberoi Hotel.

2. Maharaja of Jaipur converted his palace Ram Bagh to Hotel.
3. Maharaja of Udaipur was third in line (Taj) Lake Palace in Pichola Lake.
4. Later Jodhpur Palace (Oberoi), Jaisalmer Palace and Bikaner Palace were also converted into hotels.
5. Lakshmi Vilas Palace of Jaipur (of Maharaja Bhupal Singh).
6. Lalitha Mahal Palace of Mysore and Halcyon Castle of Travancore Maharaja.
7. Ushakiran Palace of Gwalior.
8. Hotel Jai Mahal Palace, Jal Mahal and Raj Mahal Palace in Jaipur are also converted or being converted to hotels.
9. Chamundi Hill Palace has also been converted to a hotel.
10. Bolghathy Palace near Cochin Port (Residence of former British Resident of Southern States) is also being converted into a hotel.

Many economists have often described "Hotel Business" as unique and different from many other businesses. Hotel is selling both goods and services. It not only provides both tangible and intangible services, but one of its unusual characteristic is also that it is one of the very few places where production and consumption occur simultaneously; for example, ordering and subsequent preparation, services and consumption of food items. Both the products and services are offered on credit transaction. No other business allows the customer an immediate line of credit, for example, the moment he registers, his credit purchase starts with the room and a sequence of financial charges throughout the facilities without immediately paying for them at the "point of purchase". For example, purchase of food in restaurant, drinks in bar, valet services, etc. No other business offers as varied a range of services and products at the same place as hotel business. Customers choose one establishment from another for a variety of reasons. Some such factors are service standards, amenities, products, building location, economy and staff attitude etc. Factors like location and building are of course beyond the control of the hotel but factors such as decor, creation of atmosphere, service standard and attitude etc. can be adapted to suit the customer and hence give him satisfaction. A satisfied customer is one who is not only likely to come back but is also expected to speak good about the hotel to his friends and relatives, etc.

Each hotel must offer lodging, food and protection to their guest and assume a liability for guest property, provide a high standard of hygiene, cleanliness and sanitation and should confirm to the minimum requirements of the state regarding safe hotel construction such as height of the building, municipal by-laws, fire and safety standards, etc. Hotel managers must analyse the wishes and needs of their patrons regarding accommodation, services and facilities and should plan their operations to satisfy these wishes of the guests.

The present day modern concept of the hotel is not just a place to provide accommodation, food and beverage, but is like a city within a city and offering to its guests every possible facility, accommodation, service and convenience, such as rooms, restaurants, bars, cocktail lounges, banqueting facilities, convention and conference facilities, telephones, radio and TV, laundry, valets, cigars, cigarettes, book shops, banking, parking, florists, chemists, gym, beauty parlours, travel agents, business centre, etc. Apart from these a vast shopping arcade providing various items like jewellery, men's wear, ladies' wear, toys, books, news stands and magazine, etc. are also provided. In addition to these, personal services like baby sitting, private detectives, planning of tour itineraries, railway/air booking and accommodation, booking in other hotels may also be provided. Further additional services as given below may also be given:

1. Fruits, flowers, and vegetable garden
2. Club and night club
3. Health club
4. Bank services (foreign exchange)
5. Swimming pool
6. Theatre
7. Hospital
8. Library
9. Service station

10. Post office
11. Poultry farms
12. Car rental and chauffeurs
13. Cinema ticket

All these facilities may occasionally be without additional charges to the guest but generally specifically charged.

Five Star deluxe hotels go all out to provide every conceivable service and amenities to their guests in the hotel and their rooms. Following is a list of all such services which are provided these days:

1. Airport greets and meets.
2. Limousine pick-up and enhanced limousine services and also drop by limousine.
    - Hot and cold towels
    - Cola and mineral water and chocolate service
    - General Managers' welcome address/audio cassette
    - Brochures/Magazines
3. On arrival at the hotel—welcome by name by the Lobby Hostess and escort to the lobby.
4. Express personalized sit down check-in and personalized in-suite check-in and express check-out and late check-out.
5. Tastefully furnished pre-assigned and pre-checked rooms with initialized linen, jacquise, tea/coffee dispenser, electronic safe (Elsafe).
6. Escort to room.
7. Champagne check-in.
8. Round the clock butler service.
    - Food and beverage service
    - Laundry service
    - Mini bar, shoe-shine, ice-bucket service and 24-hour room service
9. International newspaper—Times Fax, round-the-clock international news-scan.

10. Complimentary fruit basket and three tier amenity tray and cheese platter, etc.
11. Complimentary American breakfast.
12. Complimentary tea/coffee hour and also in-room tea/coffee maker.
13. Cocktail hour with hot snacks.
14. Personalized leather folder and stationery, welcome letter and personalized docket and designer toiletries.
15. Valet service—ironing of one or more dress or one or more suit complimentary once during guest stay.
16. Freshen-up service.
17. Usage of the exclusive club or any lounge in the hotel and library.
18. Stay linked amenities.
19. Use of board room.
20. Entry to exclusive health club and fitness centre.
21. Entry to the discotheque.
22. Flight reconfirmation service.
23. AT&T telephone exchange with electronic voice mail.
24. Well-equipped communication centre open round-the-clock.
25. Lounges at international/domestic airport.
26. CCTV/channel music and satellite television.
27. In-house laundry and dry-cleaning facilities.
28. International Subscribers Dialling.
29. Bank safe deposit and 24-hours money changes.
30. Take-away gifts.
31. Bon voyage complimentary at the airport lounge.

Various Departments in a Large Hotel

1. Sales
2. Personnel
3. Laundry
4. Housekeeping

5. Maintenance
6. Credit
7. Computer centre
8. Security
9. Purchases and receiving
10. Main stores
11. Horticulture
12. Accounts
13. Health club
14. Production
    (i) Main kitchen
    (ii) Satellite kitchens
    (iii) Bakery
15. Food and beverage service
    (i) Restaurants
    (ii) Banquets
    (iii) Coffee shop
    (iv) Room service
    (v) Bars
16. Front office
    (i) Reservation
    (ii) Reception
    (iii) Information
    (iv) Cash
    (v) Bell desk
    (vi) Telephone

Some common problems that a hotel faces are as follows:

To determine whether there is demand for a hotel in the area where the site is located, certain very important factors must be considered such as:

(i) determine if the existing tourist capacity is adequate or not,

(ii) find out if the location of the hotel is a positive factor or a negative factor in creating demand,

(iii) find out if it is worthwhile to invest further in increasing the number of rooms over and above the existing number in the area,

(iv) determine if the present guest structure is future-oriented, and above all

(v) determine if the national and international economic situation allows to expand the business or not.

Problem of labour is very important in hotel industry. For successfully developing new hotel projects it is the lack of adequate labour supply which creates problems rather than the problem from labour such as their demands etc. For this the two important points to study are union situation and the labour wage trend.

This is another very important factor and a big problem. Arranging of finances and control of credit line is a very serious problem confronting business today.

The Major Sources of Financing are:

(i) Long term mortgages.

(ii) Loans provided by government, semi-government and/or tourism promotion bodies.

(iii) Loans provided by financial institutions such as banks etc.

Hotel Guest

Hail Guest! We ask not what thou art:

If friend, we greet thee, hand and heart,

If stranger, such no longer be,

If foe, our love shall conquer thee.

—ARTHUR GUITERMAN- Old Welsh Door Verse.

As per Oxford Dictionary, a "Guest is a person who is invited to another person's house, on a visit or to dine together". The guest and the host hold a social relationship where a person is invited and entertained as a social obligation or with a motive. We extend warmth and welcome to our friends, relatives, near and dears in order to impress upon them our hospitality and good nature and make the experience as pleasant as possible. In India there is an old Sanskrit saying *"Atithi Devo Bhava* " meaning the guest is like God and as a person offers his best to God we shall also offer the best to our guest. There are numerous examples of the same in Hindu mythology and folklores.

A hotel customer/client is called a guest because the hotel offers homely and professional service to him, and establishes an immediate relationship with him. Thereafter it ensures satisfaction by providing nothing less than 'A Home Away From Home'. It is like projecting, 'what is an economic relationship as a personal relationship'. Unlike other business 'a guest-hotel transaction even when complete in all respect is futile, if the guest is not satisfied'. The hotel guest is the one who buys rooms, meeting space, food and beverage services and other services and amenities, etc. from the hotel. He is an important person to the hotel and is not just a cold statistics, but a thinking, feeling human being made of flesh and blood and has feeling and emotions like our own. He has certain needs and wants which he would like to fulfil. He is someone who, in his or her own mind, is always right, and is the reason for business, rather than an interruption to our work; a person who brings us his wants. It is our job to handle him profitably for him and for ourselves. He is a valued customer who is willing to pay fair price for a quality product and wants to be neither overcharged nor underserved. The guest is not dependent upon us; on the contrary, we are dependent on him. The guest is not someone to argue with or match wits with, nobody ever won an argument with a guest; even if you win, you and your hotel both loose.

Treat the guest in the hotel as you would treat a guest in your house. Make him feel welcome, and help him feel comfortable.

Hotel guests may be defined as "people who have, who are, or who will be availing the services of hotel, for a particular period in order to satisfy their demand for accommodation, food and beverage or entertainment, for which they are willing and able to pay."

As per the famous writer Dale Carnegie, "A man's name is to him the sweetest and most important sound." This also applies in full for every guest and all hotel employees must remember it and should not leave any opportunity to keep repeating the guest's name. The receptionist should concentrate on the name of the guest when he hears it by listening to the sound. Don't hesitate to ask if you miss the name in the first instance. Associate or link the person's name with his appearance, business or some other interest. Tie his name to his height, hair, mouth, attitude, clothes and shoes, etc. or to any other thing that strikes you. Repeat the guest's name during conversation as many times as possible, but make sure you don't make it very obvious.

Guest relation is an integral part of the hotel. It is a means for the management to reach out to the guest and convey to him the feeling of warmth and welcome.

Initially a guest/customer comes to a hotel for its good name and reputation about service and food, second time he comes to confirm his experiences and then further keeps on coming for its comfortable and emphatic atmosphere and becomes a regular customer, because by now he is pretty confident about the hotel.

As compared to other industries, hotel industry which is a service industry and a part of hospitality industry, requires greater personal touch and courtesy. A hotel guest is a customer and unlike a family or social guest, he pays for his stay, food and beverage consumption at the hotel. Why is he referred to as a guest instead of a customer? The idea behind referring to hotel customer or client as guest is offering homely as well as professional service in order to keep him happy and satisfied and make his experience as memorable as possible. The special treatment of allowing a line of credit for various services and products offered by hotel industry gives a special status to the guest of the hotel. Guest satisfaction is a very relative term. It basically means knowing and understanding guest needs and then providing them at least to that standard which he expects.

Once a visitor or caller is identified as a prospective user of hotel services, he may be studied under different headings such as:

Guests on the Basis of Status: For example, (i) an expected guest, (ii) an in-house guest and (iii) check out guest.

Guests on the Basis of Recognition : Such as, (i) regular guest, (ii) V.I.P., special attention and distinguished guest and (iii) new guests, and

Guests on the Basis of Revenue: For example, (i) paying guests, and (ii) complimentary guests.

Unlike other organizations and industries where the customers are very specific in nature, the customer profile in hotel business varies greatly. For example the facilities and services needed by a sportsman, a honeymoon couple, and a business executive staying at the hotel would be greatly different, and it is always useful to group customers as per their profile.

The guests will usually be on holiday and the objective of their visit will generally be relaxation and enjoyment. They would be looking for friendly, informal and relaxed services to suit their mood and leisure service and facilities such as swimming pool, health club, sports facilities like tennis, golf, water games, etc.

Hotels where the guest does not need to sign a lease and can register for a day or even less. Generally fully equipped business centre, convention centres, conference and meeting rooms, audio and visual equipment etc. are essential. Mostly this group of hotels are situated downtown.

A guest coming to a hotel expects a unique and attractive property with friendly, courteous and competent service. He expects clean and well appointed rooms and public areas as per the standard, safe quality food with personal touch and safety to him and his belongings. He also expects trained, skilled, and caring staff, good entertainment programmes, floor shows, etc. He expects TV, radio, and telephone etc. in the room. He appreciates hassles free and speedy check in and check out. Further, some added frills such as efficient room service, newspaper, wake call, shoe shine, laundry, valet services, car parking and video films etc., are expected by the guest.

The personality of the person coming in contact with the guest is very important. He should have friendly and positive attitude i.e. he should be tolerant, willing to accept the responsibility and should be people oriented. He should be helpful to the guests and should be in the business with his body and spirit. He should have neat appearance. He should be courteous and efficient.

Sometimes the guest may make special requests. Special requests of the guest can be classified into two groups.

Such as roll away beds, banquet table in the guest room, bed boards, additional blankets, pillows, iron and ironing boards, hair driers, hangers, special equipment for handicapped guest.

Such as split folio, wake calls, transportation arrangement, reservation in airlines, hotels and for entertainment shows, cinema and theatre, etc., special newspaper, etc.

Some important factors that the guest keeps in mind while returning back to a hotel are *price, cleanliness, good service, facilities, convenience/location, quiet and private accommodation.*

A hotel guest's significance can be seen from the fact that all activities and innovations in a hotel revolve around one term—*guest satisfaction.* Basically guest needs can be classified as follows:

Related to protection against heat, cold, rain etc. in the form of room and related to his appetite/thirst and special food requirement.

Value for money i.e. is he getting returns worth the value of money spent by him? How much can he afford?

Attending functions and gatherings, to meet others, going out with friends.

Enhancement of self-pride, the need for variety.

This can be usually because of two reasons classified as follows:

Such as unhelpful staff, cramped conditions and lack of choice of product i.e. type of accommodation and other service available for offer to the guest.

Factors such as location, the weather, other customers and transport problems.

Guest satisfaction shall ensure repeat business, increased clientele and maximized revenue for the establishment.

Better known as *Guest Relation* in hotel industry, it undoubtedly cannot be anything but providing hospitality to the guest of the hotel. It can be achieved by using procedures which will improve guest sales factor. It is important in this connection that we understand the basic principle that service is a two-sided coin and we must also understand the marketing concept which involves identification and satisfaction of guest needs.

There are two sides to service:

(i) Operational side, and

(ii) People side.

Most of the hospitality operations do understand the importance of providing basic levels of physical services such as good food (food to be served hot, etc.), clean rooms and standard facilities etc.

But it is the 'people side' where the major shortfall tends to be. For a serious understanding of marketing concept and hence satisfaction to guest it may be said that the service provider (staff) is some kind of an amateur psychologist. Human needs can be arranged according to priorities. Needs like hunger and thirst come first and must be taken care of first, and other needs follow this. Coldness, rudeness or being ignored leaves some powerful human needs—the needs to be accepted, to belong to, feel secure, to have status, to have recognition, and to be wanted—unsatisfied.

Service of hospitality involves creating a feeling of well being and appreciation in the customer. This feeling can be brought in by good physical and operational delivery of service and at the same time good psychological delivery.

It requires understanding of:

(1) customer's need for recognition,

(2) importance of smile,

(3) a positive attitude,

(4) genuineness, and

(5) an understanding of the importance of customer's expectation

It is vital to pay attention to customers and to demonstrate that you are paying attention. Aim at individualizing the customer, for example, by the use of the customer's name.

Smile is contagious like anger. No smile goes waste. No matter how bad you feel, you must keep smiling. Staff must be friendly. Hire right staff with right attitude for your customers.

Make sure your staff has positive attitude. They take their lead from you. Treat your staff in a friendly and fair way. Don't tell your problems to your customers; it does not help in building a happy and successful image of your establishment.

Genuineness can't be preached and taught. It comes from within like positive attitude. Wherever possible address the guest by name. Use self-involvement techniques such as address the guest by name, etc. Genuineness means accepting the guest for what he is without judgment or censor.

It is a very important point because normally a customer dissatisfaction is not related to the actual level of service provided but to the fact that the customer did not get what he expected and perceived.

The above points are very important in providing psychological service and hence maintaining good guest relation.

Often in large hotels there is a position called Guest Relations Officer. He/she is directly under either the Front Office Manager or the General Manager. It is a sales oriented position. His job is to create an image of credibility which will go a long way in building up business, specially repeat client etc. He is also expected to know the likes and dislikes as well as complaints etc. of the guest and to keep a record of these. As a part of the process of maintaining guest relation, the Guest Relations Officers should see that welcome drink and welcome activities such as *pooja, aarti,* and applying of *tika* and garlanding, etc. is done. Photographs of VIPs are to be taken and published in House Magazine. A personal check of the room of expected VIP arrivals should be done by the Guest Relations Officer. Frequent calls to check the comforts of the guest should be made. Complaints and enquiries and feed back are also very important.

Key Terms	
Hospitality market	Guest needs
Chalets	Inns
Taverns	Hostel
Guest satisfaction	Choultry
V.F.M. (Value for Money)	Boatels
Motels	Roatels
Loatels	

The Division : Since the hotel industry comprises of numerous hotels, and they provide numerous services, facilities and goods, the hotel industry lacks a single identity. Although the basic concept of hospitality, food and accommodation are same, yet hotels may have different characteristics and assets and each hotel would like to attempt to cash on its assets and develop its share of the particular market, and gain more and more recognition because of that asset. Placing a hotel into a particular group is not easy because of the diversity of services, facilities and amenities provided or not provided. Most of the hotels don't fit in any specific well-defined category. Nonetheless, several general classifications do exist.

Hotels are classified into several distinct categories to help the prospective guest in identifying the right type of hotel matching his standard and requirement. However, for the sake of convenience, we shall put them under four broad categories as given below.

1. On the basis of size.
2. On the basis of star system.
3. On the basis of ownership.
4. Other categories.

Classification on the basis of size refers to the number of rooms (bed capacity) and should not be confused with the building height, or the area of the property, or the gross sales etc. The term number of rooms refers to the lettable rooms and does not include those rooms which are converted for other use such as for manager, house keeper, accounts etc. and rooms on the ground floor and basement which are generally used for offices, rentals, support services or other operational facilities leased for businesses and associations.

Usually the distribution is :

(i) a hotel of 25 rooms or less is called a *small hotel,*

(ii) one with 26 to 99 rooms is an *average hotel,*

(iii) from 100 to 299 it is called as *above average,* and

(iv) a hotel of more than 300 rooms is classified as a *large hotel.*

Different Parts : This system is one of the most commonly understood, accepted and recognised systems in India. This is also an official system of classification. In this system hotels are classified on the basis of facilities which the hotels have and the services which the hotels provide to the guests. Based on the number of services and facilities and their quality and standards, which may vary from a basic bedroom to a luxury room with modern fittings and equipment, the hotels are awarded stars ranging from one to five star deluxe.

The classification of new and functioning hotels is done by the Ministry of Tourism. The department forms a committee called as Hotels and Restaurants Approval and Classification Committee (HRACC) which is headed by D.G. Tourism/ADG Tourism and comprises of members from hotel industry, Travel Agents Association of India, Department of Tourism and the Principal of Regional Institute of Hotel Management, Catering Technology and Applied Nutrition etc. This is a permanent committee to classify hotels into five categories i.e. from 1 to 5 star and also into a Five Star Deluxe category. The committee inspects once in three years the existing hotels which have been classified to confirm that the hotels are sticking to the standards.

A hotel applies on a prescribed application form to the Director General of Tourism, Transport Bhawan, Parliament Street, New Delhi (in case of 4 star, 5 star and 5 star deluxe category) and to the Regional Director of the concerned Govt. of India tourist office at Delhi/ Mumbai/Kolkata/Chennai, in case of 1, 2 and 3 star category giving basic details such as: 1. Name of the hotel, 2. Name of the promoter's, 3. Address, 4. Details of the site such as area, title, distance of hotel from railway station, distance from airport, distance from main shopping centre, 5. Details of hotel project such as category applied for, number of guest rooms and their area, their type with or without bathroom, details of public areas like lounge, lobby, restaurants, bars, ·shopping arcade, banquet/conference hall, health club, swimming pool and parking etc. 6. Details of air conditioning, 7. Approvals from government bodies such as Municipal or Corporation authorities, MRTP Act, Urban Land Ceiling Act, DGCA and any other concerned local authorities, 8. Proposed capital structure, 9. Want to avail of any or all of the following benefits of Income Tax Act-61 against each of the following provision — Section 80L, Section 80 H-H, Section 32 (i) (ii a), Section 32 (i) (v) and Section 33. The application fee which varies from 1 star to 5 star and 5 star deluxe is also sent along with the application.

The hotel is supposed to fill up a questionnaire containing details of facilities, features, amenities and services and their standards in the form of questions which are divided into three categories—desirable, necessary and essential—and have marks allotted to them for a hotel to be considered for classification. All items marked under essential category must be there in the hotels, two items marked under necessary may be condoned while the items marked under desirable may or may not be there.

On a pre-notified date the HRACC team members visit the hotel personally and inspect the hotel, and finally on the basis of the report of the committee and the marks scored by the hotel, the hotel is either approved or rejected for the applied star category. Approved hotels become eligible for various fiscal reliefs and benefits. The department interacts on behalf of such hotels whenever necessary to ensure that their needs get priority consideration.

To be eligible to apply for classification, a functioning hotel must fulfil the following minimum basic requirements:

(i) The hotel must have at least 10 lettable bedrooms.

(ii) Carpet areas in respect of rooms and areas of bathrooms should by and large adhere to the following limits:

Category of Hotel	Area Standard for Bedroom/ Bathroom
5-Star/5-Star Deluxe Hotels	
Single	180 sq. ft.
Double	200 sq. ft.
Bathrooms	45 sq. ft.
4-Star and 3-Star Hotels	
Single A/C and Single Non A/C	120 sq. ft.
Double A/C and Double Non A/C	140 sq. ft. (Extra area may be provided if twin beds are to be provided)
Bathrooms	36 sq. ft.
2-Star and 1-Star Hotels	
Single A/C and Single Non A/C	100 sq. ft.
Double A/C and Double Non A/C	120 sq. ft. (All rooms should have proper ventilation and ceiling fans)
Bathrooms	30 sq. ft. or subject to local bylaws.

Failure to satisfy the above conditions will disqualify a hotel for consideration.

A classification fee (at the existing rate) is payable by the hotels applying for classification.

The classification fee is payable by means of a demand draft drawn in favour of the Pay and Accounts Officer, Department of Tourism, New Delhi. For reclassification, fee will be 50% of the fee payable at first time.

Application form for the particular star category applied for can be had from the Member Secretary, H.R.A.C.C. Department of Tourism, Government of India, 'Transport Bhawan', New Delhi.

The powers to classify hotels in 1 and 2 star categories have been delegated to the respective State Governments/Union Territories w.e.f. 1.1.1986. A hotel applying for 1 or 2 star category is, therefore. required to approach the concerned State Government/ Union Territory.

The general features, facilities and services expected of hotels in the different star categories, are broadly described below:

A hotel which applies for 5 star deluxe category has basically the same number of features as a five star hotel but is superior in quality of service, amenities and facilities etc. to a five star hotel's requirement.

Five Star Hotels : The facade, architectural features and general construction of the hotel building should have the distinctive qualities of a luxury hotel of this category. The locality including the immediate approach and environs should be of highest standards and of international standard and should be suitable for a luxury hotel of this category. There should be adequate parking space for cars. The hotel should have at least 25 lettable bedrooms, all with attached bathrooms with long baths or the most modern shower chambers. All public rooms and private rooms should be fully air-conditioned and should be well equipped with superior quality carpets, curtains, luxurious furniture of high standards, fittings, etc. in good taste. It would be advisable to employ the services of professionally qualified and experienced interior designers of repute for this purpose. There should be an adequate number of efficient lifts in buildings of more than two storeys (including the ground floor) with 24 hours service. There should be a well-appointed lobby and ladies' and gentlemen's cloakrooms equipped with fittings and furniture of the highest standard, adequate parking space and swimming pool.

There should be a reception, cash and information counter attended by highly qualified, trained and experienced personnel and conference facilities in the form of one each or more of the conference rooms, banquet halls and private dining rooms. There should be a shopping arcade and bookstall, beauty parlour, barber shop, recognized travel agency, money change and safe deposit facilities, left luggage room, florist and a shop for toilet requisites and medicines on the premises. There should be a telephone in each room and telephone for the use of guests and visitors and provision for a radio or relayed music in each room. There should be a well-equipped, well-furnished and well-maintained dining room/

restaurant on the premises and wherever permissible by law, there should be an elegant, well-equipped bar/ permit room. The pantry and cold storage should be professionally designed to ensure efficiency of operation and should be well equipped. There should be dancing facility and orchestra in dining hall.

The hotel should offer both international and Indian cuisine and the food and beverage service should be of the highest standard. There should be professionally qualified, highly trained, experienced, efficient and courteous staff in smart, clean uniforms, and the staff coming in contact with guests should understand English. The supervisory and senior staff should possess good knowledge of English and staff knowing at least one continental language should be rotated on duty at all times. There should be 24 hours service for reception, information and telephones. There should be provision for reliable laundry and dry cleaning service, 24 hours housekeeping at the hotel should be of the highest possible standard and there should be a plentiful supply of linen, blankets, towels etc. which should be of the highest quality available. Each bedroom should be provided with good vacuum jug/thermos flask with ice cold, boiled drinking water except where centrally chilled purified drinking water is provided. There should be a special restaurant/dining room where facilities for dancing are also available.

Questionnaire For 5-star Category Hotel

Form 5-Star

Government of India
Ministry of Tourism, Department of Tourism
Hotel and Restaurant Approval and Classification Committee (H.R.A.C.C.) Questionnaire for 5-Star Category Hotel

Name of the Hotel: ....

....

Questionnaire to be answered by hotels applying for 5-star category:

PART-I

Name and address of the Hotel:..

....

In order to be assessed for 5-star category, a hotel should have the following basic features and the absence of any one of these will disqualify it from consideration for the 5-star category:

1. The hotel should have at least 25 lettable bedrooms. Please state the number of guest rooms:
   (a) Single
   (b) Double
   (c) Suites Total

   Note: Please furnish a list showing carpet area of each bedroom and area of bathroom.

2. The locality including the immediate approach and environs should be suitable for a hotel of this category.

   Please indicate:
   (a) Distance from airport
   (b) Distance from railway station
   (c) Distance from main shopping areas
   (d) Please describe briefly the neighbourhood in which your hotel is located.

3. All public rooms and private rooms should be well appointed and fully air conditioned (except in hill stations where there should be heating arrangements).Please indicate:
   (a) Are all your public and private rooms air-conditioned?
   (b) Is your hotel centrally air-conditioned? If so, please give the tonnage and also the total floor area/cubic space.

4. All rooms must have well appointed attached bathroom with long baths or should be equipped with most modern shower chambers. (In the case of cabana rooms, adequate shower facilities will be acceptable).
   (a) Do all your rooms have attached bathrooms? If so, how many have long baths?
   (b) How many are fitted with most modern shower chambers?

5. The kitchen, pantry and cold storage should be professionally designed to ensure efficiency of operation and should be well equipped. Please state who designed your kitchen, pantry and cold storage and when?

6. There should be ladies' and gentlemen's cloakrooms and the cloakrooms should be spotlessly clean and equipped with furniture and fittings of the highest standard available befitting a luxury hotel of this category.

   Do you have ladies' and gentlemen's cloakrooms attached to the public area? If so, how many?

PART-II

Maximum Marks *Marks awarded by the Committee*

1. Construction **10N**

The architectural features and general construction of the building should have the distinctive qualities of a luxury hotel of this category.

2. Maintenance **20N**

Maintenance of all sections of the hotel (i.e. building, walls, gardens, surroundings, etc.) should be of the highest standard.

3. Parking **5D**

There should be adequate parking space for car. Please state:

(a) How many cars can be parked in the parking space owned by your hotel?

(b) How many extra cars can be locally parked in the capacity of your hotel?

(c) How many cars can be parked by the guests/visitors of the hotel when such space is most required?

4. Swimming Pool **10N**

There should be well designed and properly equipped swimming pool (except in hill stations).

(a) Does your swimming pool have its own system for filtration, chlorination and changing of water?

(b) How often is the water changed?

(c) What arrangements does your hotel have for heating the pool in the winter?

5. Bathrooms **30E**

All bathrooms should be modern in design and should be equipped with fittings of the highest quality available befitting a luxury hotel of this category, with 24 hours service of hot and cold running water. The floors and walls should be covered with impervious material of elegant design and high quality workmanship. It is desirable that sockets for electric shaver should be provided.

(a) Do the bathrooms have sockets for electric shavers?

(b) Do the bathrooms have running hot and cold water for 24 hours?

6. Reception **15N**

There should be a reception, cash and information counter, attended by highly qualified, trained and experienced personnel.

Please state in detail the qualification, training and experience of the personnel employed at reception, cash and information counters. (Separate sheets provided at the end of the questionnaire may be used for answering this question).

7. Lobby **10N**

There should be a well-appointed lobby.

Please state the area of the lobby.

8. Conference Facilities **10N**

There should be one each or more of conference rooms/ banquet halls and private dinning rooms.

Please give the number of conference rooms/banquet halls and private dining rooms with area of each.

9. Shopping Facilities **20N**

There should be bookstall, left luggage rooms, barber shop, recognized travel agency, beauty parlour, money changing and safe deposit facilities.

Note:

1. There should be a florist in a hotel of 100 rooms and above.
2. A store selling toilet requisites and medicines should be available in the premise.

(a) Is there a bookstall in your hotel? Yes/No

(b) Is there a left luggage room in your hotel? Yes/No

(c) Is there a barber shop in your hotel? Yes/No

(d) Is there a recognized travel agency in your hotel? Yes/No

(e) Is there a beauty parlour in your hotel? Yes/No

(f) Are there money changing facilities in your hotel? Yes/No

(g) Do you have safe deposit facilities for guests? Yes/No

(h) Is there a florist in your hotel? Yes/No

(i) Is there a store selling toilet requisites and medicines in your hotel? Yes/No

10. Lifts **10N**

There should be an adequate number of efficient lifts in buildings of more than two storeys including the ground floor, with 24 hours service.

(a) How many floors are there in the building?

(b) How many lifts are there in the building?

(c) Please state their speed and capacity.

(d) Are these available 24 hours?

11. Furnishing of Bedrooms **25E**

All guest rooms should be comfortable and spacious and well furnished with good quality, properly hung curtains, carpets etc. in good taste.

Note: New hotels are advised to employ the services of professionally qualified and experienced interior designers of repute in the designing and decoration of bedrooms.

12. Lighting **10N**

Lighting arrangements and fixtures in the rooms/bathrooms/ public rooms/corridors etc. should be so designed as to ensure aesthetic as well as functional excellence.

13. Telephones **10N**

There should a telephone in each room and telephone for the use of guests and visitors.

(a) Is there a telephone in each room?

(b) Is/are there a telephone(s) separately for the use of guests and visitors?

(c) How many telephone lines does your hotel have on the switchboard?

(d) What is the maximum number of operators on duty and for how many hours? Please use separate sheet provided at the end of the questionnaire for giving the educational background and training of the telephone operators, also stating their pay scales with allowances.

14. Radios **5D**

There should be provision for radio or relayed music in each room.

(a) Is there a radio in each room?

(b) Is there relayed music? If so, how many channels?

15. Vacuum Jugs/Flasks **5N**

There should be a vacuum jug or thermos flask with ice-cold boiled drinking water in each bedroom except where centrally chilled purified drinking water is provided.

16. Dining Room/Restaurant **15E**

There should be well-equipped, well-furnished and well-maintained dining room/ restaurant.

(a) How many restaurants are there in the hotel?

(b) Please give seating capacity of each.

17. Carpeting **15D**

All public and private rooms should have superior quality carpets/rags, which should be well kept at all times. If the floors are not completely covered, quality of the following will be assessed.

(a) Are all public and private rooms carpeted?

(b) Please state the areas which are not carpeted.

18. Linen/Blankets/Towels etc. **10N**

There should be a plentiful supply of all linen/blankets/towels etc. which should be of the highest quality available and should be spotlessly clean. Bed linen and towels should be changed every day.

19. Crockery **10E**

Crockery, cutlery and glassware should be of the best quality available.

Note: No piece of crockery in use should be chipped, cracked or crazed. The silverware should be kept well-plated and polished at all times.

20. Bar **10N**

Wherever admissible by law, there should be elegant, well-equipped bar/permit room with an atmosphere of comfort and luxury.

21. Entertainment **10D**

There should be a special restaurant/dining room where facilities for dancing and provision of an orchestra are available. Hotels of this category should provide evidence that they have made a serious attempt to present specially choreographed Indian entertainment.

22. Cuisine **30N**

The hotel should offer both international and Indian cuisine. (The preparation, proper seasoning of dishes and presentation to customers will be assessed). What are the various types of cuisine offered by your hotel?

23. Food and Beverage Service

(a) Restaurant Service **25N**

While assessing this item, the organization of the dining room/ restaurant, the waiters' knowledge of the menus whether in French or English, the correct laying of tables, the variety and appearance of buffet services and the methods used to keep hot dishes at the right temperature will be assessed.

(b) Room Service **20N**

The methods used to ensure speedy service and hot meals will be assessed.

(c) Beverage Service **15N**

The provision and service of alcoholic and non-alcoholic beverages including methods used to service hot and cold beverages at the correct temperature will be assessed.

24. Hygiene **20E**

The kitchen, pantry and cold storage should be clean and organized for orderliness and efficiency, scientific and hygienic methods should be used in working and for the washing of glass, crockery, cutlery etc.

(a) Is there a dishwashing machine in your hotel? If so, what is its capacity?

(b) What steps are taken to keep the place safe from all types of pests?

25. Other Services **10E**

(a) 24 hours' service should be provided for reception, information and telephones.

(b) There should be provision for reliable laundry and dry cleaning service.

(c) Does your hotel have its own dry cleaning and laundry?

(d) Does the hotel accept responsibility of the damage done in washing, dry cleaning or pressing?

26. Staff

There should be professionally qualified, highly trained, experienced, efficient and courteous staff. The overall component of trained staff will be assessed and marks given accordingly with a deduction in marks if the supervision is done by untrained staff.

(a) Manager **10N**

(b) Executive staff **10N**

(c) Other staff **20N**

(d) The staff should be in smart and clean uniforms. 10N

(e) The staff coming into contact with guests should understand English and supervisory and senior staff should possess good knowledge of English. At least one member of the senior staff knowing at least one of the continental languages should be on duty at all times.

Note: In future classifications, knowledge of foreign language by some of the staff will be essential.

Please use separate sheets, provided at the end of the questionnaire for giving bio-data of directors directly concerned with the operation of the hotel, general manager, departmental manager, executive and supervisory staff including housekeeping, cooking and maintenance. The bio-data should include name, age, professional qualifications, on-the-job training and its duration and experience giving in detail the positions held and the duration of each and telephones.

27. Housekeeping **10N**

Housekeeping should be of the nicest possible standard.

28. Fire

I hereby solemnly declare that the information given above is correct to the best of my knowledge and belief. In the event of any of my statements found to be untrue, I fully understand that my application for approval/classification is liable to be rejected.

Signature of the Proprietor/
Managing Director/
General Manager
authorized to sign on behalf of the hotel

The Committee's Final Assessment:

Four Star Hotels : The facade, architectural features and general construction of the building should be distinctive and the locality including the immediate approach and the environs should be suitable for a hotel of this category. There should be adequate parking facilities for cars. The hotel should have at least 25 lettable bedrooms, all with attached bathrooms. At least 50% of the bathrooms must have long baths or the most modern shower chambers, with 24 hours service of hot and cold running water. All public rooms and private rooms should be fully air-conditioned and should be well furnished with carpets, curtains, furniture, fittings etc. in good taste. It would be advisable to employ the services of professionally qualified and experienced interior designers of repute for this purpose. There should be an adequate number of efficient lifts in buildings of more than two storeys (including the ground floor). There should be a well-appointed lobby and ladies' and gentlemen's cloakrooms equipped with fittings of standard befitting a hotel of this category.

There should be a reception, cash and information counter attended by trained and experienced personnel. There should be a bookstall, recognized travel agency, money changing and safe deposit facilities and a left luggage room on the premises. There should be a telephone in each room and telephone for the use of guests and visitors and provision of a radio or relayed music in each room. There should be a well-equipped, well-furnished and well-maintained dining room/restaurant on the premises and wherever permissible by law, there should be an elegant, well-equipped bar/permit room. The kitchen, pantry, cold storage should be professionally designed to ensure efficiency of operation and should be well equipped.

The hotel should offer both international and Indian cuisine and food and beverage service should be of the highest standards. There should be professionally qualified, highly trained, experienced and efficient and courteous staff in smart, clean uniform and the staff coming into contact with the guests should possess good knowledge of English. It will be desirable for some of the staff to possess knowledge of foreign language and staff knowing at least one continental language should be rotated on duty at all times. There should be 24 hours service for reception, information and telephones. There should be provision of reliable laundry and dry cleaning service. Housekeeping at the hotel should be a plentiful supply of linen, blankets, towels etc. which should be of the highest quality available. Similarly, the cutlery and glassware should be of the highest quality available. Each bedroom should be provided with vacuum jug/flask with ice cold, boiled drinking water. There should be a special restaurant/ dining room where facilities for dancing, orchestra are provided.

Three Star Hotels : The architectural features and general construction of the building should be of a very good standard and the locality, including the immediate approach and environs should be suitable for a very good hotel and there should be adequate parking facilities for cars. The hotel should have at least 20 lettable bedrooms, all with attached bathrooms with bathtubs and/or showers and should be modern in design and equipped with fittings of a good standard, with hot and cold running water. At least 50 per cent of the rooms should be air-conditioned and the furniture and furnishings such as carpets, curtains, etc. should be of a very good standard and design. There should be adequate number of lifts in buildings with more than two storeys (including the ground floor). There should be a well-appointed lounge and separate ladies' and gentlemen's cloakrooms equipped with fittings of a good standard.

There should be a reception and information counter attended by qualified and experienced staff, and a bookstall, recognized travel agency, money changing and safe deposit facilities on the premises. There should be a telephone in each room (except in seasonal hotels where there should be a call bell in each room and a telephone on each floor for the use of hotel guests) and a telephone for the use of guests and visitors to the hotel. There should be a well-equipped and well-maintained air-conditioned dining room/ restaurant and wherever permissible by law, there should be a bar/permit room. The kitchen, pantry and cold storage should be clean and organized for orderliness and efficiency.

The hotel should offer good quality cuisine both Indian as well as continental, and the food and beverage service should be of good standard. There should be qualified, trained, experienced, efficient and courteous staff in smart and clean uniforms and the supervisory staff coming in contact with the guests should understand English. The senior staff should possess good knowledge of English. There should be provision for laundry and dry cleaning service. Housekeeping at the hotel should be of very good standard and there should be adequate supply of the blankets, towels, etc. of good quality. Similarly, cutlery, crockery, glassware should be of good quality. Each bedroom should be provided with vacuum jug/ thermos flask with cold, boiled drinking water. The hotel should provide orchestra and hall room facilities and should attempt to present specially choreographed Indian dance.

Two Star Hotels : The building should be well constructed and the locality and environs including the approach should be suitable for a good hotel. The hotel should have at least 10 lettable bed rooms of which at least 75% should have attached bathrooms with showers and a bath room for every four of the remaining rooms and should be with modern sanitation and running cold water with adequate supply of hot water, soap and toilet papers. At least 25% of the rooms should be air-conditioned (where necessary there should be heating arrangements in all the rooms) and all rooms must be properly ventilated, clean and comfortable with all the necessary items of furniture. There should be a well-furnished lounge.

There should be a reception counter with a telephone. There should be a telephone or call bell in each room and there should be a telephone on each floor unless each room has a separate telephone. There should be a well maintained and well equipped dining room/ restaurant serving good, clean, wholesome food and a clean, hygienic and well-equipped kitchen and pantry.

There should be experienced, courteous and efficient staff in smart and clean uniforms. The supervisory staff coming in contact with guests should understand English. There should be provision for laundry and dry cleaning services. Housekeeping at the hotel should be of a good standard and clean and good quality.

One Star Hotels : The general construction of the building should be good and locality and environs including immediate approach should be suitable. The hotel should have at least 10 lettable bedrooms of which at least 25% should have attached bathrooms. Bathrooms should have western style W.C. All bathrooms should have modern sanitation and running cold water with adequate supply of hot water, soap and toilet paper. The rooms should be properly ventilated and should have clean and comfortable bed and furniture.

There should be a reception counter with a telephone and a telephone for the use of guests and visitors. There should be a clean and moderately well equipped dining room/restaurant serving clean, wholesome food, and there should be a clean, well equipped kitchen and pantry.

There should be experienced, courteous and efficient staff in smart and clean uniforms and the senior staff coming in contact with guests should possess working knowledge of English. Housekeeping at the hotel should be of a good standard and clean and good quality linen, blankets, towels etc. should be supplied. Similarly crockery, cutlery and glassware should be of good quality.

The Department of Tourism has introduced a new category of 'Heritage Hotels' in Rajasthan, which is proposed to be extended to other States in due course. It covers running hotels in palaces/castles/forts/havelies/residences of any size.

The guidelines for this additional new category in Rajasthan and application form for this particular star category (applied for Heritage Hotel category in Rajasthan) can be had from the Member Secretary, HRACC, Department of Tourism, Government of India.

All hotels approved by the Department of Tourism are required to furnish the following information.

1. The hotel will furnish documents relating to its legal status i.e.
    (a) If the company is incorporated under the Companies Act, a copy of its Memorandum and Articles of Association.
    (b) If it is a partnership firm a copy of the partnership deed and the certificate of registration under the partnership Act.
    (c) If it is a proprietary concern, name and address of the proprietor etc.

2. The hotel will submit the following information to the Director General, Department of Tourism so as to reach on or before 31st May each year for the preceding financial years:

   (a) A bank certificate in regard to foreign exchange deposited by the hotel.

   (b) Total bed capacity offered by the hotel as under:

      (i) Single rooms:

      (ii) Double rooms:

      (iii) Suites:

   (c) Number of rooms occupied on a permanent/semi-permanent basis by residents/staff/ offices, etc.

   (d) A specimen copy of the current tariff card.

   (e) List of the names of the following officers with their designation, experience, etc. (department wise).

      (i) Senior executives

      (ii) Junior executives

      (iii) Other staff

   (f) Total number of persons employed, indicating separately the number of Indian and foreign staff.

   (g) Annual report of the hotel and a statement showing the audited balance sheet and profit and loss account within 4 months of the close of the financial year.

   (h) Statistical returns in regard to the number of guests, rooms, occupancy, income and employment on regular basis as prescribed by the Department of Tourism from time to time. Release of exchange, issue of import licences, grant of approval for fiscal benefits including income-tax relief etc. will be cleared only if the concerned hotel has submitted updated statistical returns.

3. The Regional Director/Director/Manager of the Government of India tourism offices of the region and the Director General, Department of Tourism should be kept informed

from time to time of facilities introduced or withdrawn and of any additions or alterations made in regard to the bed capacity of the hotels.

4. The hotel tariff should be fixed in consultation with the Department of Tourism. Prior approval of the Department of Tourism should be obtained for any revision of hotel rates. The hotel tariff should be prominently displayed in each room. This card shall also indicate sales tax, service charges, etc.

5. Normally, no rooms will be let out for purposes other than residential. However, with the prior permission of the Department of Tourism not more than 10 percent of the rooms in a hotel can be let out to any person or company for residential or commercial purposes.

6. Any licence and/or approvals required from the local administration/police and or other concerned authorities for the construction/operation of the hotel should be obtained directly by the promoters from the concerned authorities. The approval by the Department will not in any way substitute for them. The Department's approval will be deemed to have been withdrawn in case of violation of this condition when brought to its notice.

7. In the event of the promoters making any changes in the plans of the project as submitted earlier, the approval of the Department will have to be applied for afresh.

8. In case the hotel is required to provide guides for tourists, only approved guides of the Department of Tourism should be employed.

9. The hotel should at all times adhere to the high standards of maintenance and services for which it has been recognized and in all dealings with its guests observe business practices worthy of an establishment of repute.

10. Officers of the Department of Tourism or any other officer deputed by the Department to inspect the hotel premises from time to time will be allowed free access with or without prior notice.

11. As a project which has been approved from the point of view of its suitability for foreign tourists, the promoters will be entitled to grant of loan from Central/State financial institutions and priority in the procurement of building material, telephone and telex connections etc. However, this approval should not in any way be construed as an assurance for the grant of these facilities since this would fall within the jurisdiction of the concerned authorities.

Form of Acceptance of Regulatory Conditions

To,

The Director General	The Regional Director
Department of Tourism	Govt. of India Tourist Office
Transport Bhavan	....
1, Parliament Street	....
New Delhi-110001	....

Subject: Acceptance of regulatory conditions

Dear Sir,

I have received a copy of the regulatory conditions prescribed by the Department of Tourism for hotels placed on its approved list, and wish to confirm that I have read and understood the same and hereby agree to abide by the same and such other conditions as may be laid down from time to time by the Department of Tourism for approved hotels.

Yours faithfully,
(Name in Block Letters)
Managing Director Partner/
Proprietor Name of Hotel.

Another way to classify hotels is to examine the ownership through which a hotel can be classed. The classification is as follows:

These hotels are on ownership basis and do not have any affiliation or contract through any other property. And also they do not have any tie up with any other hotels with regards to policy, procedures and financial obligations. The advantage in this type of hotel is that they need not maintain a particular image and they are not bound to maintain any set targets, but can independently adopt quickly to the changing trends.

Another type of chain organization which operate properties owned by individuals or partners are management contract hotels. The contract is entered between the owner and the operator and usually as per the contract

- owner retains the legal and financial responsibilities.
- operator pays for the operating expenses and recovers from the owner.
- owner is responsible for paying taxes, insurance and debts.

There are many single owned hotels, yet more and more hotels and motels are now getting affiliated to each other. This gives them the advantage of a large central organization providing reservation system, management aids, financial strength, expertise, manpower specialities, merchandises and promotional help.

Affiliation

(i) Two or more operations belonging to some organizations; for example, Holiday Inns, Ramada, Sheraton Corp., Trusthouse Forte, Hilton Corp., Howard Johnson, Balkantourist, Day Inns, Travel Lodge, Intercontinental Hotels, Hyatt, Marriott Corp, etc. Within one chain the type of affiliation may vary.

(ii) A "Referral Chain" is made up of independently owned and operated hotel and motel and provides shared advertisement, joint reservation system and standardized quality. Virtually no shared managements or financial functions.

(iii) Another chain operation is "Multi-Unit Company" usually with a head office and several operations across the country and abroad.

Franchise is a system in which the franchise owner grants another the right or privilege to merchandise a product or service for a specified return.

It is an agreement under which the owner operates as a member of the chain, utilizing the brand image, name, goodwill and obtaining for a certain fee some services of marketing and operating nature support from resources of a large organization, advertising, sales promotion, technical and financial help etc. Franchise can be described as the selling by the franchiser of the right to market a proven product. Hence major franchisers in hotel and motel business first established the quality of their product and their expertise in the field by operating company owned properties and only after demonstrating the success of their properties were they able to make their franchises marketable packages. Banks and lending institutions look with favour on the better known franchises, and are in fact reluctant to make time to potential investors, unless an affiliation with a referral organization has been established.

The most successful franchiser in the hotel industry is Holiday Inns. Other successful organizations in the field of franchise are Hilton, Marriott, Howard Johnson, Ramada Inns, etc.

Franchising must be looked at as a two-way benefit scheme. Franchiser provides certain services, and conveys certain rights to the franchisee and the franchisee has in turn certain obligations to the franchiser. For uniformity franchised units are generally standardized. Constituted to a specific standard of furniture and decor specification, fitting, fixture and equipment specification. Site selection and feasibility and appointment of architect.

Franchiser provide services in 3 general categories:

(i) Methods and Systems,

(ii) Technical Assistance,

(iii) Marketing Methods.

Methods and Systems

(a) Proven systems and established operating procedures of a franchiser are provided to franchisee (operating manuals are given).

(b) Training programmes and sessions conducted by the franchiser to the employees of franchisee.

Franchiser provides various technical assistance in various forms such as assistance during development and construction phases, study of potential sites and its selection in obtaining finances by introducing the financers to the franchiser, making of capital budget, feasibility studies, architectural services, purchasing services (crockery, cutlery, furniture, equipment, linen, glass ware, and consumables etc.) These may be provided for a fee (which may be consolidated or separate for each service).

Marketing techniques, name of the franchiser and its goodwill, logo, signs etc., reservation system marketing, advertisement programmes benefits (joint advertisement campaign) with franchiser, marketing packages, regional sales offices at strategic points.

Obligations of Franchisee : (i) *Definitive standard* (which define physical characteristics), for example, size of room, size of beds, type and number of furniture, T.V. etc. and also standard of swimming pool, F&B outlets, parking etc. (ii) *Operational quality standard* such as cleanliness, behaviour and attitude of staff, quality of service, tariff, frequency of changing of linen etc.

The franchisee is required to maintain both the above types of standards as per the franchiser's requirement.

Franchise Costs and Fees : (i) Payment of an initial fee which is non-refundable in the event of the termination of agreement due to the action or as a result of violation by franchisee. It is based on number of rooms. (ii) In addition to the initial fee a monthly fee is also payable to franchiser. (iii) Royalty based on room sales, advertising fees, reservation fees, training fees etc.

Methods of Computing

(i) Fixed monthly fee.

(ii) Fixed monthly fee plus an amount per reservation originating from reservation system.

(iii) Percentage of room sales.

(iv) Percentage of total sale.

(v) Fixed Rupee amount per available room.

(vi) Fixed Rupee amount per occupied room.

A combination of two or more of these is also possible.

Franchiser rent on a monthly basis the principal sign, identifying the hotel as a member of the chain rather than selling it outright.

Some Common Requirements for Franchise Membership

- Minimum number of rooms required
- Architectural design in conformation to hotel owner's requirement
- Scrutinization of location
- Certain services must be provided
- Centralized training programmes for management
- Highest calibre establishment in its category
- Certain standards regarding maintenance, operations, staffing and services.

Some Benefits of Franchise System

- Feasibility study
- Opening assistance
- OJT (on the job training) for staff
- Accounting services
- Advertising
- Central purchasing
- CRS benefits
- Financial assistance
- Discount on services and supplies
- Newsletters and brochures

Other Categories

1. On the basis of clientele: Hotels for aristocrats, sportsmen, doctors etc.
2. On the basis of location: Airport hotels, downtown hotels, suburban hotels, hotels situated on highways, motels, motor hotels and motor lodges, hotels on hill stations etc., hotels on boat—boatels and floatels, etc.
3. On the basis of length of stay: Transit hotels, residential and semi-residential hotels, etc.

4. In Europe star classification by AA (Automobile Association) is often regarded as an accepted mark of quality like in India and stars five to one are awarded.

AA Rosette are also awarded in certain cases which depend upon specially recommended food. For example:

Food standard higher than expected of the hotels of their standard. *Double Rosette:* Much higher food standard than expected of the hotels of that standard. *Three Rosette:* Outstanding standard food than expected of the hotels of that standard.

5. According to Guide Michelin symbols as follows are used—

Best hotels 2nd 3rd 4th 5th

XXXXX XXXX XXX XX X

6. In some of the European countries hotels are classified according to the standard as *deluxe, first class, second class, third class* and *fourth class* also. Another way of categorization in U.K. is as *deluxe* for *best, first class* for second grade, *middle class* for third grade and *moderate class* for fourth and fifth grade hotels.

Residential hotels are also called as apartment hotels or apartment house. Room in a residential hotel are sold on a monthly or yearly basis. Rooms may be furnished or unfurnished, single or *en suite.* Almost all residential hotels operate a restaurant, offer telephone service, laundry and valet service. Advance rents are usually collected while other charges are billed weekly. These type of hotels normally operate on European plan. Recent developments in this area include cooperative hotels and condominiums in which the tenants own the apartment and pay the management a fee for maintenance. When the rooms are not occupied by the owner the management often has the right to rent them on temporary basis, so that the hotel will contain both residential and transient guests. They are also called as *'en pension'*. Such establishments are very popular in U.S. and Europe. Long staying guests generally stay from months to year and rent may be paid per week or per month. Facilities are less then commercial hotels.

These hotels provide accommodation to guests on weekly or monthly basis like residential hotels as well as on per day basis like transient hotels. Reduced rates are provided to long staying guests. Transient guests who want to take the advantage of reduced rates for longer stay also come to such establishments.

Hotel guests who fall under the category of transient guests are those who are *en route* guests i.e. who are in the process of moving from one destination to another and stop at the hotel for a short period of time as against a terminal guest who has reached his final destination. Hence hotels, which cater to a transient/transit guest are called transient hotels. They find their origin in olden days inns. Examples of transient hotels are motels, motor hotels, airport hotels etc. The rates of rooms are fixed on *"per diem "* basis. In large cities they operate on European plan generally while in small towns they may operate on American plan. The olden days establishments such as theatrical hotels popular in rural areas are also included under this heading. Transient hotels such as airport hotels attract its clientele from layover passengers and crew members of the airlines. Such hotels are situated generally near port of entry i.e. airport or seaport, or international bus terminal etc. Generally the length of stay is short i.e. few hours to few days.

10. Resort Hotels

Resort hotels are located at resort places such as islands, exotic locations, hill stations, beaches and health resorts and spas i.e. summer resorts, winter sports resorts and all season resorts etc. with breathtaking beauty. People go to these places for relaxation, to enjoy themselves, and to get away from the hectic city or for health reasons away from hectic city life or to pursue a specific interest/activity. Generally a guest stay is long such as a week or more and normally holiday-makers, sportsmen and patients who have been advised by doctors etc. go to the resort hotels. In resort hotels, such as hill resort hotels, business is dependent on season and they have off season and full season tariff. Resort hotels have homely and informal atmosphere. No dress code is required; more social contact with guests, lot of entertainment items such as beauty contest, floor shows, cabarets, fancy dress parties and stage shows etc. are popular. In addition recreational facilities like table tennis, badminton, golf, water games etc. can be there. Growth of resort hotels in U.S. took place due to vast highway construction programmes, as more people started travelling by cars. Many resort properties are at Florida, California, Arizona, Michigan, Wisconsin and Carolina etc. Resort hotels are not very popular in India because of various causes, the main reason being highways are not very well developed in India. Fuel for cars is very costly, automobile industry is not as developed as in Europe and America and, most important, people are not so rich and don't have spare and leisure time to enjoy.

Resort hotels have facilities like

(i) Extensive entertainment program

(ii) Tennis court, golf course with trainer

(iii) Saddled horses with trainer

(iv) Car parking and garaging and service facilities

(v) Mini golf course, squash, billiards, etc.

Commercial hotels are situated in the heart of the city i.e. downtown busy commercial areas and urban areas. Mainly businessmen and commercial executives patronize these hotels. Generally duration of stay is a few days only and weekend business is slack. Best possible facilities of high standard are provided in commercial hotels. These days, business centre in a commercial hotel is a must. They must have services like facilities to meet the basic business demands, swimming pool, speciality restaurant, bar, disco, 24 hours room service, health club etc. Commercial hotels are sometimes also called *downtown hotels.*

Suburban hotels are situated in suburbs, with quiet surroundings. They have moderate to low tariff and are generally patronized by budget guests.

Hotels of this category are not popular these days. Such hotels cater to the needs of retired persons. They take care of their meals and lodging. They also offer some mild recreational activities to the senior citizens. Normally all the services are offered as inclusive package rate to the retired persons. Nowadays such establishments are called "Old Homes" and "Sandhya Houses" in India.

If we kill the environment we kill ourselves. Environment has always been a touchy subject vis-a-vis the hospitality industry. The spread of unplanned tourism and its allied evils hardly show any regard for the pristine beauty of the places identified for development and on grand plans. As a result, many rare flora and fauna that live on the thin red line of extinction are lost for ever as the sacrificial pigs of progress. Tourist activities are claimed to uproot the locals from their habitats, robbing them of their livelihood, eroding the quality of their life, disrupting their life-style, corrupting their value system, impinging on their socio-cultural ethos, polluting their soil, water and air and depleting natural resources and wreaking havoc on the region's flora and fauna.

This type of hotels are located on the surface of water such as sea, lake etc. Such hotels provide exclusive and exotic atmosphere. All the facilities of a first class hotel are there in this category of hotels. In many countries old luxury ships have been converted in to floating hotels. In India in Kashmir valley, houseboats are used as first class luxury hotels. They provide wonderful experience to a tourist.

These hotels are situated in metropolitan cities and provide modern western style luxury to their guests. They can also be called as full service hotels. Many such hotels are owned by big international chains. Such hotels find good market in commercial towns.

Motels, motor hotels and motor courts are designed to serve the needs of motorists. They must provide car parking, garage, accommodation, rest facilities and recreational facilities and hence motels are generally equipped with filling stations, motor garage, service stations, accessories, elevator service to automobile entrants, restaurants etc. The tariff is very low as compared to city hotels. They have easy access from highways, being located on highways or at road junctions. Motel accommodation is ranked with hotels in general in many countries.

Specific legislations laid down in some countries like France, Norway, Ireland, Iraq, Portugal and Turkey are regarding approval of plans, easy access for cars, minimum capacity, provision of restaurant, minimum standard of facilities and in Turkey provision of a petrol pump or service station.

In U.S.A. (original concept) motels/motor hotels/lodges originally provided simple accommodation with minimum service and formalities. Evolution of motor hotel stemmed from the need for more elaborate facilities. Rising cost of land in an around urban areas caused the development of motor hotels by substituting horizontal building with multi-storey car parking centre, sophisticated restaurants, banqueting and convention facility like that of a hotel. In general motel classification standards are similar to hotels.

These were developed in U.S.A. as low cost lodgings. The tariff was approximately $10 per night in 1974.

This includes prefabricated plumbing cases to which sanitary fittings can be easily connected, or complete bathroom units.

Motel accommodation may provide bedroom and bathroom facilities or include a large living area and a kitchenette. The latter is applicable to tourist area where longer staying guests require self- catering provisions and also for families relocated or temporary employees in that area, etc.

The focus in this type of hotels is on gambling and provision of casino. Casino hotels are not seen in India but are very popular in America, particularly in Las Vegas-Nevada. Top artists come to the hotel and give their live performances and entertain the guests.

Condominium development involves a joint ownership of a complex. Each owner purchases and has full benefit of an unit such as a guest-room, suite, apartment or a villa and shares the cost common to the whole complex such as taxes, maintenance and upkeep of buildings and grounds, parks, tennis court, swimming pools, provision of services such as security, letting and management, etc. Each owner can occupy or sell his unit independently but is obliged under the terms of contract to contribute towards the pool of common facilities and services.

Condominiums have many advantages over simply leased property. In a condominium the capital appreciates with rising value particularly on coast or lake sides. It relieves the owner of maintenance and upkeep worries. The owner can enjoy extensive recreational facilities exclusive to the complex. Condominium management look after the unit in the absence of the owner and if required, let it to provide income. In some instances letting or leaseback conditions may be written into the contract, particularly where the condominium unit in a complex may be used as a back up to a hotel operation, for example, to provide additional accommodation for conventions. It may be necessary for the developer to appoint an independent management agent in the initial stages and for subsequent control to be exercised by an association of owners. In some cases the developer may act as an estate agent and manager.

It is an apartment building also used as a residential hotel. Purchase of the apartment entitles full services of the hotel and during the period it is not occupied it can be added to the hotel pool for getting income. The concept was initially developed by Melia Coy of Spain in 1970.

It is the counterpart of inn in various countries. It represents a smaller unit which may have complimentary bar, restaurant and bedrooms for travellers. Here emphasis is given to eating and drinking facilities.

Boarding houses are establishments providing accommodation usually with meals and for a definite period of time—commonly for a week or longer. The facilities are generally restricted to use by resident guests. It can also be called a guest-house, a private hotel, and is known in Europe as 'pension' or 'pension de famille'. Distinctions in these depend variously on length of stay, location, facilities and levels of sophistication of premises.

Providing extensive recreation and sporting facilities on an inclusive basis. In multiple units and provide self-catering (individual kitchen). In Spain located in areas where contact with nature and sporting activities is possible. Provision of green zones, playgrounds, and social amenities like library, nursery, television room etc. For social tourism based on family units providing a convertible living room, bedroom, bathroom, shower room and kitchen. Wide range in sports like riding, swimming, skating, golf etc. Design of building and landscaping highly sophisticated (Village Equastere de Pompadour, Club Mediterranee, Correze-France) retaining the village atmosphere. Typical size ranges between 500-800 beds, a 600 beds capacity being considered the optimum for efficient operations with a density of between 150-200 beds per hectare or 60-80 beds per acre.

Specific regulations may apply as in Spain, holiday villages are classified in 3 categories according to amenities and services.

In France, regulatory standards apply to commercial holiday villages and to non-commercial establishments like those of the association "Villages Vacancis Families"— (v.v.f), which in 1973 was responsible for 70 villages and family lodges providing 33,000 beds.

This group includes all forms of rented accommodation other than the above mentioned categories such as youth hostels, dak bungalows, forest lodges, travellers' lodges, recreational centre for children, dharamshalas, sanitaria and convalescent centres, camping grounds—these are sites demarcated with amenities for living in the open air in a tent, trailer or any other mobile provisional type of accommodation unit. Usually camping sites fall into four main groups, those for transit, weekend, holiday and tourist use.

Also called as B & B Inns. These are lodging establishments that provide room with full breakfast. Usually they are converted residences or country estates. Main meals are not served. They are located along commercial and holiday routes and in rural and resort areas.

This concept is also becoming popular these days. This is also known as 'vacation ownership' or 'holiday ownership' concept. The concept is that for a set period which may be one week or more each year and for a number of years the person gets the right to enjoy stay and other facilities and services in an apartment or any other type of lodging in a tourist complex. It is like advance purchase of time in holiday accommodation. Purchaser has to pay a one time capital sum and then an annual contribution towards the maintenance of the property. The fee usually covers services such as cleaning and maintenance of apartment and public areas, electricity, gas and water, insurance, operation of resort facilities e.g. swimming pool, local taxes and sinking funds for redecoration and replacement of equipment etc. Time-share concept started as early as 1960. Alexander Nelte, a German who was the manager of a hotel in Ticino developed this concept and created a company called Hapimag based in Switzerland. Further in 1967 another innovative developer introduced the concept at Superdevolur ski resort. The sales slogan was "Stop renting a room—buy the hotel—it's cheaper!"

Although the time-share concept initially developed in Europe but was soon adopted by U.S. Soon the developer came to understand a serious drawback of the concept - lack of flexibility. In 1974 the solution to this drawback came with the development of the concept of exchange system RCI. In 1976 another company Interval International was formed with the same concept. Subsequently the idea trickled down to Mexico from U.S. and came back to Europe in 1980s and the British Holiday market in Canary Islands and the Costa Del Sol of Spain can be considered as the beginning of success story in Europe. The concept is also being appreciated in India and many companies such as Avelon Resorts and Sterling Holiday Resorts, Mahindra Holding, Nanda Tourist Corporation etc. are promoting this concept and the growth of time-shares at an annual rate of 15% since 1980 can be compared with that of travel and tourism overall of 4% and hotel accommodation 2% in the same period.

A new concept in India. They are different from the hotels in that each room has a distinct personality. It is a small but very expensive hotel. Professional but at the same time very personal and intimate services by staff are prominent feature to give guest a richer experience; each restaurant of a boutique hotel has a different entertainment concept which include lighting that changes with the mood of the guest. For more personalized services and attention restaurant are kept small. They are each theme based and everything from decoration to food to service must be in tune with the theme. 'Guest needs understanding' is the highlight of this type of hotel.

One of the most important knowledge that a salesman should have is the "Product knowledge". Similarly it is very important that all those involved in selling/booking of rooms such as reservation section staff and front desk staff and also the marketing and sales division staff has full and comprehensive knowledge of rooms which they are trying to sell and their availability and non-availability position. They should know what are the various types of rooms, their location and situation, and also the features of the rooms—can extra beds be provided in the rooms or not, facilities such as

TV, mini bar, telephone, bedside lights etc. in the rooms. Also knowledge of the room rates and plans which the hotel is operating on is important. Given below are some typical rooms that the hotels have:

> The term refers to a room with a standard single bed to provide sleeping accommodation to one person. The room furnishing and fixtures as well as amenities and facilities standards would depend upon the standard of the hotel. The size of a single bed is generally 6' x 3'.

Double room term refers to a room which has a double bed and provides sleeping comforts for two persons. A double bed is a large bed. The size of a double bed is generally 6' x 6'.

Twin bedded room is a room with two identical twin beds separated out by a small bed-side table. This room provides sleeping accommodation for two persons.

These are rooms which are connected to each other. They have a common wall and a door in the common wall to go from one room to another. They can be used for a family by opening the connecting door as well as can be given to two separate individual persons by closing the common door.

This room offers sleeping accommodation facilities to three persons and has either a double bed (or two twin beds) and an extra bed in it.

This room provides sleeping accommodation for 4 persons and accordingly has four beds.

This type of room has two double beds in it and provides sleeping comforts for four persons, such as a family of husband, wife and two children. Also called a family or twin double room.

The term suite refers to a set of two rooms out of which one is a bedroom and the other is a sitting room or living room. For going from one room to another the use of corridor is not required. Suite is a costly room of the hotel. There are various types of suites such as:

It is a single room with a sitting room attached to it and meant for one person's sleeping comfort.

It is a double room with a sitting room attached to it.

A large room with a partition separating the bedroom furnished from sitting area.

This type of suite has two rooms on two successive floors and is connected to each other with a common staircase. Generally the sitting room or living room is situated on a lower floor while the bedroom is on the next floor. This is one of the costliest accommodations of the hotel.

Very luxurious suite of the hotel, and is situated on the terrace of the building. Mostly hired by top executives of companies, businessmen, famous writers, film personalities and sometimes by retired people who want peaceful life. These are away from the hustle and bustle of the hotel.

These are the best possible suites that a hotel can have. May have more than one bedroom, along with a sitting room. Also sometimes these may have a small kitchenette and a small dining room, a changing room and an office room attached to them. The best possible furnishing and decoration are used in these rooms. The bathroom attached will also have the best possible sanitary fitments in it. These suites can be given exclusive names such as Presidential suite, Maharaja suite, etc. Additional facilities that may be provided are: (a) mini bar, (b) objects d'art, (c) valet service, etc.

These are rooms which are called multi-utility rooms also. They have utility furniture such as sofa-cum-bed, sofa convertible-bed, Murphy bed, closet bed or roll-away beds. The furniture is such which is used for sitting purposes during the daytime and for sleeping during the night time.

This type of rooms are situated near the swimming pool of the hotel and are normally used by people who love water games and are fond of swimming. These rooms have twenty-four hours supply of hot and cold water, and a hard bed. Some hotels have beautiful rooms decorated with bamboos.

This term is generally used by hotels which are situated on the hill stations for those rooms which have a view of waterfall or some water body or a garden from the balcony of the room.

A living or sitting room not used as a bedroom. Also called Salon in some parts of Europe.

A sort of complete self-sufficient unit in itself. Containing a bedroom, living room, dining room, a small kitchen and bathroom. For example, cottages on hill stations and also on sea beaches.

A room used for entertaining (cocktail party etc.). Can also be called function-room. This room is not used for sleeping purpose.

A room with two single beds joined together and with a common head board.

Two or more rooms side by side without connecting door between them i.e. to say rooms can be adjoining without being connected.

Provided by some hotels. Sometimes one or two floors of the hotel are taken by a company and converted to provide accommodation to its top executives. They are equipped with all the facilities and needs of the top executives such as a bar, a lounge, business centre, and may be a library.

The diversity and changing pattern of hotel use often make precise classification difficult. These days most of the hotels are deliberately designed to appeal to various market segments with the changing needs of market apart from traditional classification such as transit, residential and commercial etc. Many new forms of accommodation are being introduced such as sports hotel—as part of a sports hall complex, ski hotels—situated at ski resorts, boatels and floatels—associated with marine development, convention hotels—having one or more convention complex and allied services and facilities, motels, motor hotels and motor lodges and motor courts—designed to serve the needs of motorists and their vehicle i.e. car and should provide facilities for car parking, service and filling station and easy access from highway.

Hotels are also changing in character and operational style. More and more automation in services provided are taking place. Way back in 1971 Hotel SCHIPOL FROMMER in Holland was designed with self-operated room facilities and this helped in reducing the staff and guest ratio to 0.04:1

Another important point worth mentioning is that the age long distinction and difference between accommodation at hotels and hospitals is also getting blurred. Many modern private hospitals abroad and in India provide individual room facilities comparable and at times even better than a 5 star hotel room.

Another growing concept these days is of self-financed accommodation. With increasing affluence and improvements in travel and access facilities the trend in recent years has been towards the purchase of holiday accommodation such as apartments, chalets, villas, farmhouses etc. The development of high proportion of self-owned properties has certain disadvantages. Apart from low percentage of occupancy local employment and other benefits to the community are poor.

Existing Trends : As an alternative to hotel accommodation which are becoming costly day by day, most visitors are looking for facilities that provide a home like ambience. A number of real estate developers and hospitality providers are coming up with new concept of service apartments— a growing segment of Indian hospitality sector. The concept which initially started from Mumbai and Bangalore is now becoming popular in Delhi with apartment like Avion, Silver Oaks, Vasant Apartments, Hill view and Residency USI. A service apartment is a fully furnished studio or two to three room unit with a small pantry with housekeeping maintenance services, utility charges, fridge, microwave, heater, telephone, airconditioner and other such facilities. Also provides valet service, a cook, a kitchen (for home-like food) and a chauffeur driven car. Usually they are rented on weekly/monthly basis. They make long staying guest feel at home. This is a niche sector and has tremendous potential. Since they are economical, service apartments are a home away from home for families and transients in city for a week or more. They help avoid tiresome transactions required to lease flats. Presently these service apartments are catering basically to NRI's, foreigners and corporate clientele. They usually provide larger living space at economical price. Apart from the above mentioned service apartments of Delhi some popular ones are Lake Side Chalet, Mumbai; Home Stead, Bangalore; Tara Niwas, Jaipur; Riviere Heights, Kochi and Sand Pebbles, Goa.

'SPA' development in India, Basic concept of SPA is a place of relaxation and rejuvenation for people, who are ill Evian is

France is a very famous SPA. But with the change in time the SPA of today is a place for keeping the body fit and healthy not only though fitness centre but also supplemented by nutritionally balanced food. In this direction many SPA have come up. To mention few are Sanjay Khan a famous actor has built one on the outskirts of Bangalore. Hotel Crown Plaza Surya has launched a fitness and SPA at there health club Grand Hyatt's Oasis SPA has also began operation. A health SPA called' Anand' has been made in Rishikesh.

SPA prove essentially uses of therapeutic and physical properties of water therapy to relax tense bodies and minds, some of the centres in South India combine Ayurvedic massages with essential oils and also use aroma therapy.

Key Terms

Heritage hotels
Rosette classification
Holiday villages
Quad
Efficiency
Lanai
Roll-away bed
Auberge
SPA
Retirement hotels
Franchise Boutique hotels
Condominiums
Green hotels
Apartotel
Murphy bed
Object d'art
Gastoft

4

Tourism Administration

Planning and development set the stage for management and marketing. There is already a vast tourism "Plant" available throughout the world. The tourism "Plant" encompasses the facilities and capabilities available for tourism today and in the future. This "Plant" is to be profitably managed and thc product effectively marketed in order to realise the objectives envisioned in planning and development.

Issues in the management of tourism reflect the diversity of the resources which must be effectively combined—the human resources of labour and entrepreneurship, the vast variety of natural resources, and the capital investment which is the infrastructure and superstructure of tourism. The potential roles for government agencies and voluntary organisations and the development of human resources through training are among the issue related to management. So, too are the economies of scale needed by businesses in the industry and the potential of infrastructure to aid in the creation of a unique tourism experience. Differing management strategies will be needed and will be implemented and evaluated as management strives to serve different user groups.

Marketing, with its focus on identification of markets, product planning, and communication, is an area in which numerous tourism issues, and great future potential, exist. Identification of market segments, through such techniques as benefit segmentation and development of traveller motive profiles, is the first step in improving both product and promotion. The variety of travel products reflects the new markets believed to have potential for the future. Travel product alternatives include, among others, historical sites, cultural resources, vacation destinations, and special interest tourism.

Targeting advertising, based on identified market segments, and using the marketing communications network to inform travellers of the variety of opportunities that are available to them are explored as means of alleviating overcrowding of some and under other tourism resources.

Any system of categorising tourism concerns understates the complexities of the issues and the areas of mutual concern. Marketers and managers are as concerned with the environmental impacts—the social, cultural, political, economic, and natural resource implications of decision—as are tourism planners and developers. The familiarisation value of international and cross-cultural tourism is a social benefit accruing from the marketing of tourism. Cultural preservation and appreciation can be enhanced through a linkage with tourism marketing and management.

Methodological issues reflect not only the means of market segmentation, product development, and assessment of promotional effectiveness, but also the application of systems analysis and simulation to better understand the complex interactions of the various individual parts as they relate to the whole of tourism and the numerous environments potentially impacted by marketing and management. Management information systems and marketing information dissemination promise better marketing and management and better planning and development. Tourism is a complex interrelated system requiring planning, development, marketing and management. It requires continual monitoring and evaluation, and the incorporation of the results into subsequent planning activities. It also requires the kind of exchange of findings and ideas.

Marketing Need

Tourism is the fastest growing industry in the world and therefore the need for marketing it becomes imperative. Tourism needs to be marketed just as any other product, indeed more so, because it is an industry where the customer still has an immense variety of choice. The choice for the holiday maker is wide as more and more countries and resorts throughout the world expand their tourism industries.

Marketing for Tourism

It is a well-known fact that as long as the inherent sense of curiosity and adventure dwells in the hearts of human beings, the desire to travel in order to see new sights and experience new things, and to live under different environments, will always grow. It may be presumed that such being the case, marketing in the tourism industry is greatly simplified as part of the process has already been completed by the desire for travel in people. The best example would be that a person may or may not choose a tangible product which has been introduced by a manufacturer in the market, solely depending on his ability to afford it or his likes and dislikes. On the other hand, without exception, all human beings will always nurture a desire to travel in order to see places. The question then arises that if the desire is ever present in people to travel and experience new things, why would then tourism industry need marketing efforts at all?

The answer to the above lies in the fact that tourism is a very complex industry because of its multi-faceted activities which together produce the 'tourist product'. It is also complex because of various sub-sectors that are in themselves complete industries, if considered independently (lodging, transport, etc). Its complexity, furthermore, lies in the fact that tourism promotion in its various forms has to be directed at large number of people in various lands of different socio-economic structures, having different needs, tastes, attitudes, expectation and behaviour patterns. It is only through the efficient marketing strategy that will help understand people's tastes and preferences for travel. And hence need for marketing in tourism.

The Definition : Tourism marketing can be defined as the "systematic and coordinated efforts exerted by the national tourist organisations and/or the tourist enterprises at international, national and local levels to optimise the satisfaction of tourists, groups and individuals, in view of the sustained tourism growth." According to Krippendrof, J., marketing in tourism means "systematic and coordinated execution of business policy by tourist undertakings whether private or state owned at local, regional, national or international level to achieve the optimal satisfaction of the needs of identifiable consumer groups, and in doing so to achieve an appropriate return."

Product for Tourists

Availability of a 'product' is the prerequisite in the marketing function. Unless there is a certain 'product', be it tangible or intangible or a service, marketing is not possible. A 'product' may be defined as the 'Sum of the physical and psychological satisfactions it provides to the buyer'. 'Marketing' by definition is the development of a product to meet the needs of the consumer and then employing the techniques of direct sales, publicity and advertising to bring this product to the consumer.

For a tourist product, the basic raw materials are the country's natural beauty, climate, history, culture and the people. Other aspects are the existing facilities necessary for comfortable living such as water supply, electricity, roads, transport, communication and other essentials. In other words the tourist product can be seen as a composite product, as the sum-total of a country's tourist attractions, transport, accommodation and the entertainment which hopefully result in consumer satisfaction. The tourist product can be entirely a man-made one or nature's creation improved upon by man. Each of these components of a tourist product is supplied by individual providers of services like hotel companies, airlines or other suppliers, and is offered directly to the tourist by them. A consumer can combine these individual tourist products through a large number of ways. There would be many possible destinations, each with a number of hotels, each to be reached by more than one airline. Thus the potential choice before the consumer is very large.

Competing destinations have placed at the disposal of a

tourist a large variety of tourist products in abundant quantity. This eventually has led to the adoption of the new concept, i.e., the marketing concept in tourism by various countries promoting tourism. The important point about marketing is that it applies to situations where the choice can be limited to a relatively small number of brands giving the consumer a reasonable choice. The process of selection thus becomes easier. In the field of tourism this process is taking place by the increasing use of 'package tours'. A package tour is a travel plan which includes most elements of vacation, such as transportation, accommodation, sight-seeing and entertainment. The tourist product is a composite product, whether it is sold as a package or assembled by the individual tourist himself or his travel agent. The tourist product can, therefore, be analysed in terms of:

(a) Attractions

(b) Facilities

(c) Accessibility.

Of the three basic components of a tourist product, "attractions" are very important. Unless these are there, the tourists will not be motivated to go to a particular place. Attractions are those elements in the tourist product which determine the choice of a particular tourist to visit one particular destination rather than another. The attractions could be cultural like sites and areas of archaeological interest, historical buildings and monuments or scenic like flora and fauna, beach resorts, mountains, national parks or events like trade fairs, exhibitions, arts and music festivals, games, etc. Facilities are those elements in the tourist product which are a necessary aid to the tourist centre. The facilities complement the attractions. These include accommodations, various types of entertainments, picnic sites, recreation and so on. These are indeed important for every tourist centre. "Accessibility" is a means by which a tourist can reach the area where attractions are located. Tourist attractions of whatever type would be of little importance if their locations are inaccessible by the normal means of transport. If the tourist attractions are located at places where no means of transport can reach, or where there are inadequate transport facilities, these become of little value.

The tourist attractions which are located near to the tourist generating markets and are linked by a network of efficient transport, receive the maximum number of tourists.

Special Characteristics

Although general principles of marketing of products of other industries could be applicable to marketing of tourist product, there are certain differences in the approach. These differences are because of the peculiar character of the tourist product. The following are the peculiarities of a tourist product.

Intangible Non-Material : No transfer of ownership of goods is involved as compared to a tangible product, e.g., a motor car. In tourism, instead, certain facilities, installations, items of equipment are made available for a specified time and for a specified use. For instance, a seat in an aeroplane or a train for a journey from one point to another or a booking in a hotel through a travel agent is carried out for a customer, or services such as information and advice are provided.

Production and Consumption

The travel agent or tour operator who sells his product cannot store it. Production can only take place or can only be completed if the customer is actually present. There is a close link between production and consumption of tourist services. Most tourist services cannot be consumed incrementally. In other words, consumption, once begun, cannot be stopped, interrupted or modified at all. As a result, risk and uncertainty for the customer are higher, and his need for reliable pre-purchase information is stronger. The potential customer's decision-risk and dependence on accurate information are further increased because he cannot see, inspect, compare or try out tourist services before deciding to use them.

Assembled by Many Producers : The tourist product cannot be provided by a single enterprise. Each of the components of a tourist product is highly specialised and together make the final product. This is not so in the case of other tangible products where one manufacturer produces a total product. In tourism, on the other hand, an airline considers 'seats flown' or passenger miles to be its product, a hotel produces 'guest nights', a travel agent 'bookings', a theatre and museum or an archaeological site measures its 'production' in numbers of visitors. In the tourist's view, however, the product he buys covers the complete experience of his visit to a particular place. In other words, the tourist product is not an airline or a rail seat, or a hotel bed or a theatre ticket, but rather an amalgam of many components which together make a complete product. Because of these peculiar characteristics, coordination in marketing efforts is very crucial.

Demand Highly Unstable

The demand is influenced by factors such as seasonal demands, economy, political reasons, etc. The seasonal changes greatly affect the demand. Seasonality means the tourism plant is frequently used for a limited part of the year and therefore uneconomic. Many tourist areas have a short season—often as little as three months. A corollary of this seasonal usage is the seasonal unemployment, which is a serious problem. Some of the developing countries which have recently established tourist industries suffer particularly from seasonality. Seasonality also places strains on the transport system and other services. Thus seasonality presents a problem not only in relation to employment but also in relation to investment. On the other hand political unrest and economic instability caused by currency fluctuations and inflation, etc., greatly affect tourism demand.

Intermediaries' Role

In most industries, manufacturers have predominant control over product design, distribution, promotion and pricing. On the other hand, in tourism, sales intermediaries like tour operators, travel agents, reservation services and hotel brokers play a very dominant role and enjoy superior marketing strength. From the standpoint of tourism marketing, this strong position of the travel trade has significant implications. The travel trade determines to a large extent which services will be sold and to whom. The type of services to be offered as well as the pricing policies and promotion strategies to be adopted by tourist enterprises, are, therefore, determined not only by the needs and preferences of the customers but also by those expressed by travel sales intermediaries.

Various Motivations

It is comparatively simple to determine why people buy a certain make of refrigerator, smoke certain brands of cigarettes, use certain brands of toothpaste or prefer a certain type of packaged food. The subjective and objective reasons, expectations and desires which influence tourists' choice for a certain holiday destination, type of accommodation and vacation activities are far less evident.

Very often two people make exactly the same choices for entirely different and sometimes even mutually exclusive reasons. Travel motivations unlike motivations for buying a tangible article like a refrigerator, etc., are heterogeneous—composed of diverse elements. Tourism marketing, due to the various factors mentioned above, as compared to marketing in other industries, therefore, needs a somewhat different approach. Tourism marketing to a large extent depends on various market factors mentioned above.

Unlike the normal consumer product or service, the tourist product is marketed at two levels:

(i) The national or regional tourist organisation will be engaged in a marketing campaign to persuade the potential tourist to visit the country or region for which it is responsible. In view of the fragmentation of supply, the complementarity of tourist services, the predominance of many small and medium-sized enterprises and importance of tourism to an economy, the official tourist organisations have important functions in tourism marketing. The official tourist organisation will, however, not sell a tourist product directly to customers. It will have two major objectives. In the first place, it will seek to create knowledge of its country in tourist-generating markets and persuade visitors in these markets to visit the country. Secondly, it will seek to create an image of its country's tourist attractions in the best possible manner in tourist-generating markets so that the potential visitors are attracted.

(ii) The various individual firms providing tourist services can market their own components of the total tourist product after the national tourist organisations have launched marketing campaigns to persuade the potential tourist to visit the country or region for which it is responsible.

Process of Marketing

Initially, supply being short of demand it used to be mainly the sales management function as distinct from the market management function. The rapid industrial advancement subsequently placed at the disposal of the consumer a large variety of goods of improved quality and in abundant quantity from a large number of competing manufacturers resulting in supply exceeding demand. This compelled the manufacturers to give greater consideration to the needs of the consumers. This factor eventually led to the adoption of the marketing concept.

The marketing concept in the field of tourism comprises the following major processes or functions:

(i) Market research;

(ii) Product formulation and development;

(iii) Product distribution;

(iv) Advertising;

(v) Sales promotion or support; and

(vi) Public relations.

Research for Marketing

For successful marketing, market research is paramount. It relates to providing answers to various questions pertaining to the marketing activities. Market research can be defined as the "Systematic collection of information relating to supply and demand for a product or a proposed product in such a way that the information may be used by the organised to formulate informed decisions about its policies and its objectives." The marketing process in fact starts by finding out answers to questions like who are the potential tourists, where do they come from, what are their likes and dislikes, etc. In order to formulate any marketing strategy it is very essential for a national tourist organisation and others engaged in marketing a tourist product to know the answers to the following questions:

(i) Who are the persons who engage in tourism and where do they live?

(ii) Who are potential customers and where do they come from?

(iii) What are their income levels?

(iv) What are their likes and dislikes?

(v) What are their travel preferences and interests?

(vi) What do they buy and where do they stay?

(vii) What mode of transport do they use?

(viii) What are their entertainment preferences?

(ix) What are the trends in competition?

(x) What types of marketing programmes would be needed?

A tourist organisation's promotional efforts without appropriate answers to the above questions will not yield the desired results. To make the overall marketing efforts effective and successful, as in the case of manufacturers of consumer products, the tourist organisation in a country has to be totally aware of the international trends in the travel habits, vacation habits and most important of all, the reasons attributed to the better success of completing destination. A marketing manager cannot visualise successful marketing strategy without having an up-to-date knowledge of their markets in general. It is very important to have detailed information on all the aspects of a market. Results of such research will work as guidelines for launching a successful marketing programme.

Research Methods

There are various methods used to collect the data. Among the variety of methods used, some seem to be widely resorted to because of their advantages over others. Research techniques can be grouped as:

(i) desk research,

(ii) field research,

(iii) motivation research.

Research on Desk

Desk research includes the collection and analysis of all available data, statistics and published information on tourist trends and markets. In tourism much of the basic information about tourist trends and markets is available from existing sources. There are a number of international organisations like United Nations, UNESCO, IUOTO, WTO, IEC, OECD, IATA, PATA, ICAO, etc., which publish statistical information. Other data and statistics may be obtained from national tourist organisations, carriers, hotel companies, etc. This information proves very useful in assisting national tourist organisations to identify their markets and determine the objectives. The published information is of particular use to those countries which do not possess resources enough to undertake independent market research.

Research in Field

Field research on the other hand is the research work carried out in the tourist-generating markets itself. The special investigations in the field are to be carried out with a view to know more details of the market situation. Field research includes many methods among which the most common are *sample surveys* and the *motivation research.*

Surveys : *Sample survey* could be defined as the study of a given population through only a part or a fraction thereof. Much marketing information is obtained through the use of samples. In this method the population or 'Universe' for which information is required is defined, for example, all households in a country might be the universe or population under investigation. Then a statistically valid sample of the population is drawn and information is obtained from the sample. Sampling techniques consist of personal interviews of tourists, travel agents, carriers and hotel managers, etc., by way of personal interviews with the help of prepared questionnaires, by mailing questionnaires or through telephone contacts. Lower cost is the major reason why data are collected by sampling in place of complete enumerations.

The survey investigation can be classified by reference to the kind of information they seek to provide. There are surveys of market behaviour which record the holiday habits of the population, cross-analysed by socio-economic and other characteristics. The trends in the holiday making over many years may be seen and inferences made about the motives of holiday makers. Furthermore, surveys may be undertaken to monitor the conduct of marketing campaign.

Motivation Research : Motivational research attempts to describe and forecast the motives of the population under investigation, by use of techniques originally used in psychology. Assuming that every individual knows what he wants, motivation research is oriented to discover the needs of potential tourists in order to adopt the tourist supply accordingly and thus be able to satisfy them. In other words motivation research is the investigation into the motives behind travel. It concerns itself to answering the 'why' of human behaviour in contrast to answering the 'how' which is subject to sampling surveys. It analyses rather than describes the attitudes of both actual and potential tourists to travelling in general and to the tourist product offered in particular.

The technique used in motivation research is the depth interview method. The questionnaire to be used for this method is carefully designed, as motivation research aims at discovering the deep, sub-conscious and even unconscious of human beings.

An ill-designed questionnaire is likely to reach no deeper than the conscious level where rational factors prevail. Other techniques used are the projective methods like word association tests, sentence completion test and pictorial tests, etc., and observations to record the reactions of a person and to understand his motives.

Marketing Strategy : Developing a sound tourist marketing strategy is the next logical step after having identified the markets. It may, however, be mentioned here that the market research, as a continuous process of investigating market conditions is just a means to an end which is to develop a marketing strategy. The strategy aims at achieving certain objectives which could be an increase in the tourist traffic as well as increase in the foreign exchange receipts. The objectives should be compatible with the characteristics of the market or markets and with the capacity of the tourist "plant" and facilities available. Realistic assessment of the market—its size, conditions and trends—would, therefore, be the first step in developing the country's tourist marketing strategy.

Market Division

The first step which a marketing organisation has to take is to identify its market. Market may be described "as a place where buyers and sellers of goods and services meet and between them the exchange transaction takes place." It may be used in connection with a particular geographical area or in connection with a particular type of service or a product. The 'market' therefore can be defined as "the totality of actual and/or potential buyers of a given product of service in a specified geographical location at a given point in time or during a given period of time." Market segmentation is the process of identifying groups of buyers of a total market with different buying desires or requirements. It identifies and analyses the socio-economic, life-styles and motivational characteristics of potential consumers into useful categories. Due to financial and manpower constraints, it is not possible for an organisation to reach the entire market. Segmentation of the market is, therefore, made in order to achieve the most efficient use of marketing resources. The main objective of market segmentation are:

(a) Developing new markets for product variations or new products;

(b) Developing defence against competitors by differentiating one's own product from theirs and matching it more closely to the requirements of a particular segment of the market;

(c) Achieving maximum effects for given expenditure on marketing activities, particularly communication activities;

(d) Developing marketing programmes and budgets on the basis of a clearer idea of the response characteristics of specific segments.

The information on the tourist markets which will assist in segmentation are:

(i) Income distribution of overseas travellers and particularly correlation between income and distance travelled and travel expenditure;

(ii) Travel expenditure data, i.e., distribution of per head expenditure on travel;

(iii) Discretionary income of households, correlated with other characteristics enabling targets to be identified closely;

(iv) Historical trends in travel in different socio-economic categories;

(v) Survey data on attitudes to and motivations for overseas travel;

(vi) Geographical dispensation of potential customers within the market;

(vii) Membership of clubs and associations associated with other characteristics which identify particular groups as potential customers;

(viii) Influence of intermediaries (travel agents, tour operators, wholesalers, carriers, etc.) on destination choice in particular markets; and

(ix) Relative importance of different intermediaries in particular markets (e.g., all relevant type of travel business concentrated among relatively few intermediaries).

The segmentation process divides the markets on the basis of several factors. The most important and commonly used bases of market segmentation include the following:

(a) Geographic segmentation

(b) Demographic segmentation

(c) Socio-economic segmentation

(d) Psychological segmentation

(e) Behavioural segmentation

(f) Product-based segmentation

Under each of the above principal variables, there are several areas which are considered while segmenting the travel markets. These are as follows:

(a) Geographical
Operational areas,
e.g., sales regions.
Sales districts such as provinces, cities, political administrative zones.

(b) Demographic
Age groups
Sex differences
Ethnic origin
Marital status
Religious affiliations.

(c) Socio-economic
Levels of income
Types of occupation
Social class
Educational level
Level of economic activity.

(d) Psychological
Individual life-styles
Personality types
Perceptual differences
Motivational differences.

(e) Behavioural
Pattern of purchase
Loyalty of fashions
Levels of brand loyalty
Benefits recognition sought

(f) Product-based
Travel purposes
Types of holiday
Average length of stay
Type of accommodation
Mode of travel
Arrangements for travel
Individual/group travel

Targeting for Market

The strategy of market segmentation in tourism recognises that few vacation areas are universally acceptable and desired. Therefore, rather than to waste promotion at resources trying to please all travellers, the best market strategy is to isolate those segments of the entire market which are likely prospects and target promotional efforts specifically at the selected groups. Thus, one of the early steps in marketing tourism is to divide the present and potential market on the basis of meaningful characteristics and then concentrate on promotion, supply and pricing efforts on serving these most prominent sections of the market—the target markets.

A market for particular area might be largely archaeologists in their middle years who have an income of over $1,00,000 per year and who live in mid-Eastern United States, or it might be largely businessmen in the age group of say 40-60 years who have an income of over $1,50,000 per year and who live in southern parts of West Germany. In tourism marketing, the total tourism market can be divided into the above major segments. A further segmentation, however, is possible within each of the above major segments for marketing purposes and includes:

Vacation Tourist : The vacation or the holiday tourist is the most common and popular tourist. He is immensely affected by changes in price, and is easily influenced by skilled and aggressive marketing effort. This type of tourist is resort-oriented. The vacation tourist market has been regarded as highly seasonal.

Business Tourist : In recent years the market for this type of tourist has increased greatly. The choice of destination of a business tourist is generally determined by the nature of his business. The marketing efforts will not influence much the choice of the business tourist. As in the case of vacation tourist who has proved to be very sensitive to price changes, the demand for business tourism is relatively price-inelastic. The demand will tend to be big city oriented. The visits are of shorter duration and relatively frequent. The trade fairs, conventions, exhibitions, conferences and similar other events attract this kind of tourists.

Common Interest Tourist : This segment comprises visits to relatives and friends, and visits for the purpose of education, for pilgrimage, etc. The demand for this type of tourism will be relatively price-elastic. The common interest tourist will not be easily influenced by the promotional efforts. The average length of stay of this type of tourist will be relatively longer. Because of his friends and relatives, he will not be a significant user of hotel and other such types of accommodation. The visits will not be frequent and expenditure relatively little on his stay as compared with other two groups.

The market segmentation, however, in itself is not sufficient. The location and identification of potential buyers of a product does not ensure that purchases will be effected. Market segmentation is merely the first step on the development of a total marketing strategy. It helps in the process of converting as many as possible, the potential buyers into the actual buyers. The information available through market research and segmentation gives the dimension of the market and determines which particular markets are crucial. This information also assists in creating a meaningful promotional strategy to achieve pre-determined goal of reaching a set target.

Endorsement of Tourism

In order to market a product, it is necessary that information about the product reaches a prospective consumer. As applied to tourism industry, the most important function of marketing is to bring about an awareness of the product in the minds of existing as well as prospective consumer in the overall market area. All this forms a part of overall tourism promotion. The basic function of all tourism promotional activities is to have an effective and meaningful communication with the consumer and the trade intermediaries. This is possible through certain identifiable methods which are being practised by all the marketing organisations. The awareness is brought about through certain methods/marketing tools these are:

(a) Advertising

(b) Public Relations

The above tools are, however, not exclusive but complementary to each other. Proper and judicious blend of these is essential for the successful marketing of a tourism product.

The Publicity

Advertising is a non-personal communication of a sales message to actual or potential purchasers of a product by a person or an organisation selling a product or a service. The sales message is delivered through a paid medium for the purpose of influencing the buying behaviour of those purchasers. The term may be defined as "any activity designed to spread information with a view to promoting the sales of marketable goods and services". As such, it operates in two ways: firstly, by spreading information among consumers, about the possibilities of consumption, and secondly, by seeking to influence their judgement in favour of the particular goods which are the subject of the advertisement. Use of certain paid media space is, however, a prerequisite. A message in the paid media must have as its purpose sale of a product or a service.

Advertising is an investment and like all investments it should produce measurable results. The first and foremost reason for setting advertising objectives is, therefore, to measure the return on one's advertising investment. The second reason is that with the availability of many alternative methods for marketing products and with customers becoming more and more value-conscious, organisations must seek the most efficient way of marketing the goods and services if they are to remain competitive.

Professor Robert Buzzell of the Harvard Business School, gives the following example of possible advertising objectives for a consumer product advertising to increase sales directly by:

(i) Encouraging potential purchasers to visit dealers or distributors;

(ii) Announcing special sales, contests or other promotions;

(iii) Securing new dealers or distributors;

(iv) Inducing professional persons (e.g., doctors, architects) to recommend a product; and

(v) distributing coupons to be redeemed on purchases;

To create awareness and interest in the company's product by:

(i) informing potential buyers about product features;

(ii) announcing the availability of new products;

(iii) demonstrating the benefits of a products use;

(iv) comparing a product with competing product;

(v) showing how a product should be used;

(vi) informing potential buyers about the company's technical skills, production facilities, technical services, etc.;

(vii) informing purchasers about where products can be obtained;

(viii) announcing changes in prices, packages, labels, etc.; and

(ix) publicising a new brand name or symbol.

The above advertising objectives for the manufacturer's consumer product advertising can be applied or the tourism product advertising to achieve the best possible results. The broad objectives in tourism advertising include making the tourist product as widely known as possible and making it as attractive as possible for the prospective consumers.

Selection of Media

The selection of the medium or media will depend upon the factors like the area to be covered, the type of audience to be reached, the appeals to be made and upon the services and facilities of the particular medium in relation to costs. The important factors which influence the media selection are:

(i) media habits of the target audience;

(ii) product characteristics: for example, TV may be the appropriate media for those products which may require a demonstration of their operation for effective impact on the target audience; and

(iii) cost of the media.

Message Choice

The message selected should be such that it retains the interest in the minds of the customer about the product. The customer must maintain his interest in the message, and secure the action desired by the seller of the product. The objective is to present the advertiser's message in such a way that the illustration may lead the reader to favourable consideration of the advertisement. The important characteristics of an effective message are:

(i) *Information:* it should be adequate for a decision,

(ii) *Interest:* it should be able to catch the attention of the largest audience,

(iii) *Authenticity:* it should avoid exaggerated claims,

(iv) *Persuasion:* it should be capable of creating a favourable conviction in the target audience, and

(v) *Memory value:* it should have something in it which can help the target audience to remember it.

The Pricing

The agency must relate the estimated cost and the results expected from advertising. Can the advertiser carry on a campaign large enough to make it effective? Are the funds available or will they become available through the sale of the product? How much does the agency spend for the advertising? The various methods commonly used are:

(i) *Affordable method:* here, the advertising budget is set on the basis of what the agency can afford;

(ii) *Percentage of sales method:* in this case, the agency sets the advertising budget on the basis of specific percentage of sales;

(iii) *Competitive parity method:* here the company sets its budget to match those of its major competitors;

(iv) *Objective and task method:* in this the advertising budget represents the outlay required to perform the various tasks which are necessary to achieve the properly defined advertising objectives of the company. This method is considered the most rational.

Advertising Effect Assessment

It is very important for the agency to ensure that the money spent on advertisement does bring returns by way of increased sales. This could be done by way of evaluating or testing the effectiveness of advertising. Test may be applied before advertisement has been run. Pretesting of an advertisement prevents expenditure that would not be profitable and leads to expenditure that give the best results. In determining advertising effectiveness the commonly used methods are:

Coupon Response: Answer-back coupons, with some inducement, are incorporated in many advertisements. The amount of response is an indication of the effectiveness of the concerned advertisement.

Recall Tests: Here the respondents are shown the magazine cover or any other media vehicle in which the concerned advertisement had appeared. They are then asked to tell which advertisements in that publication they remember.

Recognition Tests : Here the respondents are shown the advertisement and asked if they have read them.

Sales Tests: Here, the actual sales results before and after the concerned advertising are examined. The sales results in the selected 'test markets' are also compared to those in some chosen 'control markets', i.e., the markets where the concerned advertising is not done. In the field of tourism, advertising is mainly used to create initial awareness and interest in the tourist service or destination to be promoted and motivates potential tourists to decide to make further enquiries about costs, bookings, facilities, etc. It implies indirect communication with selected target groups—the potential tourist—through paid messages designed to promote a particular destination or an area. For a country which is trying to attract tourists, there can be two forms of advertising: (i) consumer advertising, and (ii) trade advertising. To reach a wide a number of consumers, such media as newspapers, radio spots, TV prime time are used. However, this form of advertisement is very expensive. It is extremely difficult to afford such a type of advertisement because of financial constraints. Trade advertising on the hand is an indirect form of advertising and is less expensive.

In marketing a tourist product advertising plays a very important role. If the right combination of conditions is present the effect of advertising would be to increase the demand for the particular country's tourist product. Among the factors favourable to the successful use of advertising are the rising trend of demand in the particular product and an opportunity to stimulate selective demand, i.e., preference for the particular product. This is most likely where there is a possibility of product differentials, and where consumer satisfaction depends largely on hidden qualities that cannot easily be judged at the time of purchase, or where strong emotional buying motive exists as in the case of tourism.

Contact to People

Public Relations is the "art and science of planning and implementing honest, two-way communication and understanding between a company or an organisation and the many different groups with which it is concerned in the course of its operation." It is also defined as "continuous and consistent representation of an organisation's policies to the public at large to sections of the public who have a special interest in the organisation's activities, e.g., to various strata of employees, shareholders, actual and potential customers as well as its local and national governments. *Public Relations News,* a weekly newsletter written for the PR profession in the United States of America, defines PR as "a management function that evaluates public attitudes, identifies the policies and procedures of an individual or an organisation as they affect the public interest, and executes a programme of action to earn public understanding and acceptance." The internationally accepted definition of PR however is that it is "the deliberate, planned and sustained effort to establish and maintain mutual understanding between an organisation and its public."

The main function of public relations is to inform the public about the activities of an organisation. In other words, it is a part of an organisation's total communication effort. Its purpose is to create the best possible reputation for the organisation by way of presenting facts. The field with which PR is most closely identified is advertising. However, advertising pays for the print space, air time or electronic space in order to sell a specific product, while on the other hand, public relations which may include some forms of advertising as its tools, covers a much wider and broader range.

Public Relations in Tourism : Public relations assumes a special significance in the field of tourism because of the peculiar nature of the product. The need for making complete information and facts available to both potential and actual tourists assumes special importance. It involves measures designed to create and improve the image for the tourist product, create a more favourable climate for its advertising and sale support activities, especially in regard to travel trade intermediaries and news media. Favourable acceptance of any tourist destination by the public is of utmost importance. Public relations in tourism is used to create and maintain a positive image for a country, a tourist destination in the minds of people who are in a position to influence public opinion (journalists, editors, travel writers, etc.), or in the minds of sales intermediaries (travel agents, tour operators, etc.). It is oriented towards creating and maintaining an atmosphere whereby the travelling public at large is convinced of the advantages of visiting the country concerned.

Public relations is one of the important functions of the tourist organisation. In fact, tourist organisations primarily are public relations organisations. The objectives of public relations in the field of tourism are twofold: firstly, the dissemination of information, and, secondly, the creation of a favourable image for the tourist product.

Public Relation Techniques : Public relations make use of several communication techniques. These includes:

(i) News and feature stories

(ii) Press releases

(iii) Films and slides

(iv) Booklets and brochures

(v) Photographs, displays and exhibits

(vi) Advertising

(vii) House journals

(viii) Newsletters

(ix) Stockholder reports.

Public relations consist of a number of interrelated activities oriented towards creating and maintaining a favourable positive image for the tourist product. The main tools of public relations in tourist promotion are as follows:

(i) Organising familiarisation tours for travel writer, editors, travel agents, photographers and other key personnel from different parts of the world as guests to visit the country and to get first-hand knowledge about it. These persons then write about the country visited in the well-known travel and other general interest magazines.

(ii) Organising radio and television contests featuring the destination country.

(iii) Organising press releases and arranging press conferences with key personnel connected with the tourist field with a view to disseminate information about the destination.

(iv) Arranging seminars and workshops at a place where the tourist promotion office is located.

(v) Organising cultural programmes, musical and folk shows, TV interviews, exhibitions and national friendship weeks in the country where the national tourist office is located.

(vi) Organising various types of contests about the country.

(vii) Encouraging large departmental stores, organisers of fashion shows and manufacturing companies to project the country or a part of the country as a promotion showcase in their premises.

Public relations planning and organisation should be an integral part of an organisation's management strategy and must be conducted on a continuing basis. Public relations function of an organisation cannot be considered as an end in itself or something which can be introduced at a short notice to cope with a crisis situation. An organisation should have a positive and planned public relations policy. It is no coincidence that most of the national tourist organisations devote considerable effort to their public relation programmes.

5

Functional Aspects

Unlike 'management' the term 'organisation' has also been used in a number of ways. Broadly speaking, the term 'organisation' is used in two different senses: as a process and as a structure of relationships.

Nature and Goal

Organisation is treated as a dynamic process and a managerial activity which is essential for planning the utilisation of the company's resources plant and equipment materials, money and people to accomplish the various objectives. To coordinate the employee's activities in an orderly and efficient manner is very essential for bringing unity and harmony of their efforts in the pursuit of common objectives. The definitions of organisation provide by Allen, Theo Haimann, Koontz and O'Donnell, Oliver Sheldon and G.E. Milward, etc. can be can be classified under this grouping viz.

According to Allen an organisation may be defined, "as a process of identifying and grouping the work to be performed, defining and delegating responsibility and authority and establishing relationship for the purpose of enabling people to work most effectively together in accomplishing objectives."

According to Harold Koontz and O'Donnell, "Organising involves the grouping of activities necessary to accomplish goals and plans, the assignment of these activities to appropriate departments and the provision for authority delegation and coordination."

According to Prof. Haimann, "Organisation is a process of defining and grouping the activities of the enterprise and establishing the authority relationship among them."

Organisation refers to the structure of relationship and among position jobs which is created to achieve certain objectives. The definitions of Henery, UrDavis, Mooney and Reily, Chester Barnard and Bakke, etc. come under this group, for example:

> According to Mooney and Reily, "Organisation is the form of every human association for the attainment of a common purpose."

In the words of Chester Barnard, "A system of cooperative activities of two or more persons is called organisation."

Thus, from the above definitions, it may be concluded that the organisation is the mechanism developed by management to unite the efforts of the people (employees) in order to realise the set objectives.

The following are the salient features or steps involved in organising a business enterprise:

Born with the enterprise is its life-long objectives of profitable manufacturing and selling its products. Other objectives must be established by the administration from time to time to aid and support this main objective. The objectives should be clear, precise and complete because the entire organisation structure is to be built around the firm's objectives clearly. By knowing and defining objectives, it is possible to:

(a) Weigh the necessity of the organisation and the possibility of its success.

(b) Decide if they harmonise with other objectives.

(c) Estimate what financing and personnel are needed.

(d) Break the objectives into functional parts to be assigned to a particular department for accomplishment.

After the objective is selected, management has to identify the total task involved and its break up into closely related component activities that are to be performed by an individual or division or a department. All functions of a similar type are separated and concentrated into four basic functional departments—finance, sales, production and accounting.

When activities have been grouped according to similarities and common purposes they should be assigned to a particular department. Within the department, the functional duties should be allotted to particular individuals.

The authority and responsibility should be well defined and should correspond to each other. A close relationship between authority and responsibility should be established. For establishing a sound and effective organisation structure, the delegation of authority is essential.

After assigning the duties and delegation of authority, the establishment of relationship is done. It involves to decide who will act under whom, who will be his subordinates, what will be his span of control and what will be his status in the organisation. Beside this formal relationship, some informal organisation should also be developed. This organisational relationship is very important, Peter F. Drucker aptly opines— "An institution is like a tune, it is not constituted by individual sounds but by the relations between them."

From the above discussion it is clear that the nature of an organisation is two-fold:

(i) First, it is a process of coordination of employees activities in an orderly manner. In this way it is a managerial job. It specifies how work or duties shall be divided among the departments in the company, the policies to be followed while accomplishing the work, who is to do the work, the scope and limits of responsibilities, the relationship of one job to another, etc.

(ii) Secondly, it is a framework of interior relationships. It defines the relationship between person to person, position to position, job to job and so on. It specifies the orderly channels of communications between the various levels of responsibilities in an enterprise. It defines their authority and responsibility in a formal manner.

The Importance

The importance of a sound organisation for any enterprise can hardly be over- emphasised. It is the edifice of managerial success. An organisation is definitely the backbone of management through which operations of an enterprise are run. It sets the relationship between people., work and resources to get productive results. Without good organisation, a one-man enterprise cannot successfully grow beyond the limits of the owner's strength and ability. As a matter of fact, a good organisation can contribute greatly to the continuity and success of an enterprise. A good organisation brings in functions, encourages specialisation, motivates the workers and makes ways through internal friction and lost friction and lost motion; it fails to retain and develop good men and invite into its membership new men of high quality.

Kenneth C. Towe opines, "A sound form of an organisation is the answer to every business problem; that a poor organisation could run a good product into the ground and that a good organisation with a poor product could run a good product to the market."

In the same way, explaining the significance of the organisations, the world famous industrialist of USA, Mr Andrew Carnegie once said, "Take away all our money, our great works, our mines and cock ovens but leave us our organisation and in a few years, I shall have reestablished myself." Really, there is no substitute in the whole world for a good organisation.

Significance of the organisation in any institution may be discussed as below:

> An organisation is an important and the only tool to achieve enterprise goals set by administration and explained by management. A sound organisation helps the management in a number of ways. It increases their efficiency, avoids delay and duplication of work, increases managerial efficiency, increases promptness, motivates employees to perform their responsibility. That's why in advanced and modern business units, an Organisation Analysis Unit is established separately in order to improve the organisational structure of the enterprise.

Without an organisation, an enterprise is just like a man without a body, leaving head and mind (Management & Administration) only. Good organisation contributes greatly to the continuity and success of the enterprise. It contributes to the growth, expansion and diversification of the enterprise. All such programmes can be successful to the extent the organisation structure permits.

It establishes persons with different interests skills, knowledge and viewpoints. A sound organisation brings harmony in their efforts, places right persons in the right positions, improves the communication network and motivates the employees to contribute their best to the goals of the enterprise.

A sound and well conceived organisation structure is the source of creative thinking and initiation of new ideas. Delegation of authority provides sufficient freedom to the supervisors at different levels. It develops a sense of responsibility in them and provides a recognition of their competence and expertise.

A good organisation provides for optimum use of technological improvements. It accommodates new ideas in respect of organisational relationships while retaining its basic structure. It provides for the use of new automatic techniques of production, control devices and data processing, etc.

In a good organisation, the different departments perform their functions in a closely related manner. Different jobs and positions are welded together by structural relationship of the organisation, the organisational pressures exert their due and balanced emphasis on the coordination of various activities.

The pattern of an organisation structure has strong influence on the development of executives. Managers at different levels are continuously trained, developed and tested for assuming greater responsibilities and meeting new challenges of managerial positions. If an organisation is to survive beyond the life of its existing managers, there is bound to be proper management development programme in the enterprise.

A good organisation promotes mutual goodwill and cooperation among workers also. It disposes of conflict between individuals and the enterprise, enterprise and the economy as a whole. It gives proper recognition to the contribution of each individual, values their cooperation, hence gaining their sincerity and loyalty. Good organisation removes red-tapism and corruption, prevents duplication of work, makes communication easier, provides a sound basis for workers participation in management.

Thus, we see that the organisation helps to improve the operations of the business as a whole. It is not simply an organising function of management, it is more than that. To sum up, it is the only means to carry out the policies and programmes of the enterprise. That is why, it is generally said that the organisation is the machinery of management for its achievement of the ends determined by administration.

Patterns and Methods

In organising an enterprise, it is necessary to adhere to certain basic principles of organisation, which should serve as guidelines for action. These are as follows:

An enterprise must have a clearly defined objective (or objectives). It must be realised that an enterprise is a means to an end, and not an end in itself.

As a corollary, each unit in the enterprise must have an objective which should logically be related to the overall objective. (Its contribution to the common goal.)

An organisation structure is effective if it facilitates the contribution made by all individuals in the enterprise to the attainment of the objectives of enterprise. All should contribute harmoniously to the achievement of the common goal of the business and also of the good of the individual members of the business. The common goal includes primary objectives such as, producing, selling or profit-making, and secondary objectives like job satisfaction, payment of wages, having good communication, joint consultation, etc.

People working towards a common objective must coordinate their efforts. In a typical organisation, a manager will have:

(i) a boss

(ii) subordinates, often 4 to 6 in number; and

(iii) colleagues, often of his own status.

The structure within a department is often called a chain of command, e.g., *A* is the boss, *B* is his subordinate, C is *B's* subordinate, D is C's subordinate and so on.

Each superior (or boss) in the chain of command is responsible for coordinating the work of those under him and his own efforts. The work of others on his level are in turn coordinated by their common superior.

One of the essentials of coordination is good communication flow, vertically and laterally, e.g., from superior to subordinate and to people of the same level throughout the enterprise.

Coordination committees are usually formed for this purpose (e.g., General Management Committee, Budget Coordination Committee, Planning Committee, etc.).

The organisation should be planned so that the objective can be attained with the lowest possible cost, which may be either money cost or human costs or both.

There should be one head (or chief person) and one plan of action for each group of activities having a common objective and everyone must work in accordance with the plan towards the objective in one common direction.

Each person should receive orders from only one superior and be accountable only to him, i.e., he should have only one boss. If a person receives orders from more than one boss, the orders may conflict, thereby confusing him and often leading to conflicts arising from divided loyalties.

As far as possible, the work of each person should be confined to a single function. In other words, he should not be a "jack of all trades." Since this is not always possible to achieve, it is generally held that related functions should be grouped together under a common superior.

The organisation must have a supreme authority and a clear line of authority should run from that person (or group) down through the hierarchy, e.g., from the Chairman—the Managing Director—Plant Manager—Production Manager— Foreman-rank and file of employees. The more clear the line of authority (from the ultimate authority for management to every subordinate position) the more effective will be the responsible decision-making and organisation communication. This is usually called the scalar principle because the hierarchy is like a scale. The resulting hierarchy is known as the "Chain of Command."

If the chain of command is short, it will enable better communication at various levels within the enterprise and cause fewer delays and bring the top decision-maker to grassroot levels (i.e., the operating personnel).

Should commensurate with each other, i.e., a man must have sufficient authority to fulfil his responsibilities. Conversely, if a man has the authority, he should be willing to take the responsibility for the results.

Decision should be made at the lowest competent level. For this purpose, authority (or powers for decision-making) should be delegated as far down the line as possible.

There are various parts of an enterprise (e.g., Sales, Production, Accounts, Personnel, etc.) which functions in close coordination to meet the objectives of the enterprise. A continuous survey should be made to ensure that there is a reasonable balance, the size of the various parts should be in balance and none of the functions should be given undue emphasis at the expense of others. A continuous survey should be made to ensure that there is a reasonable balance in the size of the various departments, between standardisation of procedures and flexibility, and between centralisation and decentralisation. Imbalances between departments occur as a result of new technology, new products, new marketing plans, etc.

There should also be a balance between the principle of the span of control and the principle of short chain of command.

The application of principles and techniques must be balanced in the light of overall effectiveness of the structure of the enterprise in meeting its objectives.

Change is one unchanging characteristics of an organisation. In other words, an organisation should be flexible and capable of adjusting to change, it cannot be rigid. It has to be flexible to take care of changing circumstances.

The enterprise after it has reached a certain position may well be split up into a series of separate semi-autonomous enterprises, to each of which responsibility is delegated.

Varied Sorts : On the basis of relationship, an organisation may be divided into two broad categories: (i) formal and (ii) informal. Both types of relationship are necessary for any group action just as two blades are essential to make a pair of scissors workable.

A formal organisation refers to the structure of well defined jobs, each bearing a definite measure of authority, responsibility and accountability. The structure is consciously designed to enable the people of an organisation to work together for accomplishing common objectives. Thus, a formal organisation is created through the coordination of efforts of various individuals. Every member is responsible for the performance of a specified task assigned to him on the basis of authority responsibility relationship in an organisation. According to Edwing O'Stone, "formal organisation is a number of persons who systematically and consciously combine their efforts for the accomplishment of a common task."

Informal organisation refers to the relationship between people in an organisation based on personal attitudes, emotion, prejudices, likes and dislikes, etc. These relations are not developed according to procedures and regulations laid down in the formal organisation. Generally, large formal groups give rise to small informal groups. These groups are not pre-planned but they develop automatically within an organisation. In the words of Bernard, "an organisation is informal when the aggregate of interpersonal relationships are without conscious joint purpose."

Informal organisation is very important in all enterprises. It brings cohesiveness to formal organisation. It brings to the members of a formal organisation a feeling of belonging, of status, of self-respect and of gregarious satisfaction. Informal organisations are important means of maintaining the personalities of the individual against certain effects of formal organisation which tend to disintegrate personalities. An informal organisation is created because of limitations of a formal organisation. Sometimes to keep a personnel, who is indispensable for the organisation, the changes are brought in the formal organisation. Sometimes new departments and sections are created for such a personnel.

Rising Part : In a formal organisation, there is lack of sense of belongingness and personal satisfaction, but an informal organisation fills this void by constantly emphasising and reinforcing each members individual personality and self-image.

In the daily work routine there are many opportunities for tension and frustration. In such situations a worker seeks a sympathetic ear of a friend in the informal group who can share and understands his troubles.

In case of accidents or illness, members of an informal group help one another. They may protect one another from authoritative action. They may increase group's efficiency by changing work assignments or by increasing the specialisation of their task beyond what is prescribed in the job description.

By enabling members to modify the job situation more to their liking, the informal organisation creates the necessary environment for individual innovation and originality. The individual can experiment with his ideas. News travels quickly via informal groups. They are the clandestine transmitters and receivers of information before it is officially released.

Informal groups provide all its members a set of norms or guides to correct behaviour. Members are expected to conform to those norms.

Informal group forces the manager to plan and act more carefully than he would otherwise. Informal organisation is a check and balance on unlimited use of authority by a manager.

Informal group is self-policing. This relieves the management of much of the burden of supervision. A manager is encouraged to delegate and decentralise his authority to members of an informal organisation.

The information gives the manager much feedback about employees and their work experiences thereby increasing his understanding of what he needs to do. It also helps interpret management to the workers so that they may be more supportive. It makes up for any management failures in communication.

Dawning Part : Following are the limitations of an informal organisation:

> An informal organisation is bound by customs, conventions and culture. The organisation resists those management decisions which threaten its culture or existing relationships among the members.

In an informal organisation, everyone works towards the same objectives. But when informal groups with different interests and needs develop the quest for achieving group goals they may lead members away from the organisation objectives. Members put their own group objectives ahead of organisation's objectives. Hence, the organisation suffers.

An informal organisation sometimes functions as a carrier of rumour.

Workers become loyal to their groups. They believe that what they seek must be good because the group has decided so. Thus, there develops a delusion of righteousness.

An informal organisation develops on its own, management cannot order the informal group out of existence. The logical course therefore is to harmonise it with formal organisation. A number of steps can be taken for this. Firstly, where informal rules are acceptable they should be institutionalised. Secondly, if informal lines of communication exist they should be used by management. Thirdly, informal leaders should be appointed to positions of formal authority.

Effective Areas : The term 'span of control' represents a numerical limit of subordinates to be supervised and controlled by a manager. It is an important principle of a sound organisation. This principle is based on the theory of relationships propounded by V. A. Graicunas, a French management consultant. Graicunas analysed superior-subordinate relationship and developed a mathematical formula based on the geometric increase in complexities of managing as the number of subordinates increases. But he failed to give factors which govern the actual span of control. Thus, his theory is not of much help in the practical life of managers.

Span of control or supervision refers to the number of subordinates, an executive can supervise. The concept is central to the classical theory of an organisation. Proper span of control is considered a necessity for effective coordination. The bias in the traditional theory has been that a small group is better than a large one because an executive must have intimate and direct contact with his subordinates. But in recent years the wide use of delegation and the transformation in the style of decision-making have had an inevitable bearing on questions relating to the number of people an executive can supervise.

Following are the factors which determine the span of control:

> Individuals differ in various qualities like leadership, decision-making and communication. The span may be wider if an executive possesses these skills in greater degree as compared to others.

It is said that span should be narrow at the higher levels. This is because of the fact that top managers have less time available for supervision. They have to devote the major portion of their time in planning, organising, directing and controlling.

When the spans are narrowed, the levels in the organisation increase. This involves delegation of authority and responsibility. If the work is of a routine and repetitive nature, it can easily be delegated to the subordinates.

If the subordinates are skilled, efficient and knowledgeable, they will require less supervision. In such a case, the superior may go in for a wider span.

If there is an effective communication system in the organisation, it favours large number of levels because there will be no difficulty in transmission of information in spite of a large number of intervening layers.

The span of control also depends upon the control practices being followed. Control may be followed either through personal supervision or through reporting. The former favours narrow-span and the latter favours a wide-span of supervision.

Staff functions such as training, recruiting and quality control free the managers from frustrating routine work and permit them to increase their span. Expert advice and staff assistance enables a manager to carry a greater load and handle more subordinates.

The lesser coordination needed, the broader the span. Similarly the lesser the planning required, the larger the span. Activities like launching a new product, surviving in a highly competitive environment demand careful planning whereas activities like filing, indexing, despatching require little planning.

The closer a work group is located physically, the larger the span. It is much easier for a manager to control the affairs of a large group working under the same roof, in one place.

The more similar the functions performed by the work group, the larger the span. The more a subordinate's job involves unpredictability, variety, discretion and responsibility, the smaller the span is likely to be. Office managers generally enjoy a larger span of control.

It can be concluded that every manager should be expected to supervise a reasonable number of subordinates. What is reasonable depends on a variety of factors like individual differences in managers, number and capacity of subordinates, the nature of work, ease of communication, internal checks and controls, and degree of decentralisation in an organisation. If the span of control is narrow there will be more organisational levels, which in turn may impede communication, but if the span of control is widened, the supervisory load may become too heavy. Sound organisation requires a proper balance between supervisory load and organisation levels.

Departmentation means "group of activities and employees into departments." It is, as Allen wrote a means of dividing the large and monolithic functional organisation into smaller, flexible administrative units.

Departmentation, therefore, refers to the organisational device of classifying the activities or operations of an undertaking into functionalised categories. Modern enterprises tend to be larger in size and complex in technological operations. All the activities cannot be managed by a single individual or the Board in a common sweep. Therefore, departments or sections are created for all major activities of the undertaking to bring the administrative and operational functions within compact compass of specialisation and in the range of managerial convenience.

The size of an undertaking may be large but departmentation solves the problem of management by compartmentalising the big-sized undertaking into manageable units based on functions, area, product or process. Hence the departmentation enables large firms also to derive the benefits of small functional organisation and at the same time softening the disadvantages that normally arise due to increasing size and diversity. Departmentation, limits the number of persons to be managed by inducting them into different departments. Thus, ensuring suitable span of control. It makes direction and control effective by confining the managerial focus to well-knit and functionally conceived units product-wise, process-wise or area-wise. Costs and revenues can be determined only if the enterprise is parcelled out into departments for administrative convenience. Allocation of duties, selection of specialised staff, fixation of responsibility will have decisive character under departmentalised organisational set-up, sharing of authority and spreading of responsibility are the underlying factors of departmentation subject to coordinating authority of the top management.

Departmentation is done through the following processes:

(a) Identification of tasks or duties.

(b) Analysis of detail of each task.

(c) Description of the functions.

(d) Entrusting the groups of functions to separate specialist heads and providing them with suitable staff.

(e) Delineation of scope of authority and responsibility of departmental heads.

Departments can be made on the basis of:

(a) Functions, e.g., sales, production, personnel, planning, transport, etc.

(b) Products, e.g., air-conditioners, accounting machines, electronic calculators, etc.

(c) Territory, region, or geographical area, e.g., Northern Railway, Western Railway, N.E. Railway, etc.

(d) Customer, e.g., wholesaler, retailer, government.

(e) Process.

(f) Appropriate combination of any of these types.

The functional structure is the most common. In most companies, unless they are giant corporations, this is the form of the organisation. The departmental heads will report to the Chief Executive. A typical department, say Production Department, will have the following structure:

Managing Director

Production Manager

- Production Planning Manager
- Production Engineering Manager
- Industrial Engineering Manager
- Maintenance Manager
- Works Superintendent

Under each of these five managers, there will be subordinate managers and under them, the subordinate staff.

The Advantages

(i) It is a logical reflection of functions.

(ii) It follows the principle of specialisation.

(iii) Maintains power and prestige of major functions.

(iv) Inter-departmental coordination is facilitated.

(v) The structure is simple, logical and easy to understand.

(vi) Provides a good means of control at the top.

The Disadvantages

(i) Responsibility for profits tends to be at the top.

(ii) There may be chances of heavy centralisation in decision-making.

(iii) Where geographical centralisation is desirable or required, this form becomes unsuitable.

(iv) This is not very suitable where product lines have to be emphasised.

(v) There is a lower potential for manager development.

Product wise departmentation is resorted to where specialisation is required in respect of specific products of the company. For example, a company may deal with eight or nine product lines, e.g., chemicals, drugs, foodstuffs, cosmetics, etc. and each under a separate division, e.g., Chemicals Division, Foodstuffs Division, etc.

The Advantages

(i) Places greater effort on individual product line.

(ii) Better customer service arising from greater product knowledge.

(iii) Simplifies departmentation of profitability of each product line. Responsibility for profits is at the Division level.

(iv) Improves coordination of functional activities.

(v) New department may be added without difficulty. Permits growth and diversity of products and services.

(vi) Detailed information on markets for specific products will be generated.

(vii) Extremely suitable where product lines are complex or vary greatly.

(viii) Furnishes measurable training ground for Managers. Some of the disadvantages inherent in such departmentation are:

  (i) A customer has to deal with different salesmen or managers for different products of the same company.

  (ii) Extra costs of maintaining separate sales force for each product.

  (iii) Duplication of costs on travel, etc.

  (iv) Tends to make maintenance of economical central services difficult.

  (v) Results in increased problems of the top management control.

Such departmentation is especially attractive to large-scale enterprise or others having activities physically or geographically spread out. Such departmentation is proper when its purpose is to encourage local participation in decision-making and to take advantage of certain economies of localised operation.

The Advantages

(i) Regional expertise is generated and managers can tackle customers or competition better. Places responsibility at lower levels.

(ii) Proximity will reduce costs of operation and administration.

(iii) Places emphasis on local markets and problems. Local conditions might warrant different types of selling. This is possible only in territorial departmentation.

(iv) Improves coordination at the regional level.

(v) Better face to face communication with local interests in mind.

Better Manager Development

(i) Involves higher costs of coordination and control from headquarters.

(ii) Results in more managerial levels which increases overhead costs.

(iii) Unsuitable for departments like Finance, where no gains are possible by specialisation on local factors.

(iv) Increases problems of the top management control.

Departmentation by customers places greater emphasis on the customers and distinguishes one type from the other. For example, the division could be industrial buyers, whole-sellers, government, and public undertakings, agriculturists, etc.

Some advantages of this type of structure are:

(i) Greater specialised customer service.

(ii) Where marketing channels are considerably different for various types of customers, this type of structure is very useful.

Some Disadvantages

(i) May not be enough work for certain types of customers. Hence, under employment of facilities and manpower specialised in terms of customer groups.

(ii) Problems of coordination might pose difficulties.

(iii) Unequal development of customer groups.

This structure is used where the machines used need special skills for operating them or have technical facilities which make concentrated location desirable. This type of structure is mainly motivated by cost and economic considerations. For example, a factory might have two processes—electrolytic and the other chemical process.

Some writers use the word 'Divisionalisation' instead of 'Departmentation' and distinguish the two words as follows:

A company has several departments, say Sales, Production, Planning, etc. When it breaks up into Divisions, each Division may have Chemicals Division and Drugs Division which are both autonomous.

The head of a Division is responsible for both production and marketing of a given product or family of products. Just below the chief executive, there is functional structure, i.e., they have functional authority over the staff in the Division—which means, the authority to recommend general policies, which acquire the force or rules if they are approved by the Executive of the Corporation.

Some companies are divided by products, e.g., petroleum, chemicals, etc. The other is geographical divisionalisation. Others may have a combination of both.

The movement towards divisionalisation comes mainly out of an interest in decentralisation of decision-making which becomes necessary because of the increasing size of many companies and the increasing diversification of their activities, both of which increases the burden at the top.

In its extreme form, divisionalisation amounts to this creation of semi-autonomous units.

A basic consideration in divisionalisation is that the output of the division should be able to produce enough revenue to cover the cost of setting it up and running it and produce a substantial contribution to profit.

In product divisionalisation, technological factors are very important.

The location of resources and customers is another important factor in geographical divisionalisation (brings production/distribution closer to customers).

Some centralisation is necessary because production facilities are labour bound. Some advantages of divisionalisation are:

(i) Greatly reduces the burden of the top management.

(ii) Helps in fixing accountability.

(iii) Brings decision-making close to the scene of action.

(iv) Divisional Manager becomes more of a generalist than a specialist in one function.

(v) More effective performance can lead to greater profitability.

Some of the Disadvantages

(i) Division may become too independent that it may begin to work against the company as a whole.

(ii) Division may maximise short-run gains at the expense of corporate long-run goals.

Potent Factors : Management in designing departmentalised organisation should bear the following factors in view for operating the entire undertaking in fulfilling the basic business objectives:

Division of labour should permit persons to become specialists in specific types of work. If the specialised skill and knowledge are crucial to success of the enterprise than functional departmentation becomes essential.

Departmentation should be thought of in terms of effectively regulating and evaluating the operation of the varied activities of the undertaking. It is said that departmentation makes it easier for management to measure performance and to hold people accountable for results.

Departmentation should not create insoluble problems of coordination. Therefore departments should be created in such a way that mechanism for coordination can be built into the very structure of the organisation. There should be administrative arrangements whereby all departments report to a common authority who can take timely steps to bring in sequential or functional coordination.

Pattern of departmentation should not imply top heavy expenditure on capital equipment, establishment, incidental expenses, etc. Certainly it will require more expenditure to organise multiple departments. But the benefits of specialisation—increased sales, better servicing, etc. expected of departmentation should outweigh the additional costs that need to be incurred.

There should be sufficient preparation before departmentation is decided upon. Administrative preparation for departmentation should include a full measure of decentralisation of authority. This will enable vitalisation of the independent administrative units conceived under the departmentalised set-up.

This chapter described the basic concepts regarding organisation such as its meaning, scope, nature and importance. The important elements of an organisation are; (a) Outlining the objectives (b) Identifying and enumerating the activities (c) Assigning the duties (d) Defining and granting the authority and (e) Creating authority relationship. It also concisely described the principles of organisation and concepts such as formal and informal organisation. Formal organisation refers to the structure of well defined jobs, each bearing a definite measure of authority, responsibility and accountability. Whereas, an informal organisation refers to the relationship between people in an organisation based on personal attitudes, emotion, prejudices likes and dislikes, etc. Further it provided glimpses into important concepts of span of control and the process of departmentation. Departments can be made on basis of business functions, products, geographical territories, on customer focus, and process definition.

Management Skill

In order to make it possible for people to work effectively towards accomplishing goals, an intentional structure of roles must be designed and maintained. This is the purpose of the managerial function of organising. For a meaningful role to exist, it should incorporate verifiable objectives, an understood area of authority or discretion, a clear concept of the major activities or duties involved and a clear understanding of the relationships of that role with others, where coordination is required. To make a role fully operational, these structural requirements must be additionally provided with the required, information, wherever and however it may be obtained.

It is in the sense of a structure of roles, that a formal organisation is conceived. The connotation, implied in organising refers to the grouping of activities necessary to attain objectives, as also, the assigning of each group to a manager with the authority necessary to supervise it, and the provision for coordination, both horizontally and vertically in the enterprise structure. An organisation structure should be designed to clarify the environment so that everyone knows who is to do what and who is responsible for which results, the obstacles to performance caused by confusion and uncertainty of assigning of tasks are removed, and there is a furnished decision making communication network, reflecting and supporting the enterprise's objectives.

What is Mean ? According to Haimann, an authority on management, "Organising is the process of defining and grouping the activities of an enterprise and establishing the authority relationships among them. In performing the organising function, the manager defines, departmentalises and assigns activities so that they can be most effectively executed. Organisation is concerned with the building, developing and maintaining of a structure of working relationships in order to accomplish the objectives of the enterprise. Organisation means the determination and assignment of duties to people, and also the establishment and the maintenance of authority relationships among these grouped activities. It is the structural framework within which the venous efforts are coordinated and related to each other."

Organisation means several things to different people. Its meaning or connotation changes with a change of context or application. Generally, the following are considered to be the characteristics of an organisation:

a. An organisation can be construed as consisting of behaviours of a set of participants.

b. It could be equated to a network system of social and cultural relationships.

c. It could be thought of as an enterprise, such as Infosys or Tata Steel.

However, to most practitioners of management, it is a formalised intentional structure of roles or positions. An institutional structure is devised with an intent to optimise the cohesive working of people in a productive group manner. Also, every organisation is a state, a culture, a social, rational and sentient system.

The organisations culture is typically defined as the major tenets that help its members to understand what the organisation stands for, how it does things, and what it considers important. Culture can generally be deduced from what members say, do, and think within an organisational setting. Culture also involves the collective learning and transmission of knowledge, beliefs, and patterns of behaviour developed over a period of time. Organisational culture is an important dimension of the organisation's internal environment and sets the tone for managerial behaviour.

Importance of Establishment : The importance of organisational culture can be succinctly described as follows:

- It sets the tone for conduct of an organisation and establishes implied rules for the way people should behave.
- It is a powerful force in a organisation that shapes its overall effectiveness and long term success.

Determinants of Organisational Culture

- The top leadership of an organisation has a strong influence on developing organisational culture through determination of ideology to permeate everyday decisions.
- A clear vision develops a commitment oriented culture.
- Participative processes of decision making and goal setting create a culture of belongingness.

According to Harrison and Handy, organisation culture are of the following types:

a. Power culture

b. Role culture

c. Task culture

d. People culture

Power culture typically has a central hub of power with functional influences emanating as spokes. In such a culture, the powerful hub exercises control through a group of key individuals. The general atmosphere is power oriented and there is a general lack of restraint for risk taking among employees.

Role culture works by logic and rationality. In such culture, roles and rules dominate. This sort of culture is likely to succeed in predictable and subtle operating environments.

Task culture is job or project oriented. This culture is cross functional with project teams made of individuals of different levels of expertise. Organisations with this type of culture often adopt matrix structure.

In people culture, the individual is all important. In such an organisational culture, the organisation is subservient to the needs of the individuals in it. Typically, groups of professionals, such as architects, lawyers, doctors, and consultants may associate themselves with this type of culture.

Another classification of culture is provided by Deal and Kennedy. They classify organisation culture as follows:

a. the tough guy, macho culture;

b. the work hard, play hard culture;

c. the Bet-your-company culture;

d. the process culture.

This classification is typically based on the degree of risk and the speed of feedback, as major factors. It can be represented by the following grid:

Degree of Risk

	High	Low
Rapid	Tough guy,	Work hard,
	macho culture	play hard culture
Slow	Bet-your-company culture	Process culture

Organisational climate refers to the day-to-day morale of the employees. While one may have a culture stating that, "Our people are the most important part of our business", there may be certain niggles in the environment or management philosophy that can significantly lower the morale.

A research carried out at the Harvard University suggests that 50 to 70% of an organisation's climate can be traced to its leadership or management style. In other words, good managers create good climates.

Generally, most of the organisations conduct organisation climate surveys. At the organisational level, there are three strategies for measuring climate:

- By observing work in progress.
- By carrying out interviews with key members of the work-force.
- By conducting a survey of staff members, using questionnaires.

Difference between Organisation Climate and Culture

- Changing an organisation's climate can provide quick wins and boost productivity dramatically.
- While changing an organisation's culture can often be a long term activity, climate change has a short time span and the payback is immediate.

The following administrative problems are created by organisational weaknesses:

This can be caused by a failure to define responsibilities, assigning too much of responsibility, or incompatible duties, or failure to designate an alternative to act in the absence of an employee.

This can be caused by overlapping responsibilities or prevalence of committees.

This can be caused by overlapping responsibilities, overload of work resulting from inadequate delegation or improper or incomplete job specification.

This can be caused by poor definition of responsibility, too much supervision, and uncertainty of supervisory responsibility.

This can be caused by overload of work resulting from inadequate delegation or too great a diversity of duties delegated.

This can result from failure to define targets and failure to define limits of responsibility.

This will result from an excessive use of committees or other joint effort, overlapping responsibilities and misunderstandings of the relationships.

This results from an excessive or improper delegation, faulty definitions of responsibilities and assignment of duties, and disproportionate skills.

The ten commandments of good organisation were formulated by M.C. Rorty, formerly a Vice president of International Telephone and Telegraph Corporation. Shortly after he became the president of the American Management Association (AMA) in 1934. AMA, in 1941, issued these in a commemorative form. They are as follows:

(i) Definite and clear responsibilities should be assigned to each executive, manager, supervisor, and foreman.

(ii) Responsibility should always be coupled with corresponding authority.

(iii) No change should be made in the scope or responsibility of a position, without a definite standing to that effect on the part of all persons concerned.

(iv) No executive or employee occupying a single position in the organisation, should be subject to definite orders from more than one source.

(v) Orders should never be given to subordinates by passing the executive to whom they are responsible. Rather, the officer efforts should be supplemented.

(vi) Criticism of subordinates should not be done in public. In no case should a subordinate be criticised in the presence of executives or employees of equal or lower rank.

(vii) No dispute or difference between the executives or the employees regarding authority or responsibility, should be considered too trivial for prompt and careful adjudication.

(viii) Promotions, wage changes, disciplinary action, should always be approved by the executive immediately superior to the one for against whom these are intended.

(ix) No executive or employee should be assistant to and at the same time a critic of the person he is assistant to.

(x) Any executive whose work is subject to regular inspection should, whenever practicable, be given the assistance and facilities necessary to enable him to maintain an independent check of the quality of his work.

Rules of Functioning : However, the ten principles of objective as enunciated by Urwick are also very popular and have been extensively quoted in management literature. These are as follows:

> Every organisation and each part of every organisation, must be an expression of the purpose of the undertaking concerned, or it becomes meaningless and therefore, redundant. One cannot organise in a vacuum, one must organise for something.

The activities of every member of any organised group should be confined, as far as possible, to the performance of a single function.

The purpose of an organisation per se, as distinguished from the purpose of the undertaking, is to facilitate coordination and the unity of efforts.

In every organised group, the supreme, authority must rest somewhere. There should be a clear line of authority from the supreme authority to every individual in the group.

The responsibility of the superior, for the acts of his subordinates, is absolute.

The content of each position, both the duties involved, and the authority and responsibility contemplated, and the relationships with other positions should be clearly defined in writing and published for all concerned.

In every position, the responsibility and authority should correspond with each other.

No person should supervise more than five, or at the most six, direct subordinates whose duties interlock.

It is essential that the various units of an organisation should be kept in balance.

Reorganisation is a continuous process in every undertaking and specific provisions should be made for it.

Organising consist of establishing relationships (responsibility and authority) among the components (personnel, functions and physical factors) for the purpose of structuring (line, line and staff functionalised, project) and directing them towards some common objective. Thus, the elements of the organisation process are:

1. Establishing objectives
2. Determining the functions that need to be accomplished
3. Assessing personnel requirements
4. Determining the physical resources necessary to achieve the objectives (inputs)
5. Grouping the functions, physical resources and the personnel into a coordinated organisation structure
6. Assigning authority and responsibility
7. Determining the levels of accountability of personnel within the established structure
8. Determining the work activities.

Once the objectives have been established, it is then necessary to determine the type of functions that must be performed within the organisation. A function is the work that can be identified and distinguished from other work.

The basic function or activities can be defined in any business, government or educational organisation. For instance, the major functions of a manufacturer would be production, marketing and finance.

Organisation design refers to the process by which managers create a structure of tasks and authority. It is through the process of decision-making that managers evaluate the relative benefits of alternative tasks and authority structures. This process may be explicit or implicit, it may be one shot or developmental, it may be done by a single manager or by a team of managers. Structure refers to relatively fixed relationships that exist among the jobs in the organisation. This fixed relationship results from the following decision processes:

1. The total task of the unit is broken down successfully into smaller jobs. That is, the task is divided or specialised among the persons in the unit. This is the issue of division of labour.
2. The individual jobs are recombined and grouped together. A common basis for the combined job is defined to rationalise the grouping; this is the issue of departmentalisation.
3. The appropriate size of the group reporting to one superior, must be determined; this is the issue of control.
4. Authority is distributed among the jobs or group of jobs. This is the issue of delegation.

The form and characteristics of an organisation's structure vary depending upon the attributes of each of the four sub problems. Conceptually, each of the four can vary along a continuum as shown:

Specialisation____________________________

Division of Labour :

High Low

Basis

Departmentalisation : ____________________________

Homogeneous Heterogeneous

Number

Span of control: ____________________________

Few Many

Delegation

Authority : ____________________________

Centralised Decentralised

Generally speaking, organisational structures will tend towards one extreme or the other, along each continuum. Structures tending to the left are characterised variously by such terms as formalistic, structured, bureaucratic, system and mechanists. Structures tending to the right are termed informalistic, unstructured, non-bureaucratic, system 4 and organic.

The issues associated with division of labour are concerned with the extent to which jobs are specialised. All jobs are specialised to a degree and the ability to divide work among many job holders is a key advantage of organisations. Rather than having a book-keeper in a hospital, performing emergency room tasks, the work is divided so that the book-keeper concentrates on preparing bills, and the emergency room clerk concentrates on admitting patients.

A major decision in developing an organisational structure involves determining how much division of labour should exist. Advocates of dividing work into smaller tasks, often cite the advantages of specialisation. Two of the major advantages are:

1. If a job contains few tasks, it is possible to train replacements easily for personnel who are terminated, transferred or absent. The minimum training effort results in a lowering of the training cost.
2. When a job entails only a limited number of tasks, the employees can become proficient in performing these tasks. This high level of proficiency is reflected in better quality of output.

Specialisation of labour is normally accomplished by the process of departmentalisation or departmentation. Departmentalisation is defined as the process of grouping related functions or major work activities into manageable units to achieve more effective and efficient overall coordination of organisation resources. The primary means of departmentalisation are by:

1. Function, 2. Product, 3. Customer, 4. Territory, 5. Project.

Departmentalisation by function is the most common means of grouping related functions. Departmental lines are drawn on the basis of specialised functions such as production, marketing, engineering, finance, and personnel. This assists management in efficient utilisation of the resources of the organisation. However, departmentalisation by function may create problems for management in the sense that personnel in these specialised functions may become more concerned with their own department, than with the overall company.

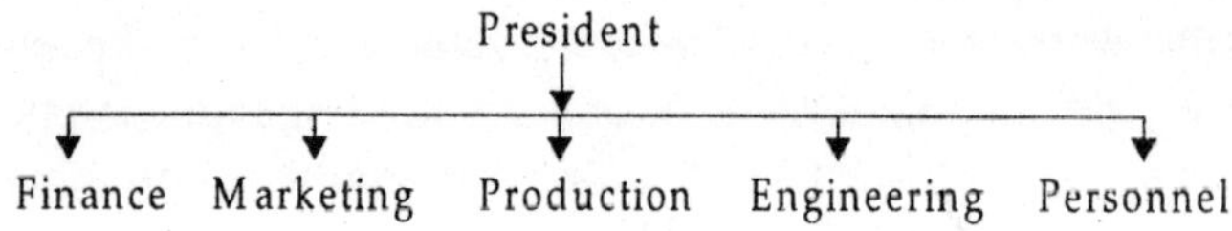

Departmentation by function

This form of departmentalisation is concerned with organising, according to the type of product being produced or sold by the firm. It enhances the use of specialised knowledge of particular products or services and is often used by rather large, diversified companies. Shown below is a large electronics firm organised into three product divisions.

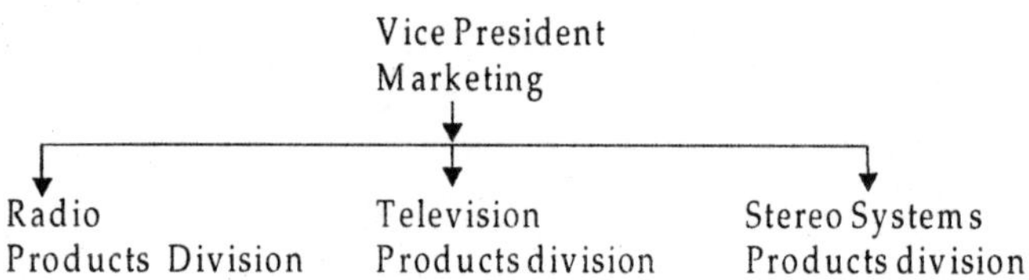

Departmentation by product

Departmentalisation by customers is used by organisations that have a special need to provide better service to different types of customers. As illustrated in the following figure, a diversified manufacturing company has an industrial, government and consumer product divisions. Large retailers and banks use departmentation along customer lines, to provide better service to different customer groups.

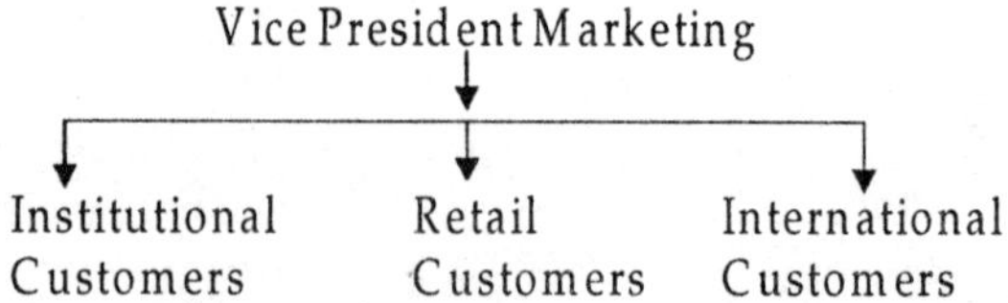

Departmentation by Customer

Grouping activities according to geographic territory is used by organisations that have physically dispersed and/or independent operations or markets to serve. The marketing functions of the company shown in the figure below are organised into the Southern, Western, and Eastern regional divisions. Geographic departmentation offers the advantages of better service with local or regional personnel, often at lesser cost.

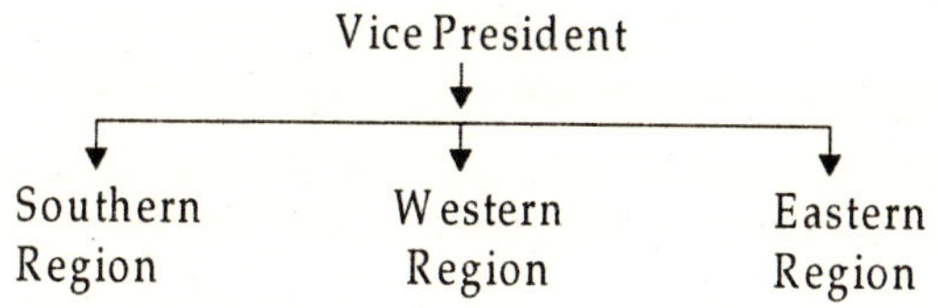

Departmentation by Geographic Territory

Departmentalisation by project is a method of bringing together personnel with different work backgrounds to form a team. This form of organisation has received considerable usage in recent years by the construction and aerospace industries.

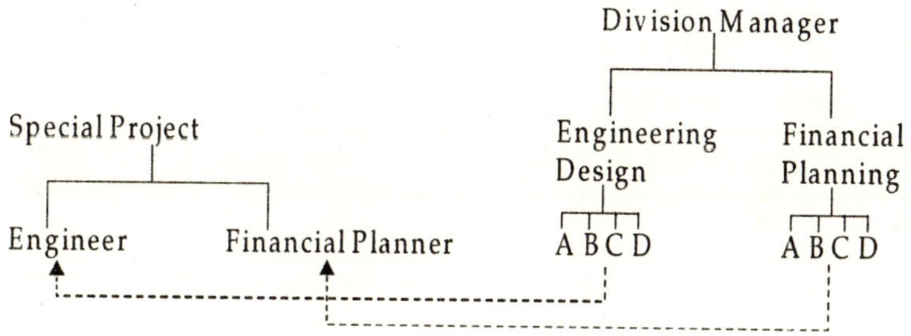

Departmentation by Project

Most organisations make use of several different basis for departmentation. In the example of the manufacturing company is departmentalised by type of function performed, i.e., production, engineering, marketing, etc. type of product industrial and consumer and by geographic territory.

An emerging organisation design, termed matrix organisation, attempts to maximise the strengths and minimise the weaknesses of both, the functional and product structures.

The matrix organisation form achieves the desired balance by superimposing or overlaying a horizontal structure of authority, influence, and communication.

Matrix structures are found in organisations which require responses to rapid change in two sectors, viz., technology and markets, which face uncertainties, that generate high information processing requirements, and which must deal with financial and human resources constraints.

The matrix organisation arrangement can be described as shown below; personnel assigned in each cell belong not only to the functional department, but also to a particular product or project. For example, manufacturing, marketing, engineering, and finance specialists will be assigned to work on one or more projects or products namely, A, B, C, D, E and F. As a consequence, personnel will report to two managers, one in their functional department and one in the project or product unit. The existence of a dual authority system is a distinguishing characteristic of a matrix organisation. Traditional functional and product based organisations maintain a strict chain of command, wherein, each employee reports to only one superior.

Projects, Products	FUNCTIONS			
A	Manufacturing	Marketing	Engineering	Finance
B				
C				
D				
E				
F				

Requirement and Importance : The following are the major advantages of matrix organisation.

Matrix organisation facilitates the utilisation of highly specialised staff and equipment. Each project, or product unit can share the specialised resource with other units, rather than duplicating it to provide independent coverage for each. This advantage is particularly so when projects require less than the full time effort of the specialist. For example, a project may require only half the time of a computer scientist. Rather than having several unutilised computer scientists assigned to each project, the organisations can keep fewer of them, fully utilised by shifting them from project to project.

Timely response to change requires information and communication channels which can efficiently get the information to the right people at the right time. Matrix structures encourage constant interaction among project unit and functional department members. Information is channelled vertically and horizontally, as people exchange technical knowledge. The result is quicker response to competitive conditions, and technological breakthroughs. (and other environmental conditions).

Technical specialists interact with other specialists while assigned to a project. These interactions encourage cross fertilisation of ideas such as when a computer scientist discusses the pros and cons of electronic data processing with a financial accounting expert. Each specialist must be able to listen, understand and respond to the views of the other. At the same time, specialists maintain an on going contact with members of their own discipline because they are also members of a functional department.

An initial stimulus for the development of matrix organisations is that top management increasingly becomes involved with day to day operations. Matrix organisation makes it possible for top management to delegate on going decision making thus, providing more time for long range planning.

The opportunity to participate in key decisions fosters high levels of motivation and commitment, particularly for individuals with acknowledged professional orientation.

Members of matrix organisations are provided considerable opportunity to develop their skills and knowledge. They are placed in groups consisting of individuals representing diverse parts of the organisation. They have the opportunities to learn something of other specialities. Engineers develop knowledge of financial issues, accountants will learn about marketing. The experience broadens each specialist's knowledge, not only of the organisation, but also of other scientific and technical disciplines.

Matrix organisation forms can be depicted as existing in the middle of a continuum which has functional organisations at an extreme and product. Organisations at the other as shown in figure below:

Organisations can move from functional to matrix forms or from product to matrix forms. Ordinarily the process of moving to matrix organisation is evolutionary.

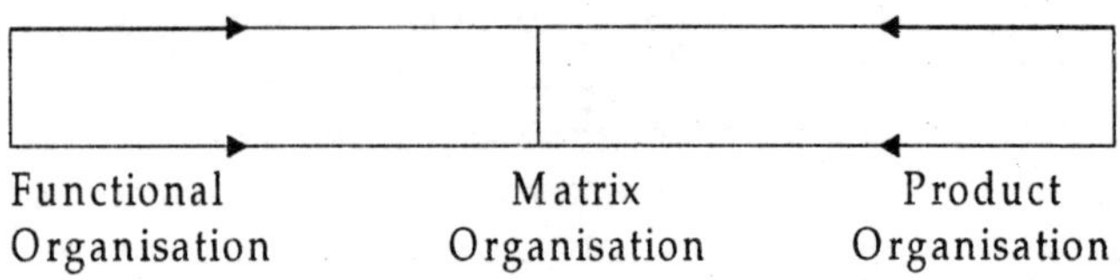

Alternative Matrix Organisation Forms

Galbraith describes the evolutionary process as moving in successive steps from task force to product management departments.

When a competition markets a new product that quickly captures the market, a rapid response is necessary. The convenient approach is to create a task force of individuals from each functional department and charge it with the responsibility to expedite the process. The task force achieves its objectives and dissolves, as members return to their primary assignment.

If the product or technological break through generates a family of products which move through successive stages of new and improved products, the temporary task force concept is ineffective. A typical next step is to create permanent teams which consists of representatives from each functional department the teams meet regularly to resolve inter departmental issues and to achieve coordination. When not involved with issues associated with new product development, the team members work on their regular assignments.

If the technological breakthrough persists such that new product development becomes a way of life, top management will create the roles of product managers. In a sense product managers chair the teams, but they are now permanent positions. Ordinarily they report to top management, but they have no formal authority over the team members.

The final step in the evolution to matrix organisation is the creation of product management departments. Figure below depicts the organisation which has a product manager reporting to top management and with sub product managers for each product line.

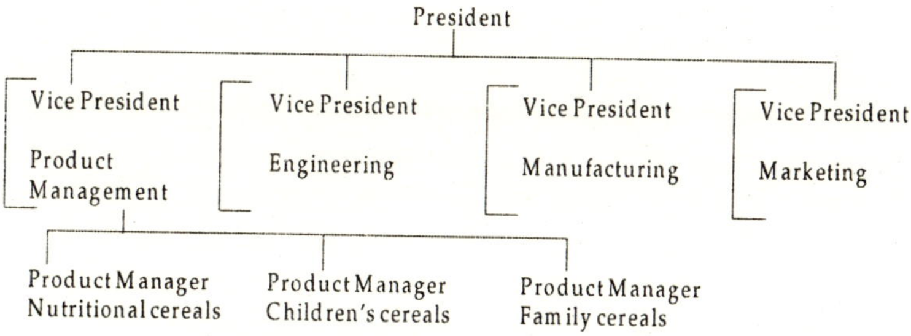

Fully involved matrix organisation

Prominent Factors

The following factors are to be taken into consideration in departmentation:

> Departmentation should be such as to yield the advantages of specialisation which is the most widely recognised characteristics of modern enterprise.

Departmentation should simplify the executives task of control. Departmentation should have a direct bearing on independence of checks, clear-cut accountability, telling comparison of results, or ease of supervision.

Quite different activities may be grouped under a single executive because they need to be coordinated.

An unusually important activity for the success of the enterprise should be given a special recognition in the organisation, for giving it greater attention than other activities, it may be placed in a separate division and also at a higher level in the administrative hierarchy according to its importance.

The departmentation should take into consideration local conditions at the places concerned.

The expense involved in creating separate departments for any activity is an important factor and should be kept in mind.

In addition to select alternative methods of grouping activities into departments at the outset as detailed above, the executive is confronted from time to time with the problem of deciding where to fit in a new activity and where to shift an old one. The first need is usually that of recognising a function. A second need is that of combining function so as to realise efficient performance and balanced operation without increasing the number of management levels through creation of splinter departments. Each major department consists of a combination of subsidiary activities narrower in scope. Essential activities of purchasing, inventory control, and production scheduling may well be combining under one individual in a simple organisation. Accounting finance statistics and business economics might all be grouped under a high level controller in a large organisation.

A third need is that of developing principles where by activities may logically be combined.

Two widely recognised principles of underlying departmentation are: (i) Similarity of function (ii) Closeness of association.

Similarity of function is useful primarily as a basis for classifying activities at the lower levels of organisation structure where duties are not yet highly differentiated. Grouping of typists into a general typing pool is an example. Salesmen, machinists, and of office workers are often grouped into their respective departments by reason of similarity of function.

The principle of similarity has narrow limitations and diversity must be coped within grouping most activities.

Titles and Charts : An organisation chart is prepared to show formal organisational relationships which are intended to prevail. It shows who supervises whom and how the various units are related to each other. It also shows the main line of communication, the downward flow of authority, and the upward flow of responsibility. It enables the top management to assign responsibility by designating different persons entrusted with certain jobs.

The assignment of responsibilities within a sound organisation structure serve several purposes.

(a) It acquaints all members of the enterprise with their own responsibilities and with the responsibilities of others whom they must deal.

(b) It permits greater decisiveness of action by restricting duplication of effort.

(c) It eliminates frictions and playing of politics.

(d) It eliminates unnecessary functions.

(e) It stimulates the execution of activities and the development of individual capacities by providing an understandable framework of authority within which to carry on the activities.

(f) It provides executives with more time for planning and policy formation by assuring them that all operating details are provided for.

(g) It adopts the "principles of organisation" to individual company needs.

To accomplish these purposes it is necessary to define the titles of members and relate them to authority and responsibility. The titles may be such as Production Manager, Works Manager, Factory Manager, Plant Superintendent, General Foreman, Foreman, Supervisor and Department Head, and should be defined and placed in their proper relationship to the whole. The title should not be changed very often. After all, titles are labels which define segment of work. They should be helpful to those out side the organisation and they should build an internal system of procedure.

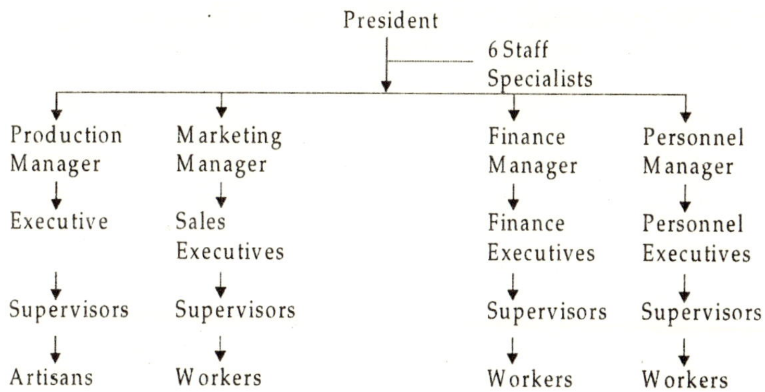

Span of control also called span of management supervision indicates the number of people directed or managed effectively by a single executive or supervisor. Stated differently, it refers to the number of subordinates reporting directly to a single manager who is accountable for their activities. Thus, if a general manager has 5 managers reporting to him directly in a firm employing 10,000 employees, the span of control of the General Manager is 5 not 10,000.

While there is a limit to the number of employees a manager can effectively supervise, the precise span of control varies according to the situation.

The number of potential relationships between a manager and subordinates can be calculated by the formula:

R = n [2n-1+n - 1]

where, R = the number of relationships; n = number of subordinates.

The calculation assumes that the managers must contend with three types of relationships:

(1) Direct Single (2) Direct Group (3) Cross.

Thus, as shown in figure below a manager with two subordinates has 2 direct relationships, two cross relationships and two group contacts for a total of six possible relationships.

The potential relationships with number of subordinates are shown below:

No. of Subordinates	***No. of Relationships***
1	1
2	6
3	18
4	44
5	100
6	222
7	490

Contd..

No. of Subordinates	No. of Relationships
8	1,080
9	2,376
10	5,210
11	11,374
12	24,708

The practical solution to the span of control problem is to identify the specific factors which are important in a particular situation. One such solution was undertake at Lockheed Missiles and space company where a model for determining the optimal span was deviced. Following variables must be considered in establishing the span of control:

1. Similarity of functions.
2. Geographical closeness of subordinates.
3. Complexity of functions.
4. Direction and control required by subordinates.
5. Coordination required.
6. Planning importance, complexity and time required.
7. Organisational assistance received by supervisor.

Each of these variables should be assigned weights. The weighting reflect the importance of each of the variables and are summarised in the following table.

The most important variable is direction and control with a maximum weight of 15. The weight values were based on the common sense, experience and experimentation with 150 different situations in Lockheed. Every management position was evaluated, and point values for each of the variables were assigned. The values were summed and the resultant figure was termed the supervisory index. The index reflects the supervisor's burden arising from the type of work of the unit. The higher the index the greater the burden consequently the narrower and appropriate span.

Span factor					
Similarity of functions	Identical	Essentially alike	Similar	Inherently different	Fundamentally distinct
	1	2	3	4	5
Geographic contiguity	All together	All in one building	Separate building 1 plant location	Separate locations 1 geographic area	Dispersed geographic area
	1	2	3	4	5
Complexity of functions	Simple repetitive	Routine	Some complexity	Complex varied varied	Highly complex
	2	4	6	8	10
Direction and control	Minimum Supervision and training	Limited Supervision	Moderate Periodic Supervision	Frequent Continuing Supervision	Constant Close Supervision
	3	6	9	12	15
Coordination	Minimum relation with others courses	Relationships limited to defined controlled	Moderate relationships easily relationships.	Considerable close relationships	Extensive mutual non recurring
	2	4	6	8	10
Planning	Minimum Space and complexity	Limited scope and complexity	Moderate scope and complexity	Considerable effort required	Extensive effort requited
	2	4	6	8	10

Middle Management Indexes and Span of Control

Supervisory Index	Suggested Standard Span
40-42	4-5
37-39	4-6
34-36	4-7
31-33	5-8
26-30	6-9
25-27	7-10
22-24	8-11

The Lockheed study revealed that when the span of control was increased, the number of supervisory levels was often reduced.

The principle is that wider the span of management, the less direct supervision and the narrower the span, the greater the number of managers necessary and therefore, the higher the cost.

Tall organisations are costly and less effective communication. Narrow spans of management require not only mare supervisors but also the added expense of executive offices, secretaries, and fringe benefits. In all organisation decision and communication process takes longer and is of poorer quality. This results not only in inefficiency but also in demoralisation among the lower level subordinates.

Small organisations generally have a higher level of employee morale and productivity than the large organisations.

Hierarchical Setup : The scaler concept is also known as a chain of direct superior subordinate relationships throughout the entire organisation. In this regard, it seems realistic to consider the scalar concept as a series of steps which establish a clear line of authority from the top of an organisation to the bottom. Adherence to the chain of command is sometimes difficult. A continued violation of scalar relationship, may result in breakdown in coordination, a misunderstanding of managerial positions and general inefficiency. As a general guide all organisational should normally follow prescribed communication channels, however, good judgement should be exercised when time is of the essence. By passing certain managers in the chain of command may be necessary in some instances, but these managers still be kept informed through follow up communication that are initiated as soon as possible.

The principle of unity of command states that no member of an organisation should report to more than one superior on any single function. The application of this principle is easy in pure line organisation, in which each superior has general authority, however it becomes a complex problem in actual cases in which some form of staff and/or functional organisation is used. In practice, instructions may be received from several sources without loss of productivity. The problem is to avoid conflicts in orders from different people relating to the same subject. The principle of unity of command may be useful in the planning of an organisation if it helps to keep relations between superior and subordinate simple and direct, it is not realistic if it is interpreted as an immutable law that would eliminate useful relationships among a number of managers.

The exception principle states that recurring decisions should be handled in a routine manner by lower level managers, whereas problems involving unusual matters should be referred to higher levels. This principle emphasises that executives at the top levels of an organisation have limited time and capacity and should refrain from becoming bogged down in routine details that can be handled as well by subordinates.

The exception principle can be very useful to a manager by focussing his attention on those matters that should receive his attention first. It is applicable to all levels, and if kept in mind, can help the inexperienced manager compensate for a human tendency to concentrate on the immediate, concrete, and detailed problems at the expense of more fundamental, difficult and abstract issues.

Detailed organisation structure varies widely from company to company, even in the same industry, and within a given company, especially if it is of large size, the relationships of functions and sub-functions usually under go continuing change, to conform to changes in environment, objectives, and needs. Traditionally recognised, however, there are five principal organisation proceedings.

(i) Line, (ii) Line and staff, (iii) Pure functional, (iv) Line and functional staff, (v) Committee.

A business controlled under the line form of organisation may act more quickly and effectively in changing its direction and policy than any other form of organisation. Authority is passed down from the owners through a board to directors to a general manager, to whom the heads of the various departments respond. Each department in importance is a complete self substaining unit, its head being responsible for the performance of its particular process, product or function. This means that the foreman must (1) Direct its techniques, (2) Formulate the necessary work specifications, (3) Sometimes purchase materials, (4) Plan and schedule the work, (5) the necessary materials handling and (6) Keep the necessary shop cost and production records. The procedure would be repeated in all other departments with complete control centered in each head subject only to the will of the general manager, whatever little research, planning or central record keeping is required fall upon general manager.

Each department has got responsibilities and is working as self supporting unit.

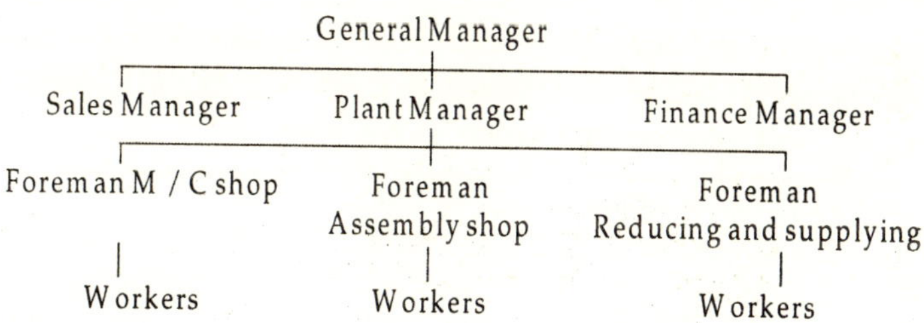

Advantages: (i) It is simple. (ii) There is a clear cut division of authority and responsibility. (iii) It is extremely stable, (iv) It makes for quick action. (v) Discipline is easily maintained.

Disadvantage: (i) The organisation is rigid and inflexible. (ii) Being an autocratic system it may be operated on an arbitrary, opinionated and dictatorial basis. (iii) Department heads carry out orders independently and often in accordance with their own whims and desires. (iv) As division of labour is only incidental crude methods may prevail because of lack of expert advice. (v) There is unique reliance upon the skill and personnel knowledge of operators. (vi) Foreman may offer resistance to much needed changes. (vii) Key men are loaded to breaking point. (viii) The loss of one or two capable men may cripple the entire organisation. (ix) Difficulty of operation occurs in large or complex enterprises.

This admits the fact, that today in any industrial enterprise, the functions of directive and controlling any business are so complex, that it is not feasible for any man, may be highly qualified, to handle the situation smoothly. Therefore, overall responsibilities of the enterprise divided according to the functions to be done. This concept was introduced by F.W. Taylor. He was in favour that all the industrial activities should be done and supervised by experts. Taylor contended that a foreman could be specialised in everything, he was expected to do.

Therefore instead of having one single superior, as in the line organisation, Taylor arranged for a group of specialists to boss the workers in various aspects of the business. Office work is separated from the shop work. Thus Taylor separated the mental and clerical functions from the production functions. This type of organisation, employing the principle of specialisation is based on individual's proficiency and specialised knowledge. Each executive is controlling and thus he becomes the expert in his field.

In this scheme ample scope and opportunity will be provided for proper expansion and development:

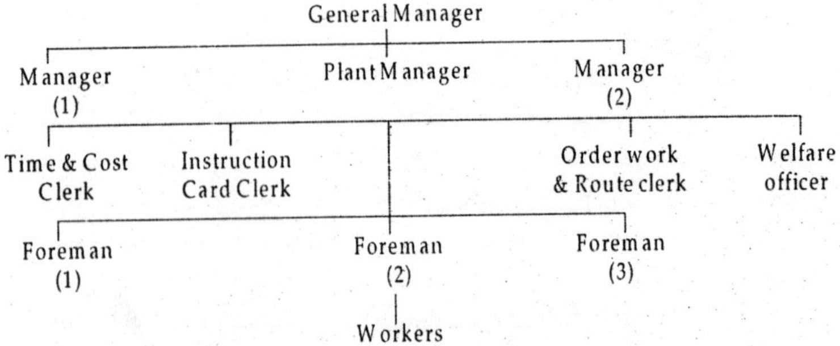

Advantages

(i) Functional organisation is based on expert knowledge.

(ii) Division of labour is planned, not incidental.

(iii) The highest functional efficiency of each person is maintained.

(iv) The manual work is separated from the mental-aspiration initiated by Taylor.

Disadvantages

(i) A relative lack of stability is manifest.

(ii) The coordinating influences needed to insure a smoothly functioning organisation may involve heavy over head expenses.

(iii) The inability to locate and fix responsibility may seriously affect the discipline and morale of the workers through apparent or actual contradiction of orders.

(iv) Overlaping authority may give rise to friction between foreman and supervisor.

(v) The initiative of supervisors may become like a stiffer man may become more automations and routine may become very complicated.

The two systems which are discussed above give evaluation of third one, which has got all the good features of both. Today most of the industries in India and abroad are using this form of organisation. Individual industry may bring certain changes in the above said organisation system depending on the size of the industry and the situation.

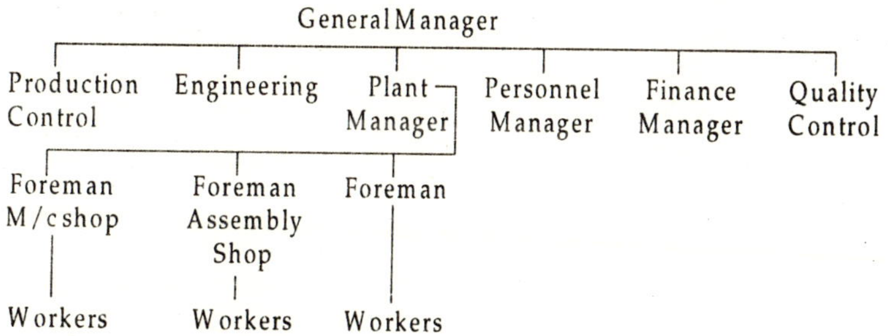

Basically it is the form of line organisation where some experts are introduced at different levels in the line organisation. These experts help in carrying out the work of line executives and thus their work is lightened.

It is very difficult to express the relationship between the line executives and staff executives, but in a very simple way the concept of the duties can be expressed. Line executives do while the staff executives advice how it is to be done. In any organisation the staff executives offers four types of services.

(i) Advice (ii) Control (iii) Service (iv) Coordination.

The whole idea of this system is that the specialised work in connection with analysis, research, labour, standardising, costing, material, equipment etc. should be left to experts who can solve the problem of high technical standard and thus the departmental managers are free to organise, control and supervise the productive activities.

Advantages

(i) It is based upon manned specialisation.

(ii) It brings expert knowledge to bear upon management and operating problems.

(iii) It provides more opportunity for advancement for able operators, a great variety of responsible jobs are available.

(iv) It makes possible the principle of undivided responsibility and authority and at the same time permit staff specialisation.

(v) It repays its added costs many times over through the savings resulting from increased efficiency of operation.

Disadvantages

(i) Unless the duties and responsibilities of the staff members are clearly indicated by chart and manuals, there may be considerable confusion throughout the organisation as to the functions and positions stage members with relation to line supervisors.

(ii) The staff may be ineffective for lack of authority to carry-out its functions or intelligent backing in the application of its recommendation.

(iii) The inability to see each other viewpoint may cause difficulty and friction between the line supervisors and members.

(iv) Although experts information and advice are available, they reach the operators through line officers and thus run the risk of misunderstanding and misinterpretation.

Under the pure line and staff organisation the work of the staff is not regarded as a specific managerial function, but under this plan, however specialists become more than just advisers, they become executives in charge of single techniques which are common under several units of the works. The entire organisation is divided so that no activity is left out and there is no duplication in the allotment of activities to different departments. Under this system the weakness of the pure functional plan is eliminated and no employee is placed under more than one boss. It is really the line and staff type of organisation through functions.

The most important advantage of this system is that it helps mass production by standardisation and specialisation. It makes for organisation growth, because each man grows in his own speciality. If not carried too far, coordinations through cooperation and leadership is easily achieved.

Steps Towards Goal : The staff system when used with line system corrects to some extent the incfficacies of the pure line system, it also comments the lack of coordination inherent in the pure functional form of organisation. But this is not enough. As every piece of work in any department in any enterprise has some connection with a piece of work in other departments, group participation is essential to ensure coordination and to promote cooperative relationship committees are formed for the performance of special duties, and may be either permanent or temporary, formed to serve a temporary function only. As many problems in an enterprise are plant wide, a high degree of cooperation, which is paramount to success can be achieved through committees, which promote the pooling of knowledge.

A committee is a group of people usually on the same authoritative level specially designated to perform a managerial act and a committee meeting is gathering of these people for the purpose of talking over hinge they have to do. Thus the function of a committee is the assignment of a task to a group rather than to one or more individuals.

Advantages

(i) Under a strong executive chairman, a committee may quickly marshal many valuable points of view, since two heads are better than one.

(ii) In conducting investigations, the several phases of various questions may be quickly assigned to responsible members with a reasonable assurance of speedy action if a time schedule and proper follow up are instituted.

(iii) Decisions are impersonal, leaving the chairman free from the personal criticism so often levelled at an aging executive.

(iv) There is stimulus toward cooperative action.

(v) The members of the committee know better what is going on in the plant so that they can spread the information and team up with other individuals or departments.

Disadvantages

(i) Committee may be too large for constructive action. The number of members should seldom exceed three.

(ii) Committees are expensive in time and usually have to be prodded to prevent delays.

(iii) Important executives may be called too frequently from their work for meetings that the operations of the enterprise slow down.

(iv) The members of the committee offer are unfamiliar with important details of questions at issue and therefore may make wrong or ineffective decision.

(v) Action often be superficial because of lack of time or the disinterestedness of committee members.

(vi) Committee weakens the individual responsibility and makes for compromise instead of clear cut decisions.

(vii) The decisions often are made to conform with what it is assumed some executive wants or to enable the members to avoid direct responsibility for any bad results.

(viii) Aggressive and outspoken members may dominate committee meetings and unduly influence the action often adversely.

The most common use of the committee in industrial organisations is in policy-making. When so used, it is known as the executive or administrative committee.

Line and staff are two terms that are often used in ways that are loose and unclear. Attempts have been made in some organisation to dispense with them, and thus "operating" is frequently substituted for line and "auxiliary" and service are common substitutes for "staff." Clarification will be achieved if we examine the terms in the light of work done and authority exercised.

A line or operating organisation unit is one that is actually doing the work that represents the primary mission of the larger organisation unit of which it is a part. For example, an assembly department in the manufacturing division or a selling branch in the sales division.

A staff or service organisation unit is any unit which is helping to do its work, or making it possible for the line to do its work, but is not actually engaged in the work itself. Examples: a purchasing unit, a time study unit, a payroll preparation unit, in service training unit etc.

Misunderstandings arise from failure to realise that whether an activity is "line" (operating) or "staff" (service) depends upon whose shoes you are putting on and when you are looking at the operation. Thus, the total organisation headed up by a controller render service to all of the other organisation units in the entire company. Those other units therefore look upon this organisation unit as staff or service. The controller however, looking at his own operations can consider the various units with in his organising units as far as he is concerned. He may, however, within his own organisation, set up staff units (perhaps an economist to advise him or a special analysis devoted solely to improving procedures in his own department).

It is frequently said that a member of a staff unit can not tell a manager or a member of line unit to do any thing rather he can only inform or suggest or advise or offer his specific services. This is largely true, but there are exceptions. For example, a safety engineer may shut down a line activity as quality inspector. Similarly it is often said that a line manager can not issue direct orders to staff or service man. This is an over simplification.

Following are seven distinct types of line and staff relationships.

Here the staff unit is one that offers advisory help only an operating manager may or may not avail himself of it. He may request it, but the staff unit can not foist itself from him. However, the staff unit may volunteer suggestions on the basis of observations made, even though uninvited.

This relationship is similar to the above, but involves services rather than advise or suggestions. The relationship of the staff personnel is similar to that of an outside contractors personnel—their "boss" is their own staff unit head.

Staff services rendered to an organisation unit as part of fulfilling the units mission supplied on a programmed basis, for example, there may be certain periodic specialised technical services rendered by a head quarters engineering unit to customers served regularly by a customers' service department working out of a branch plant. There should be no question about lines of direct supervision—the direct chain of command of these specialists or technicians is to the head of the central staff unit, and the latter is responsible for the quality of their service and their mode of operating. The head of the customers' service department at the branch can not attempt to supervise the specialists, but he can communicate directly with the head of the central staff unit if he questions the quality of their work, their adherence to schedule etc. At the same time, the head of the central staff unit cannot dictate the degree of utilisation of the services since this is stipulated by an over all programme previously authorised at a higher level.

Accounting and procurements are examples. The supplying organisation unit has the right to insist that the operating organisation follow officially specified rules having to do with reporting, requisitions or other information necessary to rendering the service. If established procedures are not complied with, personnel of the service unit after normal courtesies in the form of requests to the operating personnel; have the right to insist to the operating supervisor that corrective action be taken. Personnel of the using organisation unit can communicate directly with the supplying unit to request service or information about service as long as specified initiating or confirming paper work is executed.

Functional relationship between a central staff unit and personnel in a counter part staff unit attached to an operating organisation unit.

Examples are a central quality control department which operates through a quality control department at each plant, and a central personnel department which operates through a personnel department at each plant. On organisation charts a "dotted line relationship" is shown between such central staff units and the counterpart units in the operating organisation. A solid line goes up from the operating organisation is staff unit through the local operating chain of commando, and its ultimate boss is the head of the local operating organisation. However the central staff unit has responsibility for the professional conduct of the work and its personnel can make suggestions for improvement. They do not give direct orders to the counterpart professional people in the local operating organisation's staff unit. If they have strong feelings about the way something is or is not being done, they can make strong suggestions to the head of the operating organisation's staff unit and failing action can only proceed higher in the operating chain of command.

Relationship between a department head and personnel assigned to them by a staff unit—specialised personnel are often assigned to an operating unit by a staff unit which is responsible for their training and for the quality of their professional work. They are considered as being permanently attached to their home staff unit, even though their assignment may be of relatively long duration. But they are under the administrative command of the head of the operating unit and for accounting purposes may be on the operating unit's pay-roll. They are under the "professional command of the head of their staff unit". Professional command means that the staff unit head and not the operating unit head lays down the procedures and sets the standards with respect to their professional work.

Relationship between an operating executive and an advisory

or service staff person or unit directly reporting to him and relationship between the staff personnel and other personnel in the organisation units under the operating executives.

The staff man or unit only supplies information and advice and recommends. The operating executive is the one who must make the decisions and take action. The staff unit can act only in the name of that executive-it can not tell other employees what they must do or must not do.

Recent Trends : Since the early 1980s, organisation designers have been focussing on to effect new structural changes in organisation designs which can enable the organisations to compete effectively. Four of such new organisational designs are : the team structure, the virtual organisation, the boundaryless organisation and the feminine organisation.

Teams are an important means to organise work activities. When management uses teams as its central coordination device, we have a team structure. The main characteristics of the team structure are that it breaks down departmental barriers and decentralises decision making to the level of the work team. Team structure also requires employees to be generalist as well as specialists. In small companies, the team structure can define the entire organisation. In such companies teams have full responsibility for most operational issues and customer service.

Many large organisations have also made extensive use of team structure, for example companies like Motorola and Xerox improved productivity at the operational level through self managed teams. Such teams are generally composed of 10 to 15 people who take on full responsibility of work related decisions and their outcomes. Members of such teams do their own scheduling, determine work assignments, rotate jobs on their own and even select their own members and evaluate their performance. Also, while designing a new product or to coordinate major projects, organisations can structure activities around cross functional teams. These teams are made up of employees from about the same hierarchical level, but from different work areas to coordinate complex projects, develop new ideas and solve problems.

The virtual organisation is a small, core organisation that

sources out major business functions. It is a highly centralised organisation, with little or no departmentation.

The virtual organisation creates a network of relationships which allows them to contract out manufacturing, distribution marketing or any other business function where management feels others can do it better or cheaper.

In a typical bureaucratic organisation, which has many vertical levels of management, research and development is carried in-house, production occurs in company owned plants, and sales and marketing are performed by the company's own employees. In contrast, the virtual organisation outsources many of these functions and concentrates on what it does best.

One of the major advantage to the virtual organisation is its flexibility. One needs just an innovative idea and little money to successfully compete against large companies. The disadvantage to this structure is that it reduces management's control over key parts of its business.

The Boundaryless Organisation is an organisation that seeks to eliminate the chain of command, have limitless spans of control, and replace departments with empowered teams.

In such organisations, management flattens the hierarchy by removing vertical boundaries and minimises status and rank. Such organisations also emphasise participative decision making and function in cross hierarchical teams which include top executives, middle managers, supervisors and operative employees.

Such organisations also eliminate horizontal boundaries by replacing functional departments with cross functional teams that work in a single process instead of around narrow functional teams that work in a single process instead of around narrow functional tasks.

Some boundaryless organisations also go to the extent of breaking the barriers to external constituencies and barriers created by geography. Globalisation, strategic alliances, customer-organisation linkages and telecommunicating are few examples of such organisations.

In the early 1980s, many organisation theorists studied the

relationship between values and structural preference. It was found that women had preferences for those organisations that emphasised relatedness and connecting with others. They argued that since women have been socialised for their role in the family, that teaches the value of supporting and nurturing others, therefore they prefer to work in organisations which value human relationships, and are based on care and trust.

Joyce Rothschild developed a model of the feminine organisation that has the following characteristics :

1. Members are valued as individual human being.
2. Relationships are seen as possessing value in themselves and not just means to achieve organisational goals.
3. Career success is defined in terms of service to others.
4. Create extensive opportunities of personal growth for their members.
5. Members are closely knit and have trust and care for each other.
6. Emphasise on participative decision making.

Organisation design is the process by which managers create a structure of tasks and authority. The form and characteristics of an organisational structure vary depending upon the attributes such as division of labour, departmentalisation, span of control and authority.

Division of labour is the extent to which the organisation's work is separated into different jobs to be done by different people.

Departmentalisation is the process of grouping the related functions or major work activities into manageable units to achieve more effective and efficient overall coordination of organisation can be departmentalised on the basis of function, product, customer, territory and project.

Span of control indicates the number of people directed or managed effectively by a supervisor. However, organisations must give due consideration to similarity of functions, geographical closeness of subordinates, complexity of functions, direction and control required by subordinates etc., in establishing the span of control.

The authority is the legal power to command or extract action from others. Since managers get work done through others, authority constitutes the key to the manager's job authority in this sense is thus shared by the manager with the right to command.

Delegation of authority takes place when organisational power is given to subordinates by a superior. It plays an important role in the organisation as it relieves the manager from performing rest time duties, provides motivation to the subordinates and thus develops the subordinates. However, certain amount of centralised control is essential as it provides a feeling of prestige to the manager, powers cost, tightens control and results in greater uniformity of policy and practices.

The new organisation design developed in the recent years to enable the organisations to compete effectively are the team structure, the virtual organisation, the boundaryless organisation and the feminine organisation.

Different Kinds : One of the important components of the organisation process is the creation of an appropriate organsation structure. The organisation structure represents the hierarchical arrangement of various positions in the enterprise. It helps in allocating authority and responsibility formally. But there is no best structure of the organisational relationship which may be suitable, for enterprise has to evolve its own organisation structure based on the nature of activities and business competence of personnel and the philosophy of management. There are five types of an organisation:

(a) Line Organisation

(b) Line and Staff Organisation,

(c) Functional Organisation

(d) Project of Matrix Organisation,

(e) Committee Organisation.

Historically, this is the oldest form of an organisation. This is known by different names, i.e., military, vertical, scalar and departmental. All other types of organisation structure have mostly been modifications of the line organisation. The concept of the line organisation holds that in any organisation derived from a scalar process, there must be a single head who commands it. Although an executive can delegate authority, he has ultimate responsibility for results.

According to McFarland, "Line structure consists of the direct vertical relationship which connect the positions and tasks of each level with those above and below it." According to Allen, "Organisationally, the line is the chain of command that extends from the board of directors through the various delegations and redelegations of authority and responsibility to the point where the primary activities of the enterprise are performed."

From the above chart, the following special features of the line organisation come up:

(a) There are many levels of management depending upon the scale of business and decision-making ability of managers. Each level of management has equal rights.

(b) There is a vertical flow of authority and responsibility. The lower positions derive authority from the higher positions.

(c) There is a unity of command. Every person is accountable to only one person (his immediate boss) and none else. A person receives orders only from his immediate boss.

(d) There is scalar chain in the line organisation. The flow of orders, communication of suggestions and complaints, etc. are made as it is in the case of a ladder. One cannot defy the claim.

(e) There is limit on subordinates under one manager. A manager has control only over the subordinates of his department.

The merits of the line organisation are as follows:

It is the simplest of all types of organisations. It can be easily established and easily understood by the workers.

The authority and responsibility of every person is clearly defined. Everyone knows as to whom he can issue orders and to whom he is accountable. Further it is easier to fix up the responsibility if there is any lapse anywhere in the performance of activities.

Because of direct authority responsibility relationships, discipline can be maintained more effectively. Direct supervision and control also helps in maintaining strong discipline among the workers.

Since the orders are given by one superior, there is no confusion, among the subordinates. This ensures better understanding and quick action.

As the superiors enjoy full authority, quick decisions are taken by them. Such decisions are executed promptly also.

Since each departmental head has sole responsibility for his department, he can easily adjust the organisation according to the changes in business situation.

The demerits of the line organisation are as follows:

> Since the departmental head has to look after all the activities of his department, hc is over burdened with work. He may neglect some of the duties and there may be some inefficiency in management.

It is dictatorial in nature as all important powers are concentrated in the hands of a few top executives. If they are not able the enterprise will not be successful.

The line organisation suffers from lack of specialised skill of experts. It is extremely difficult for one person to handle activities of diverse nature. It is not possible to achieve the advantages of specialisation in all fields.

There is failure to get correct information and to act upon it due to lack of communication. Although there is communication from top to bottom there is usually no communication from the lower ranks to higher ranks and executives. They are not provided with an opportunity to put forward their viewpoint or problems or suggestions to persons at the top level. Thus, they lose their capacity for independent thinking.

Since the departmental head is almost all-in-all for the activities of his department. There is scope for favouritism. There may be a good deal of nepotism and jobbery and personal prejudices. The executive may appoint and promote his own men in various positions ignoring the claim of efficient persons.

Despite these drawbacks, the line organisation is still considered as very ideal for small enterprises where the work involved is not of a very complex nature and number of people are small. It is also, ideal where automatic machines are in use or where talented and capable executives are at the head of various departments. But it is not very successful in large concerns.

The line organisation suffers from three main drawbacks, i.e., heavy burden of work on the line executive, too much concentration of power in the hands of a low line executive and lack of specialisation. In view of these drawbacks, the idea of the line and staff organisation was introduced.

Normally staff means those elements of an organisation that help the line of work most effectively in accomplishing the primary objectives of the enterprise. The staff authority support those executives who hold the line authority. The staff authority consists of experts and specialists in various fields. The main function of the staff is to help the line executives in such activities which require expert and specialised knowledge. The role of the staff is purely advisory and not authoritative. They have to recommend but have no authority to enforce their preference on subordinates or to issue orders to them. In fact, the function of the line executives is to act and that of the staff is to think and suggest.

In short, the line and staff organisation refers to a pattern in which the staff specialists advise the line managers to perform their duties. Thus, in a firm engaged in the manufacture of dyes and chemicals, the works manager, marketing manager and the finance manager are line officials while functions like personnel management, quality control, public relations and accounting are staff functions. Thus, the line and the staff are two types of organisational relationships.

Following are the characteristics of the line and staff organisation:

1. Managers are of two types—Line Managers and Staff Managers.
2. The Line Managers perform the functions of decision-making, issuing orders and controlling while the Staff Managers perform the functions of advising, assisting and providing expert and specialised services.
3. There is a unity of command.
4. There is a scalar chain.

This from of organisation came to existence as an improvement over the line organisation. The line and staff organisation has removed serious drawbacks of the line organisation.

It is based on planned specialisation. The line managers get the benefit of specialised knowledge of the staff specialists at various levels.

The growth of an enterprise depends largely upon various research and development programmes. The staff provides this service to the line departments.

The line managers may not have specialised knowledge in all areas and due to this line managers may sometimes give wrong orders or pass wrong judgement. The suggestions and advice given by staff manager help them in making rational judgement and balanced decisions.

The staff managers relieve the line managers from the botheration of concentrating on the specialised functions like accounting, selection and training of employees, public relations, etc. Thus, there is less burden on line managers. Many problems that are ignored or poorly handled in the line organisation, can be properly covered. It is more flexible.

Demerits of the line and staff organisation are as follows:

It is very difficult to clearly establish the authority and responsibility relationship between the line and staff executives. This creates confusion.

The role of the staff is purely advisory. Since they do not have the power to get their recommendations implemented, the staff services may prove to be ineffective.

There is generally a conflict between the line and staff executives. The line authorities feel that staff executives do not always give right type of advice and therefore reject even some very good schemes. Line authorities do not want to give an impression to management that they are in any way inferior to the staff. Thus, there is always a conflict between the line and staff organisations.

The line and staff organisation structure has gained popularity because certain problems of management have become so complex that in order to deal with them, expert knowledge is necessary which can be provided by the staff officers. Whatever drawbacks are there, they are mainly due to its wrong application.

In the functional organisation, all activities in the enterprise are grouped together according to certain functions like production, marketing, finance and personnel and are put under the charge of different persons. The person-incharge of a function follows it throughout the organisation and also controls the individuals working in that functional area. This means that if a person performs several functions, he will be under the direct charge of several persons-incharge of these functions. The functional incharge is an expert in his own field. It is rare to find a pure functional organisation. However, many business enterprises follow functional plan to some extent to carry out the primary functions.

Functional organisation may be at different levels. At the top level, it leads to formation of departments each for a common major activity like purchases, sales, production, finance, etc. Each department looks after its function common to all departments. For example, the question of selection, training, promotion, etc. in purchase, sales and other departments will be decided by the personnel department. Taylor recommended functional organisation even at the shop level (lowest level). He expressed the view that a foreman should also be assisted by a number of specialists.

Following chart shows the functional organisation:

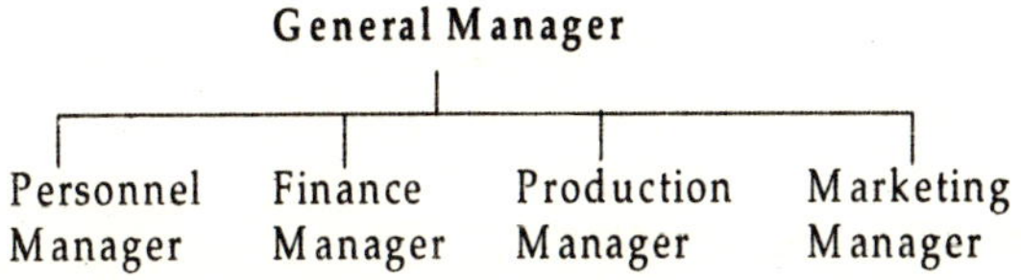

The above discussion brings out the following characteristics of functional organisation:

1. The work is divided into specialised functions.
2. The superior specialist commands an authority and therefore gives orders relating to his specific functions throughout the line.
3. The specialist must be consulted before any decision is taken on matters relating to his specialised area.
4. The responsibilities of functional authority are mainly discharged by other executives.
5. It is flat topped organisation in comparison to the line organisation. A specialist can supervise a large number of employees while in the line organisation, a specialist supervises a limited number of subordinates.

The merits of the functional organisation are as follows:

It ensures a greater division of labour and enables the concern to take advantage for specialisation of functions.

Efficiency of workers is increased as the workers and other have to perform a limited number of operations and they get suggestions and instructions from specialists.

It ensures the separation of mental and physical functions. This ensures better control of the working of the different sections.

Standardisation and specialisation in various fields facilitates production on a large scale resulting in economy in production.

It offers a greater scope for expansion as compared to the line organisation. It does not face the problem of limited capabilities of a few line managers. The expert knowledge of the functional managers facilitates better control and supervision in the organisation.

The demerits of the functional organisation are as follows:

The operation of functional organisation is too complicated. Workers are supervised by a number of bosses. This results in overlapping of authority and thus creates confusion in the organisation.

Under this, the work is divided into parts and sub-parts. It poses difficulties in coordinating the functioning of different parts. Thus, it is difficult to take quick decisions.

Because of multiple authority, responsibility for poor performance cannot be fixed easily on a particular person.

Supervisory staff of equal rank may not always agree on certain issues. Therefore, there may be frequent conflicts which may lead to non-performance.

This type of organisation is suitable for all kinds of enterprises irrespective of their nature or size. But it can be practised more successfully at the higher levels of the organisation than at the lower levels.

This is one of the latest types of organisational design. It has teen developed to establish flexible structure to achieve series of project objectives. Matrix organisation, also known as grid, is an answer to the growing size and complexity of the undertaking, which require an organisation structure more flexible and technically oriented than the line and staff and functional structures.

The matrix organisation is a combination of the project organisation and the functional organisation. Authority flows vertically within functional departments, while authority of project managers flows horizontally crossing vertical lines. Thus, matrix organisation is created, "when project management is superimposed on a stable hierarchical structure, usually of a functional nature. Here the individuals working on a project have a continuing dual assignment; to their project and to their base department."

The important features of the matrix organisation are as follows:

The matrix organisation is built around specific projects. The charge of the project is given to the project manager who has the necessary authority to complete the project in accordance with the time, cost, quality and other conditions communicated to him by the top management.

The project manager draws personnel from various functional departments. He assigns the work to the various functional groups. Upon completion of the project, the functional groups return to their functional departments for reassignment to other projects.

The project and the functional manager have different roles. The project manager exerts a general management viewpoint with regard to his project. Each functional manager is responsible for maintaining the integrity of his function. However, both the project and functional managers are dependent on each other as they have to take several joint decisions in order to execute the project. So there is proper coordination between the project and the functional groups.

Management by project objectives is paramount to the way of thinking and working in it.

The matrix organisation has many advantages. Many organisations which otherwise face problems of structural and technical complexities should adopt this type of organisation. The functional vertical relationships as well as interdependent horizontal relationships lead to operational flexibility. This makes it more adaptable to crisis and change. It provides focus on projects and retains the benefits of specialised expertise and capabilities of functional departments.

It is of a temporary nature. Further, there may be a conflict between project groups and functional groups. It requires coordination of a number of specialised skills. Project personnel entertain considerable fear that termination of a project may bring discharge rather than reassignment to a new project. Frequent movements from one project to another also create considerable anxiety about career progress.

It is very difficult to say which of the types of organisation is the best. On a careful analysis, we find that the line and staff organisation is quite popular in the business world.

There are many points of similarities between the line organisation and line and staff organisation:

(i) In both forms of the organisation, business activities are divided into many departments and sub-departments.

(ii) In both the organisations, orders and request are in linear form.

(iii) The number of subordinates under every officer is limited.

(a) Difference between the line organisation and the line and staff organisation

In spite of the above similarities, both the organisations can be differentiated on the following basis:

Basis of Difference	*Line Organisation*	*Line and Staff Organisation*
1. Services of experts	There is no provision for the services of experts	Services of experts are made available
2. Principle of specialisation is not followed	The principle of specialisation followed	The principle of specialisation is followed
3. Elasticity	In this form of organisation, the elasticity is less	In this form, the elasticity is more
4. Investigation	There is no provision for investigation	It encourages investigation

(b) Difference between the functional organisation and the line and staff organisation

In both forms of the organisation the principle of specialisation is followed but the difference between these two may be explained on the following basis:

Basis of Difference	*Function Organisation*	*Line and Staff Organisation*
1. Direct contact with workers	The workers are in direct contact with experts	The workers are not in direct contact with experts
2. Order by experts	The experts may give orders to the employees	The experts cannot give orders to the employees
3. Discipline	The discipline is lethargic	There is very hard discipline

(c) Difference between the line organisation and the functional organisation

Basis of Difference	*Function Organisation*	*Line and Staff Organisation*
1. Flow of orders	The orders flow from top to bottom	Every worker gets the orders and instructions from many officers at one time.
2. Responsibility determination	Responsibility of employees can be determined easily	It is not possible to determine the responsibility of employees
3. Specialisation	It is not based on the principle of specialisation	Based on the principle of specialisation
4. Role of experts	There is no role of experts	Experts play an important role
5. Coordination can be	It is very established in the activities of enterprise easily	difficult to coordinate different activities of the enterprise
6. Discipline	There is very hard discipline	The discipline is lethargic

The Appropriateness : In this complex business world, each activity taken out by any department, affects the work of other departments. A slight change in production policy will concern the sales department. Similarly, a new sale policy or a change in the sale policy cannot be followed by the sales managers without consulting the finance manager or the production manager. It should be well understood in this reference that such important policy decisions which concern other departments also, should not be taken by the incharge of the department concern alone but they should be referred to a committee consisting of the managers of the affecting departments. It will ensure cooperation and better coordination. Thus, committee organisation is extensively used to solve the multifaceted problems of large and complex business units.

The Approach : Committee is a group of individuals especially designated to take decision in matters referred to it through free exchange of ideas among its members. Louis A. Allen states that "A committee is a body of persons appointed or elected to meet on an organised basis for the consideration of matters brought before it." W. H. Newman defines it as "A group of people specifically designated to perform some administrative act. It functions only as a group and requires the free interchange of ideas among its members." On the basis of the above definitions, the following broad characteristics may be spelled out:

> A committee is a group of two or more persons appointed or elected.

It deals with specific problems referred to it. There are strictly defined jurisdictions within which committee is expected to justify its existence.

The members can go into details of the problems and can discuss each and every aspect of the problem concerned.

A committee may have the authority either to take final decisions or to recommend the action in the matter.

Committees may be classified in various forms. The most common are:

A committee may be permanent (standing) or *ad hoc* (temporary) in character. A standing committee has permanent existence while *ad hoc* committee is constituted for a specific purpose.

A committee may be delegated authority to make a final decision while others may merely deliberate on the problems. Some committees are authorised only to make recommendations to the line executives.

The line committee is charged with the authority of decision-making affecting subordinates responsible to it.

Formal committees are those which have been established under organisational rules, regulations and with specific authority spelling out its duties and authority. Most committees in business are formal ones. An informal committee, on the other hand, is organised without specific delegation of authority. It does not form a part of the organisation.

Main principles of the committee organisation are as under:

The number of members of the committee should not be very large. There must be maximum 5 or 6 members in the committee so that it may be managed properly.

Only those persons must be included in the committee organisation who are concerned with the particular works.

The meetings of the committee must be called in proper manner and every member of the committee must be duly informed of the meetings of committee.

The rights and duties of all the members of the committee must be clearly defined.

The liabilities of all the members of committee must be in accordance with the rights delegated to them.

The meetings must be conducted in accordance with the programme which must be predetermined.

There must be mutual trust and feeling of cooperation among all the members of the committee.

Members of committee must be liable to retire by rotation.

If the committee is set up and managed according to the above principle, it may be expected that the committee will be successful in obtaining its objects.

The committee organisation is becoming more and more popular day by day. Important merits or advantages of the committee organisation are as under:

All the important decisions are taken collectively in the committee organisation. Such decisions are more logical and sound and are affected by the skill, intelligence and experience of all the members of the committee.

The committee organisation provides a suitable stage for effective communication.

The committee organisation depends on the feeling of mutual cooperation and coordination. Thus, the committee organisation is helpful in developing the feeling of mutual trust and mutual cooperation among the members.

The committee organisation is based on decentralisation of power because in this system, the rights to take the important decisions are not centralised with any individual officer. All the members of the committee take collectively decisions.

It encourages democracy because all the decisions of committee are taken by majority.

All the decisions of the committee organisation are taken collectively by all the members of the committee. Therefore, such decisions are also not effected by personal thinking and personal opinion of any officer.

All the members of the committee organisation participate in all the functions of the committee. They make their whole-hearted contribution in the functions of the committee. In this manner, the business enterprise gets the advantage of abilities of all the members.

This is based on mutual cooperation and mutual trust. Therefore, the activities of all the members are coordinated.

The process of control becomes quite easy in this organisation because all the members take active participation in the decision-making process and they contribute their whole-hearted efforts in implementing the decision.

There are some other advantages also in addition to the above advantages. These are common directions, increased knowledge of members, etc.

In spite of the above merits, the committee organisation is considered to be defective and impractical. According to Koontz & O'Donnell, "It is an association made of the unit selected by the unwilling to do the unnecessary." Demerits of the committee organisation can be briefly discussed as follows:

> A great disadvantage of the committee organisation is that the decisions become a project and thus delayed because all the decisions are to be taken by majority. Sometimes, the decisions are so late that they become meaningless.

As the decisions are late, their implementation is late and the action gets late.

As no individual officer is authorised to take an important decision, it creates lack of motivation.

As all the decisions are taken collectively, it creates the problem of assigning responsibility to any individual officer.

A great disadvantage of the committee organisation is that the leadership of such committee is of aggressive nature because the person who speaks more and loudly dominates the committee.

As all the important decisions are taken collectively by the heads of all the departments, there is a lack of secrecy.

As the decisions are taken by the rule of majority, there are some persons against these decisions. This way, the decisions of the committee remain against such minority members.

Sometimes the committee performs some functions which are of no use to the enterprise.

As the members of the committee are the heads of their departments and these members frequently call their meetings, it causes slackness in the activities of enterprise.

In addition to the above-mentioned disadvantages, there are some more disadvantages also, as difficulty in the discharge of duties by officers, etc.

Thus, we see that the committee organisation is meaningless and useless because of the above disadvantages. Koontz & O'Donnell has stated in this regard as, "You go to purchase a horse and you come back with a camel in your hands."

The committee organisations are generally found only in big business enterprises because the organisation of a big business and industrial enterprise is possible only through the committee organisation. Some examples of misuse of the committee organisation may be as under:

> Decisions by compromise is a very common misuse of the powers of officers of the committee. The opinions

of members of committee are also different so that it becomes almost impossible to take the unanimous decisions. In this case, almost all the decisions are taken by compromise. These decisions are not very sound and effective. Sometimes these decisions are against the interests of enterprise.

A committee organisation is a very big organisation. Therefore, it is an expensive organisation. The members of the committee make many unnecessary expenses in the name of the organisation.

All the decisions of the committee are taken by the rule of majority. It means that there are some members against the decisions taken by committee. Thus, the decisions of committee are imposed upon these members which is against the interests of enterprise itself.

Theoretically all the decisions of the committee are taken by majority. All the members have right to express their opinions on all the subjects discussed at the committee. But practically the committee is dominated by a few persons who can speak loudly and fluently. Such members of committee influence the decisions of committee in undesirable manner.

The committee organisation is a big organisation. It has to perform a large number of functions, and the time is limited. There is always a shortage of time in relation to the works to be performed. Therefore, the members do not take due interest in the functions of committee and they waste their time on meaningless and fruitless discussions.

As all the decisions of the committee are taken collectively by all the members of committee, it becomes very difficult to determine the responsibilities of an individual member, if any of the decisions of committee is wrong and against the interests of enterprise.

The committee organisation may be made effective by the following suggestions:

The committee organisation must be set up only when it is felt that the advantages of committee will be more than its expenses. If, it is felt that the expenses of such committee will be more than its advantages, it should not be set up.

The size of committee must be appropriate in accordance with the size of enterprise. It is necessary so that the opinions of members of committee may be easily and conveniently exchanged.

Its success depends upon the capability of the members. Therefore, only those members must be selected as the members of committee who are capable enough to discharge their duties properly and which may represent their departments properly. The members must be capable enough to understand, analyse and decide the problems.

Success of the committee organisation depends to a large extent upon the capability of the chairman. Therefore, it becomes necessary that the chairman of the committee must be selected very carefully, the person must be an experienced person who may conduct the committee meetings properly. Chairman must be a person who can move, direct and control other members of the committee.

An important suggestion for the success of the committee organisation is that its scope must be clearly defined and properly communicated so that there may be no dispute of opinion about the functions to be performed by the committee.

Mutual trust and mutual cooperation for the members of committees is necessary for the success of committee. For developing the feeling of mutual trust and mutual cooperation, it becomes necessary that the rights and duties of all the members of committee must be clearly defined.

The committee should consider only the proper subjects. Only those matters must be assigned to the committee which are of great importance to the enterprise. If the matter is not so important, it should not be delivered to the committee otherwise it will be wastage of time, energy and money.

A programme must be determined well in advance for the meetings of committee and programmes must be properly communicated to all the members of committee so that the members can prepare themselves for the discussion and decision. It will save time and make the decisions more sound and effective.

In this chapter various types of organisation were described. These include, line and staff, functional, matrix and committee form of organisation. The concept of the line organisation holds that in any organisation derived from a scalar process, there must be a single head who commands it. In the functional organisation, all activities in the enterprise are grouped together according to certain functions like production, marketing, finance and personnel are put to under change of different persons.

The matrix in organisation has been developed to establish flexible structures to organisation has been developed to establish flexible structures to cope up with growing size and complexity of an enterprise. The distinctions between various types of organisation were also highlighted. The committee form and its need were described at great length.

6

Marketing Strategies

Evolution of the concept of tourism marketing can be associated with the various business and social changes, which have occurred since the introduction of industrialisation. Industrialisation had brought about the need for holiday and travel even in its early stages as the workers felt the need for temporary rest and relaxation after long hours of work. Industrialisation enabled societies especially in western countries, and later on, elsewhere, to produce a range of consumer products in mass quantity. The products were to be sold to the consumers to be consumed. The selling thus became an important business function.

In the early stages the concept of selling was also applied to selling travel and holidays. However, like consumer products, tourism also assumed huge proportions, resulting in a multiplicity of products and sales intermediaries trying to get maximum share of the market. This gave rise to competition industry . Today, tourism is the fastest growing industry in the world and also one of the world's most competitive industry. This competition is constantly growing as more and more destinations seek to attract tourists and more companies and organisations become involved in the highly-skilled business of destination planning, transportation, accommodation and catering for the tourists.

Like any other product, tourism needs to be marketed. Perhaps travel and tourism needs to be marketed more vigorously because it is an industry in which the customer has immense variety of choice as also varied motivations for travel. Marketing concept helps in understanding and identifying the needs and desires of holiday-makers and then satisfying the same. This aspect of marketing is particularly important to the travel and tourism industry.

Marketing and its role today has changed drastically over the years. However, markets and marketing systems were in existence much earlier. It is therefore important to understand how the markets and marketing systems were evolved before discussing marketing in the tourism industry. From the time of simple barters to the present day complex marketing systems, exchanges, have undergone a great change since the advent of the industrialised societies first in the west and, subsequently, all over the world. Most of an industrialised country's production was conducted in small manufacturing units.

In the nineteenth century the market for the goods was limited to the areas surrounding the manufacturing unit. It was rare that a particular manufacturer's product found place in other parts of the country. The main cause for products not finding wider markets was the absence of distribution channels and non-availability of products in sufficient quantities as required by these channels. The absence of quality products and the means of transport to carry these goods over to distant areas were other inhibiting factors. A large majority of people during this period had a limited purchasing power as a result of considerable unemployment. The market for goods other than the necessities of life was rather limited. Only a fraction of the population could afford to indulge in the purchase of such luxuries.

Introduction of mass production during the subsequent years in the post-industrialisation period brought about a change. There was an increase in purchasing power of a large number of people. Also, rapid industrial advancement placed at the disposal of the consumer, a large variety of goods of improved quality, and in abundant quantity, from a large number of competing manufacturers.

Supply exceeded the demand. The consumer's choice began to be limited as a result of mass production. This fact compelled the manufacturers to give greater consideration to the needs of the consumer.

The growth of communication systems as a result of rapid industrial advancement played an important role in the development of the marketing concept. The advent of the mechanised transport, first the railways, and later road transport systems, made the physical distribution of goods produced possible over much wider areas. This in turn resulted in increased production being disposed of, over a large geographic area, by means of railways and road transport networks. Subsequently, the mass communication channels like telegraphs, telephones and then circulation of newspapers, helped the manufacturers dispose their products in large quantum. All these developments eventually led to the adoption of a new concept, i.e., the marketing concept by the progressive and forward-looking manufacturing organisations.

The Approach

Several attempts have been made to define 'marketing' but so far no universally accepted definition has been devised. This is perhaps due to the fact that 'marketing' as a comprehensive management function is a fairly recent concept which effectively only started to be applied in the early 1950s. Like most innovations, marketing has been gradually adopted by increasing number of enterprises, mainly in the field of consumer products, with diverse ideas developed, as to what it should embrace and how its principles should be implemented. In the last few decades, however, marketing has become an established management process and practice in most industries.

To understand about marketing, it is necessary to distinguish between the familiar word in everyday use and the term as it is used professionally by marketing managers. There are several definitions of the term, marketing. However, the one definition which is universally quoted is by Philip Kotler. Kotler defines the marketing concept as follows :" The marketing concept holds that the key to achieving organisational goals consists in determining the needs and wants of target markets and delivering the desired satisfactions more effectively and efficiently than competitors."

Some other experts in the field have defined the concept as follows :

Philips and Duncan: "marketing includes all the activities necessary to place goods and services in the hands of consumers and industrial users, excluding only such activities as involve a significant change in the form of goods."

Carl Dysinger: "Marketing is finding out what the consumer wants and selling it to him at a profit."

Neville Teller: "as the efficient utilisation of a company's resources to match existing or future consumer demand, and the manipulation and promotion to ensure that the products of these resources are in the right place, at the right time and at the right price to meet that demand."

Colin Mclver: "marketing is concerned essentially with the prediction of people's future behaviour and an attempt to influence their behaviour in some particular way."

Eugene J. Kelly: "as a business discipline, marketing consists of systematic study of the demand generating or consumer motivating forces, the temporal and spatial considerations influencing economic transaction, and the interacting efforts and responses of buyers and sellers in a market."

Dr. William H. Kaven: "Marketing is a business process by which the existing and potential demand for goods and services is determined, cultivated, and then supplied by the seller. The process includes the efforts of all functional areas of the seller working in concert to produce at the right price, time and place the service or product that meets the market's demand and the marketer's profit goals."

All the above definitions emphasise that concept is a customer orientation backed by integrated marketing aimed at generating customer satisfaction. The important aspects of marketing which emerge are :

(i) Identification of customer needs,

(ii) Prediction of customer behaviour,

(iii) Converting customer needs and motivations into effective demand; and

(iv) Moving the product to the final consumer or user so as to achieve the objective set by the organisation.

The American Management Association has defined marketing as - "the indentification or creation of customer needs and thereafter the motivation and coordinated use of all functions within a business that can fill those needs and benefit both the buyer and the seller."

The British Institute of Marketing has formulated the following definition : "Marketing is the management function which organises' and directs all those business activities involved in assessing and converting customer purchasing power into effective demand for a specific product or service and in moving the product or service to the final customer or user so as to achieve the profit target or other objectives set by the company."

The Institute of Marketing has defined Marketing as "the creative management function which promotes trade and employment by assessing consumer needs and initiating research and development to meet them. It coordinates the resources of production and distribution of goods and services; determines and directs the nature and scale of the total effort required to sell profitably the maximum production to the ultimate user."

Application of the marketing concept has certain important benefits. *Firstly,* the management using this concept realise that customer needs are more basic than particular products. This provides a more reliable and enduring base to the operations of such managements. *Secondly,* the focus on the customer needs helps the management to spot new product opportunities more speedily. *Thirdly,* merchandising becomes more effective under this concept. This is because managements view their tasks as that of meeting customer satisfaction rather than creating demand for its products among the customers. The physical product is only a part of the satisfaction sought by the buyer because he wants, in addition, convenience, service and certain other symbolic values. *Fourthly,* the managements are able to create more harmony between their own interests and those of the society because the market orientation under this concept means that the managements build their profits through seeking better ways to satisfy customer needs.

Concept and Meaning

It is a well-known fact that as long as the inherent sense of curiosity and adventure dwells in the hearts of human beings, the desire to travel, in order to see new sights and experience new things, and to live under different environments, will always grow. It may be presumed that such being the case, marketing in the tourism industry is greatly simplified as part of the process has already been completed by the desire for travel in people . The best example would be that a person may or may not choose a tangible product which has been introduced by a manufacturer in the market, solely depending on his ability to afford it or his likes and dislikes. On the other hand, without exception, all human-beings will always nurture a desire to travel in order to see places. The question then arises that if the desire is ever-present in people to travel and experience new things, why would the tourism industry need marketing efforts at all?

Tourism is a very complex industry because of its multi-faceted activities which together produce the 'tourist product'. It is also complex because of various sub-sectors that are in themselves complete industries, if considered independently (lodging, transport, etc.). Its complexity, furthermore, lies in the fact that tourism promotion in its various forms has to be directed at large numbers of people in various lands of different socio-economic structures, having different needs, tastes, attitudes, expectations and behaviour patterns. It is only efficient marketing strategy that will help understand people's tastes and preferences for travel, And hence the need for marketing in tourism.

How to Define ? Tourism marketing is defined in a number of ways. It could be defined as the "systematic and coordinated efforts exerted by the National Tourist Organisations and/or the - tourist enterprises at international, national and local levels to optimise the satisfaction of tourists, groups and individuals, in view of the sustained tourism growth."

According to Krippendorf, J., marketing in tourism means "systematic and coordinated execution of business policy by tourist undertaking whether private or state owned at local, regional, national or international level to achieve the optimal satisfaction of the needs of identifiable consumer groups, and in doing so to achieve an appropriate return."

Products for Tourists

Tourism marketing and marketing in general both emphasise consumer orientation and satisfaction. The concept of consumer orientation, however, makes it necessary to understand the components of the tourist product from the point of view of the consumer. The product for the tourist covers the complete experience from the time he leaves home to the time he returns.

Availability of a product is the prerequisite in the marketing function. Unless there is a certain product, be it tangible or intangible or a service, marketing is not possible. A product may be defined as the 'Sum of the physical and psychological satisfactions it provides to the buyer.' 'Marketing' by definition is the development of a product to meet the needs of the consumer and then employing the techniques of direct sales, publicity and advertising to bring this product to the consumer. In the case of tourism product, the basic raw materials would be the country's natural beauty, climate, history, culture and the people. Other aspects would be the existing facilities necessary for comfortable living such as water supply, electricity, roads, transport, communication and other essentials. In other words the tourist product can be seen as a composite product, as the sum-total of a country's tourist attractions, transport, accommodation and entertainment which hopefully result in consumer satisfaction.

The tourist product can be entirely a man-made one or nature's creation improved upon by man. Each of these components of a tourist product is supplied by individual providers of services like hotel companies, airlines or other suppliers, and is offered directly to the tourists by them. A consumer can combine these individual tourist products through a large number of ways. There would be many possible destinations, each with a number of hotels, each to be reached by more than one airline. Thus the potential choice facing the consumer is very large. A number of tourist destinations have placed at the disposal of a tourist a large variety of tourist products in abundant quantity from a large number of competing destinations. This, eventually, has led to the adoption of the new concept, i.e., the marketing concept in tourism by various countries promoting tourism. The important point about marketing is that it is applied to situations where the choice can be limited to a relatively small number of brands giving the consumer a reasonable choice. The process of selection thus becomes easier. In the field of tourism this process is taking place by the increasing use of 'package tours'. A package tour is a travel plan which includes most elements of vacation, such as transportation, accommodation, sight-seeing and entertainment. The tourist product is a composite product, whether it is sold as a package or assembled by the individual tourist himself or his travel agent.

Important Characteristics

Tourism, basically, is an infrastructure based service product. The nature of the service marketed being highly intangible and perishable offers a limited scope for creating and maintaining the distinctive competitive edge. Effective marketing of tourism needs constant gearing up of infrastructure to international standards and presupposes its coordination with the tourism suppliers. In strategic terms, it calls for the action of an integrated approach to management and marketing. In operational terms, it means the implementation of a better defined, better targeted market-driven strategy for realising the defined objectives.

Marketing of tourist product has certain peculiar characteristics. Although general principles of marketing of products of other industries could be applicable to marketing of tourist product, there are certain differences in approach. Among the peculiarities of the tourist product are:

Tourism is an Intangible, Non-material Product : No transfer of ownership of goods is involved as compared to a tangible product, say for example, a motor car. In tourism, instead, certain facilities, installations, items of equipment are made available for a specified time and for a specified use. For instance, a seat in an aeroplane or a train for a journey from one point to another or a booking in a hotel through a travel agent are carried out for a customer or services such as information and advice are provided.

Production and Consumption of Tourist Services are Closely Interrelated : The travel agent or tour operator who sells his product cannot store it. Production can only take place or can only be completed if the customer is actually present. There is a close link between production and consumption of tourist services. Most tourist services cannot be consumed incrementally. In other words, consumption, once begun, cannot be stopped, interrupted or modified at all. As a result, risk and uncertainty for the customer are higher, and his need for reliable pre-purchase information is stronger. The potential customer's decision-risk and dependence on accurate information is further increased because he cannot see, inspect, compare or try out tourist services before deciding to use them.

Multiplicity of Producers : The tourist product cannot be provided by a single enterprise. Each of the components of a tourist product is highly specialised and together make the final product. This is not so in the case of other tangible products where one manufacturer produces a total product. In tourism on the other hand, an airline considers 'seats flown' or passenger miles to be its product; a hotel produces 'guest nights' a travel agent 'bookings', a theatre and museum or an archaeological site measures its production' in number of visitors. In the tourist's view, however, the product he buys covers the complete experience of his visit to a particular place. In other words the tourist product is not an airline or a rail seat, or a hotel bed or a theatre ticket, but rather an amalgam of many components which together make a complete product. Because of these peculiar characteristics, coordination in marketing efforts, is very crucial.

Highly Unstable Demand : The demand is influenced by factors such as seasonal, economic, political, etc. The seasonal changes greatly affect the demand. Seasonality means that tourism plant is frequently used for a limited part of the year and therefore uneconomic. Many tourist areas have a short season - often as little as three months. A corollary of this seasonal usage is the seasonal unemployment, which is a serious problem. Some of the developing countries which have recently established tourist industries suffer particularly from seasonality. Seasonality also places strains on the transport system and other services. Thus seasonality presents a problem not only in relation to employment but also in relation to investment. On the other hand political unrest and economic instability caused by currency fluctuations and inflation, etc., greatly affect tourism demand.

Dominant Role of Intermediaries : In most industries, manufacturers have predominant control over product design; distribution and promotion and pricing. On the other hand in tourism, sales intermediaries like tour operators, travel agents, reservation services and hotel brokers play a very dominant role and enjoy superior marketing strength. From the standpoint of tourism marketing, this strong position of the travel trade has significant implications. The travel trade determines to a large extent which services will be sold and to whom. The type of services to be offered as well as the pricing policies and promotion strategies to be adopted by tourist enterprises, are, therefore, determined not only by the needs and preferences of the customers but also by those expressed by travel sales intermediaries.

Diverse Motivations : It is comparatively simple to determine why people buy a certain make of refrigerator, smoke certain brands of cigarettes, use certain brands of toothpaste or prefer a certain type of packaged food. The subjective and objective reasons, expectations and desires which influence tourists' choice for a certain holiday destination, type of accommodation and vacation activities are far less evident. Very often two people make exactly the same choices for entirely different and sometimes even mutually exclusive reasons. Travel motivations unlike motivations for buying a tangible article like a refrigerator, are heterogeneous - composed of diverse elements.

Marketing in tourism, due to the various factors mentioned above, as compared to marketing in other industries therefore needs a somewhat different approach. Tourism marketing to a considerable extent depends on various market factors mentioned above. Unlike the normal consumer product or service, the tourist product is marketed at two levels.

(i) The national or regional tourist organisation will be engage in a marketing campaign to persuade the potential tourist to visit the country or region for which it is responsible. In view of the fragmentation of supply, the complementarity of tourist services, the predominance of many small and medium sized enterprises and importance of tourism to an economy, the official tourist organisations have important functions in tourism marketing. The official tourist organisation will however not sell a tourist product directly to customers. It will have two major objectives. In the first place, it will seek to create knowledge of its country in tourist-generating markets and persuade visitors in these markets to visit that country. Secondly, it will seek to create an image of its country's tourist attractions in the best possible manner in tourist-generating markets so that the potential visitors are attracted

(ii) The various individual firms providing tourist services can market their own components of the total tourist product after the national tourist organisations have launched marketing campaigns to persuade the potential tourist to visit the country or region for which it is responsible.

Primary Functions

Marketing Function : It is basically customer-oriented, backed by integrated marketing aimed at customer satisfaction. The focus of marketing therefore centres around a customer. Professor Kotler in his definition has also emphasised this fact and stated that achievement of organisational goals depends on determining the needs of target markets (customers) and delivering the desired satisfaction more effectively and efficiently.

From the above it follows that organisations, before achieving their desired goals, have to go through series of marketing functions; and specific understanding of both marketing functions and specific marketing tasks becomes very crucial to grasp the subject of marketing. The marketing function can be considered as a system where interaction occurs between an organisation and a customer.

The main marketing functions and the tasks these functions set for themselves are as follows :

(a) Market Research
(b) Product formulation and development
(c) Analysis and selection of target markets (segmentation)
(d) Distribution networks
(e) Product Promotion

Research Works and Surveys

Identifying the customer needs especially in a tourism industry which has very high service base content is very important. This is possible only through systematic market research and analysis. This is basic for successful marketing. It relates to providing answers to various questions pertaining to the marketing activities. Market research can be defined as the "Systematic collection of information relating to supply and demand for a product or a proposed product in such a way that the information may be used by the organisation to formulate informed decisions about its policies and its objectives." The marketing process in fact starts by finding out answers to questions like who are the potential tourists, where do they come from, what axe their likes and dislikes, etc. In order to formulate any marketing strategy it is very essential for a national tourist organisation and others engaged in marketing a tourist product to know the answers to the following questions:

(i) Who are the persons who engage in tourism and where do they live?
(ii) Who are the potential customers and where do they come from?
(iii) What are their likes and dislikes?
(iv) What are their travel preferences and interest?
(v) What do they buy and where do they stay?
(vi) What mode of transport do they use?
(vii) What are their entertainment preferences?
(viii) What are the trends in competition?
(ix) What type of marketing programmes would be needed?

Answers to all the above questions are obtainable only through research. A tourist-organisation promotion effort, without appropriate answers to the above questions, will go waste. To make the overall marketing efforts effective and successful, the tourist organisation has to be totally aware of the trends in the travel habits, vacation habits and most important of all, the reasons attributed to the better success of a competing destination. A marketing manager cannot visualise successful marketing strategy without having an uptodate knowledge of their markets in general. It is very important to have detailed information on all the aspects of a market. Results of such research will work as guidelines for launching a successful marketing programme.

Different Methods

Market research is a continuous process. Among the variety of methods used, some seem to be widely resorted to because of their advantages over others. Research techniques can be grouped as:

(i) Desk research

(ii) Field research

(iii) Sample surveys

(iv) Motivation research

Desk research includes the collection and analysis of all available data, statistics and published information on tourist trends and markets. In tourism much of the basic information about tourist trends and markets is available from existing sources. There are a number of international organisations like United Nations, WTO, EC, OECD, IATA, WTTC, ICAO, etc., which publish certain statistical information. Other data and statistics may be obtained from national tourist organisations, trade associations, carriers, hotel companies, etc. This information proves very useful in helping national tourist organisations to identify their markets and determine the objectives. This published information is of particular use to those countries which do not possess resources enough to undertake independent market research.

Field research, on the other hand, is the research work carried out in the tourist-generating markets itself. The special investigations in the field are to be carried out with a view to know more details of the market situation. Field research includes many methods among which the most common are the sample surveys and the motivation research.

Sample survey could be defined as the study of a given population through only a part or a fraction thereof. Much marketing information is obtained through the use of samples. In this method the population or 'Universe' for which information is required is defined, for example, all households in a country might be the universe or population under investigation. Then, a statistically valid sample of the population is drawn and information is obtained from the sample. Sampling techniques consist of personal interviews of tourists, travel agents, carriers and hotel managers, etc., by way of personal interviews with the help of prepared, questionnaires, by mailing questionnaires or through telephone contacts. There are certain advantages of this method. Lower cost is the major reason why data are collected by sampling in place of complete enumerations. The actual obtaining of information from the sample units (i.e., households in this case) is done by way of use of interviews and questionnaires. The questionnaire is administered to the sample population and various data obtained. The sampling place could be anywhere. Interviews may take place at homes or offices, at the place of arrival departure or temporary stay. In many countries there are a number of specialised firms which carry out sample survey enquiries, as well as government agencies similarly equipped.

The survey investigation can be classified by reference to the kind of information they seek to provide. There are surveys of market behaviour which record the holiday habits of the population, cross analysed by socio-economic, and other characteristics. The trends in holiday-making over many years may be seen and inferences made about the motives of holiday-makers. Furthermore, surveys may be undertaken to monitor the conduct of marketing campaigns.

Motivation research on the other hand attempts to describe and forecast the motives of the population under investigation, by use of techniques originally used in psychology. Assuming that every individual knows what he wants, motivation research is oriented to discover the needs of potential tourists in order to adopt the tourist supply accordingly and thus be able to satisfy them. In other words motivation research is the investigation into the motives behind travel.

It concerns itself to answering the 'why' of human behaviour in contrast to answering the 'how' which is subject to sampling surveys. It analyses rather than describes the attitudes of both actual and potential tourists to travelling in general and to the tourist product offered in particular. Motivation research provides answers to very important questions. Research in the past has shown that people from some countries, are traditional good travellers (the French, the Germans, the American and the British), while others have become a nation of travellers only recently.

The most important techniques used in motivation research is the depth interview method. The questionnaire to be used for this method needs to be carefully designed, as motivation research aims at discovering the deep, subconscious and even unconscious of human beings. An ill-designed questionnaire is likely to reach no deeper than the conscious level where rational factors prevail. Other techniques used are the projective methods like word association tests, sentence completion test and pictorial tests, etc. and observations. Means have been devised to record the reactions of a person and to understand his motives.

Production and Development

Having identified the consumers and the markets through the method of market research, the next step is the product formulation and development. The concept of consumer orientation makes it necessary to understand the various components of the tourist product from the point of view of the consumer. In the tourism industry product is what gives the consumer the various benefits they are seeking and its production and delivery. The formulation and development of a product involves factors like service, quality, range of different products offered in the market, the features and benefits it offers, and the brand name.

Availability of a 'product' is the prerequisite in the marketing function. Unless there is a certain 'product', be it tangible or intangible or a service, marketing is not possible. A 'product' may be defined as the 'Sum of the physical and psychological satisfactions it provides to the buyer. 'Marketing' by definition is the development of a product to meet the needs of the consumer and then employing the techniques of direct sales, publicity and advertising to bring this product to the consumer.

In the case of tourism product, the basic raw materials would be the country's natural beauty climate, history, culture and the people. Other aspects would be the existing facilities necessary for comfortable living such as water supply, electricity, roads, transport, communication and other essentials. In other words the tourist product can be seen as a composite product, the sum-total of a country's tourist attractions, transport, accommodation and entertainment which hopefully result in consumer satisfaction. The tourist product can be entirely a man-made one or nature's creation improved upon by man. Each of these components of a tourist product is supplied by individual providers of services like retail travel agents, tour operators, hotel companies, airlines or other suppliers, and is offered directly to the tourist by them. A consumer can combine these individual tourist products through a large number of ways.

There would be many possible destinations, each with a number of hotels, each to be reached by more than one airline. Thus the potential choice facing the consumer is very large. A number of enterprises have placed at the disposal of a tourist a large variety of tourist products in abundant quantity from a large number of competing destinations. This eventually has led to the adoption of the new concept, i.e., the marketing concept in tourism by various enterprises marketing tourism. The important point about marketing is that it applies to situations where the choice can be limited to a relatively small number of brands giving the consumer a reasonable choice. The process of selection thus becomes easier. In the field of tourism this process is taking place by the increasing use of package tours. A package tour is a travel plan which includes most elements of vacation, such as transportation, accommodation, sight-seeing and entertainment. The tourist product is a composite product, whether it is sold as a package or assembled by the individual tourist himself or his travel agent. The tourist product can, therefore, be analysed in terms of; (i) Attractions; (ii) Facilities; (iii) Accessibility.

Tourist attraction is a very important element. Unless these are there, the tourists will not be motivated to go to a particular place. Attractions are those elements in the tourist product which determine the choice of a particular tourist to visit one particular destination rather than another. The attractions could be cultural like sites and areas of archaeological interest, historical buildings and monuments or scenic like flora and fauna, beach resorts, mountains, national parks or events like trade fairs, exhibitions, arts and music festivals, games, etc. Facilities are those elements in the tourist product which are a necessary aid to the tourist centre. *The facilities* complement the attractions.

These include accommodations, various types of entertainments, picnic sites, recreation and so on. These are indeed important for every tourist centre. *Accessibility* is another important component in the tourist product. It is a means by which a tourist can reach the area where attractions are located. Tourist attractions of whatever type would be of little importance if their locations are inaccessible by the normal means of transport. If the tourist attractions are located at places where no means of transport can reach, or where there are inadequate transport facilities, these become of little value. The tourist attractions which are located near to the tourist-generating markets and are linked by a network of efficient transport, receive the maximum number of tourists.

Segmentation : Market segmentation is one of the important functions of marketing. The technique of market segmentation has been used by organisations to effectively target selected groups in the market with specially designed products and services. Market segmentation can be defined as "the process whereby producers organise their knowledge of current and potential customer groups and select for particular attention those whose needs and wants they are best able to supply with their products. According to Dibb, Simkin, Pride and Ferrell Market Segmentation is defined as :

> "The process of dividing a total market into groups of people with relatively similar product needs, for the purpose of designing a marketing mix (or mixes) that precisely match the needs of individuals in a selected segment (or segments)."

From the above definition it emerges that the market segmentation is the process of identifying groups of buyers of a total market with different buying desires or requirements. It identifies and analyses the socio-economic, life styles and motivational characteristics of potential buyers into useful categories and thereby launching advertising and promotional campaigns for these selected groups. The identification of segment of a total market is therefore of crucial importance. Due to manpower and financial constraints, it is not possible for an organisation to reach the entire market. Segmentation of the market in therefore made in order to achieve the most efficient use of marketing resources. The main objectives of the market segmentation, therefore, are :

(a) Developing new markets for product variations or new products;

(b) Developing defence against competitors by differentiating one's own product from theirs and matching it more closely to the requirements of a particular segment of the marker;

(c) Achieving maximum effects for given expenditure on marketing activities, particularly communication activities;

(d) Developing marketing programmes and budgets on the basis of a clearer idea of the response characteristic of specific segments.

The following information on the tourist markets will assists in segmentation :

(i) Income distribution of overseas travellers and particularly correlations between income and distance travelled and travel expenditure;

(ii) Travel expenditure data, i.e., distribution of per head expenditure on travel;

(iii) Discretionary income of households, correlated with other characteristics enabling targets to be identified closely;

(iv) Historical trends in travel in different socio-economic categories;

(v) Survey data on attitudes to and motivations for overseas travel;

(vi) Geographical dispersion of potential customers within the market;

(vii) Membership of clubs and associations associated with other characteristics which identify particular groups as potential customers;

(viii) Influence of intermediaries (travel agents, tour operators, wholesalers, carriers etc.) on destination choice in particular markets;

(ix) Relative importance of different intermediaries in particular markets (e.g., is all relevant type of travel business concentrated among relatively few intermediaries or it is dispersed throughout the market?).

The segmentation process divides the markets on the basis of several factors. The most important and commonly used market segmentation include the following:

A. Geographic segmentation

B. Demographic segmentation

C. Socio-economic segmentation

D. Psychological segmentation

E. Behavioural segmentation

F. Product-Based segmentation

Under each of the above principal variables, there are several areas which are considered while segmenting the travel markets. These are as follows:

Geographical : Operational areas, e.g., sales regions. Sales Districts such as provinces, cities, Political administrative zones.

Demographic : Age groups Sex differences Ethnic origin Marital status Religious affiliations.

Socio-economic : Income Levels Types of occupation Social class. Educational level of economic activity.

Psychological : Individual life-styles Personality types Perceptual differences Motivational differences.

Behavioural

Patterns of purchase.

Loyalty to fashions.

Levels of brand loyalty.

Benefits/recognition sought.

Product-based

Travel purposes.

Type of holiday.

Average length of stay.

Type of accommodation.

Mode of travel.

Arrangements for travel.

Individual / group travel.

In tourism, market segmentation is very important. The strategy of market segmentation in tourism recognises that a few vacation areas are universally acceptable and desired. Therefore, rather than waste promotional resources trying to please all travellers, the best market strategy is to isolate those segments of the entire market which are likely prospects and aim at the promotional efforts specifically to the needs of these selected groups. Thus, one of the early steps in marketing tourism is to divide the present and potential market on the basis of meaningful characteristics and then concentrate on promotion, supply and pricing efforts on serving these most prominent sections of the market - the target markets. Usually as stated earlier, the market segmentation for tourists is in terms of the following criteria: demographic, geographic, psychographic, social and economic.

For example, market for particular area might be largely archaeologists in their middle years who have an income of over $100,000 per year and who live in mid-eastern United States, or it might be largely businessmen in the age group of say 40-60 years who have an income of over $150,000 per year and who live in southern parts of West Germany. In tourism marketing, the total tourism market can be divided into the above major segments. A further segmentation, however, is possible within each of the above major segments for practical marketing purposes, and includes:

The Vacation Tourist : The vacation or the holiday tourist is the most common and popular tourist. He is immensely affected by changes in price, and is easily influenced by skilled and aggressive marketing effort. This type of tourist is resort-oriented (Rome, Bombay, New York, London, Paris are resorts as much as Venice, Goa, Pattaya, Miami). The vacation tourist market has been regarded as highly seasonal.

The Business Tourist : In recent years the market for this type of tourist has increased greatly. The choice of destination of a business tourist is generally determined by the nature of his business. The marketing efforts will not influence much the choice of the business tourist. As in the case of the vacation tourist who has proved to be very sensitive to price changes, the demand for business tourism is relatively price-inelastic. The demand will tend to be big-city oriented. The visits are of shorter duration and relatively frequent. The trade fairs, conventions, exhibitions, conferences and similar other events attract this kind of tourism.

The Common Interest Tourist : This segment comprises visits to relatives and friends, and visits for the purpose of education, for pilgrimages, etc. Demand for this type of tourism will be relatively price-elastic. The common interest tourist will not be easily influenced by the promotional efforts. The average length of stay of this type of tourist will be relatively longer. Because of his friends and relatives, he will not be a significant user of hotel and other such types of accommodation. The visits will not be frequent and expenditure relatively little on his stay as compared with other two groups.

Market segmentation in tourism has developed from the realisation that there is no such thing as a homogenous tourist market. Tourist market is composed of several homogenous sub groups having same wants, desires and behaviour etc. It is therefore advantageous for an organisation/company to serve one or more of these segments.

Marketing Segmentation

1. Delineation of the segment and identifying its potential.
2. Target market selection matching the characteristics of those segments with what you have to offer.
3. After matching the two, preparing a marketing plan or programme based on marketing mix.
4. Implementation and control or monitoring.

The Strategy

a. When the total market is diffused demographically, geographically and psychologically.
b. When the organisation has been in business for several year already.
c. When there are several competitors.
d. When most competitors employ a segmentation strategy.

It may however be mentioned here that the market segmentation in itself is not sufficient. The identification and location of potential buyers of a tourism product or service does not ensure that purchases will be effected. Market segmentation is merely the first initial step in the development of a total marketing strategy of a firm or an enterprise. It helps in the process of converting as many as possible of the potential buyers into actual buyers.

Marketing Mix

The most important objective of a tourist enterprise is to achieve the best results. This to a larger extent depends on a properly conceived marketing plan through which a strategy is to be developed to achieve the best results. Through the segmentation process appropriate targets are identified and analysed. The marketing strategy thus developed would now attempt to penetrate and persuade the target markets through a variety of tools mainly promotion and advertising. In addition, the marketing strategy will also look into the crucial question of pricing and distribution. The various tools are to be mixed in such a way that the enterprise obtains the optimal use of financial and manpower resources available at its disposal.

The mixture of various marketing tools is called the 'marketing mix'. Marketing mix is a mixture of elements which interact and complement each other to achieve targeted results. The term was first introduced by Professor Neil Bordes in the year 1953 when he got the cue from a study of Management of Marketing costs which described the marketing executive as a mixer of ingredients. Professor Philip Kotler, has defined the 'marketing mix' as the set of marketing tools that the firm uses to pursue its marketing objectives in the target market.

Tourist Marketing Mix : Tourist 'marketing mix' is largely a complex group of several factors intervening to achieve the marketing 'end product' which is increased effectiveness in demand output in relation to supply and marketing investment by tourist enterprises. Marketing mix helps the marketing manager of an enterprise whether individual or firm or an official tourism organisation to understand where marketing action can be initiated to improve the acceptability of a tourist product and stimulate the demand within the market. A tourist enterprise with a combination of specific activities can achieve the best possible results. It can decide *which* specific activity to use, *how* it is to be used, *when* and *where* to use and what resources to be allocated to them. A judicial mixture of activities at the appropriate time would give the enterprise to achieve its set marketing objectives.

The different components or elements of the mix may be seen as cooperating with or replacing each other as complements or substitutes. An example would be a policy of price reduction by an enterprise to tourist services or facilities which could be substituted by enhancing/increasing available facilities and services for the same price or by strengthening various promotion activities in view of competition offered by competitors and thereby increasing the sales output. A strategy to combine both reduction of prices and at the same time offering extra facilities or extra advertising and promotion may or may not however always be efficient or result oriented. It is therefore essential that the target markets must be clearly defined for the success of marketing mix strategy.

Main Variables : Marketing mix incorporates four core variables. The four variables or four Ps as originally used to describe marketing mix by McCarthy in the year 1960 are :

- Product
- Price
- Promotion
- Place

Each of the above variables includes within it many sub-elements. Cowell in the year 1993 however revised the marketing mix variables for service industry including the travel and tourism. According to Cowell in addition to four original elements of product, price, promotion and place, there are three more which are :

People

Physical Evidence

Process (Customer involvement variables)

The three revised variables as introduced by Cowell in 1993 are to be used for travel and tourism since being a service industry it has certain special features. The use of marketing mix in travel and tourism has both short as well as long term aspects. The short term aspects relate to meeting the immediate initiatives of the competitors and include aspects like :

a. Price reduction

b. Aggressive promotion

c. Introduction of a new product

d. Special offers

e. Incentives

Long term aspects relate to meeting the objectives set aside for future long duration plans. These are based on longer range plans and are derived from the study of all kinds of trends in the market like natural, economic, social environmental and technological. The four variables or Ps have been illustrated below with illustrations taken from a well known and a branded tourist product. 'Palace on Wheels' is a famous train with historic charm and modern conveniences. For one week it is possible to roll back the pages of Indian History. The royal train takes the tourist on a royal Odyssey bringing alive the luxury of princely travel of the bygone age of the Raj. The train has been designed to offer all the modern comforts. The journey offers a complete package and covers nine well known historic cities in north India. Most of the travelling is done during night and the days are left free for discovering the various attractions.

Palace-an-Wheels

- Various special features and characteristics of the product
- Size and facilities offered
- Service elements of the product
- Benefits it offers
- Image, reputation
- Branding
- Positioning - upmarket / down market

Price

- Normal
- Promotional
- Corporate
- Discounted
- Wholesaler
- Seasonal

Promotion

- Advertising
- Sales promotion
- Press and public relations
- Brochure / Folder
- Personal selling
- Direct mail
- Outdoor

- Sponsorship
- Point-of-sale material

Place (Distribution)

- Travel agents
- Tour operators
- Airlines
- Reservation system
- Direct from producers
- Trade fairs and exhibitions
- Clubs
- General sales agents (GSA)

7

System at Work

It is the foundation for building hotel management structure and the evolution of all forms of life of human society show the need for organisation.

It is the mechanism that enables living things to live and work effectively and efficiently together and hence organisation may be called as the arrangement of personnel and assignment of duties and responsibilities to them so the entire establishment functions as one unit. It is important that there are clear lines of authority and effective lines of communication.

For organisation to take place there must be:

Every job should be well defined and should possess a definite place in the organisation. Each man in an organisation has got a definite purpose which he should fulfil in order that things may go as desired. This is important otherwise the work of one member of the group may overlap the work being done by others resulting in chaos. A simple principle of 'One Man-One Boss' should be followed to avoid overlapping of work. Situations such as anyone reporting to more than one person, should be avoided.

Authority means having the right to acquire work from others. A supervisor or a junior manager without authority would refer all matters to their managers for decision and direction and hence will not be in a position to exercise any influence upon a worker, and as such their existence will not carry any meaning. Authority should commensurate with responsibility.

For the effective working of the organisation pattern, they are divided as (i) Direct, (ii) Lateral and (iii) Functional.

(i) *Direct relationship* exists between a senior and a subordinate and vice versa. This is also called as line relationship or vertical relationship. The relationship involved here is of instructions from the seniors and execution by the subordinates.

(ii) *The lateral relationship* exists between executives or supervisors at the same level of responsibility and holding authorities. It's also called staff/horizontal relationship.

(iii) *The functional relationship* arises in case of a specialized position contributing a service to the managers or supervisors of different departments e.g. personnel manager.

Meaning and Nature : The limit of number of subordinates—whose activities are inter-related—that a person can effectively supervise is called 'span of management' or span of control. Hotel industry requires highly qualified and professional people to be engaged so as to enable smooth operation. The manager of a hotel is needed to coordinate and monitor the activities of the group and he will require a suitable organisational structure. The manager will depend on an efficient communication network to achieve this goal. To avoid even the least possible inconvenience to the guest and the hotel management, it is very important for the hotel to have necessary staff at all time.

The organisation of a hotel will depend largely on the objectives and the size of the hotel and its type. There are as many different forms of organisations as there are different hotels, primarily because each head of the institution or the General Manager work somewhat differently. There are hotels where General Managers are qualified, trained and experienced. They have their own style of working, which is usually based on certain experiences. Each individual may design his organisation network according to his experience and qualification. The problem of physical plant and personnel grow larger and become complex as the size of the establishment increases.

From the above discussion we can say that the primary purpose of organisation is to:

1. Afford an effective framework for the delegation of management responsibility.
2. Bring about coordinated effort of personnel towards the goal.
3. Establish channels of communication.

We may say that organisations are characterized by:

1. Division of labour, power and communication. Division of responsibility, which are not traditionally designed, but deliberately planned to enhance the realization of specific goals.
2. Presence of power control centres which control the concerned efforts of organisation and direct them towards its goals. These power centres must also review continuously the organisation's performance and re-pattern its structure, when necessary, to increase its efficiency.
3. Substitution and rearrangement of personnel i.e. unsatisfactory personnel to be removed or shifted and others assigned their duties.

Concept of organisation has two aspects:

1. Technical or mechanistic aspect pertaining to activities.
2. Social or humanistic aspect pertaining to people (For personal contentment and social satisfaction of people, organisation calls for matching of jobs to people and vice-versa).

Different Types

It is one of the earliest models based on the thinking that people are like plant and machinery and they can be treated in the same style. It believes that they come to work, are told what to do, given tools to do the job, do it and go. Manager's job is to direct and impose discipline. Not a very practical approach as it is based on unrealistic assumption about the way in which people behave.

This model has rational appeal and works in most situations. The organisation is divided in a series of neat components, within each of which every one has a precisely defined role. They are thus highly specialized. The relationship with others is governed by a specific set of rules and procedures. Everyone's ability to authorize and decide is very clearly defined and limited. This system would not work if the people bring the likes and prejudices of outside world into the work structure.

The systematic approach recognizes that the organisation may have to function under conditions of change and there is no one best method in which to complete a task and that the structure must be varied according to the elements which exist in the current environs. For this theory to work, it must be assumed that every one will work with a spirit of cooperation but this won't work in conflict with the goals of the organisation. It is not possible to suggest an ideal structure which could be used to perform any task. There are many factors which need to be taken into account while designing the structure of an organisation. Organisation cannot be regarded as a static structure and it is important to recognise that it is constantly evolving and changing.

As per the dictionary the word mission means 'a vocation or life's purpose'. It is a statement setting out an organisation's policy.

A written statement stating the mission of the establishment is called as *'mission statement'*. Since hotel is also an organisation it is important to have a mission statement. Different hotels will have different mission statements because the business is such where a common profile cannot be established and hence a mission statement of a hotel defines the specific (unique) purpose that makes this hotel different from other hotels. While formulating the policies of the hotel it is the uniqueness of the philosophy that is reflected by its mission statement and this gives directions to the policy makers.

A hotel's mission statement should be made keeping in mind the interest of hotel management, guests and employees. Equal emphasis should be given to all these three factors. As far as guest interest is concerned the mission statement should be able to stress upon his basic needs such as clean and comfortable accommodation, nutritious, healthy and safe food, and professional and courteous service. As far as management is concerned the mission statement should take care of the management policies in relation to financial and social responsibilities.

This statement will help the new job aspirant to understand the philosophy and growth in the establishment and will help the existing employees in their jobs by identifying the property's basic values. Finally the mission statement of the hotel should be able to guide the employees of the hotel in understanding the requirements of both the management and the guest clearly.

The "Hotel Mission Statement" should be able to speak out of the consistent level and quality of its service and products so that the guest is satisfied and encourage him to return and improve word-of-mouths promotions (understanding the needs of the guests, defining its market, consistent delivery of goods and services of a specified standard expected by the market, and hence enhanced guest satisfaction).

For example, a mission statement may read like this:

The mission of our hotel is to:

(i) *Provide comfortable accommodation and professional and efficient service to our guests and to assure total satisfaction.*

(ii) *Provide good returns to our shareholders.*

(iii) *Have the best-trained, qualified, enthusiastic and motivated employees.*

Goals and Objectives

As per the dictionary the word objective means 'a purpose, intention or aim *(The new company achieved its objective by making a profit in the third year of operation.)*'; that is to say that in order to carry out its mission the organisation must establish certain ends and must achieve these ends. These established ends are called as objectives. Objectives should be measurable and more specific than the mission, because they will be able to guide the workers in monitoring and auditing their progress. Written objectives specifying the course of action, followed by a measurement programme should be made. For example, the objectives of front office department may be written as :

(a) over the period of coming one year the number of guest complaints to be reduced down to 25% of the existing,

(b) to increase the average occupancy percentage by 10% for the coming year,

(c) to increase the percentage of foreign guest by 5% over the last year percentage.

Since the hotel services are interrelated it may not be possible to achieve the objectives of each department individually and it may be necessary to keep in mind the objectives of the departments also and hence it is important that the objectives are stated as 'total hotel property-wide objective' and not merely as departmental objectives. Objectives are more specific than mission.

Goal means 'the object of a person's ambition or effort; an aim or purpose. *(His goal in life is to become a racing driver.)*'

Goals give direction to the managers and other workers regarding the action to be taken to achieve the mission of the hotel and also guide the managers in planning strategies for the same reason. For example,

(i) To cut down the idle time by 2 minutes for each arrival.

(ii) To meet the objective of increase in occupancy percentage, a possible goal may be to encourage more walk-ins.

After having understood the goals, objectives and mission of the hotel the managers shall now be in a position to plan strategies to achieve the above. Hence strategies are methods by the use of which the goals will be achieved. Hence keeping the above in mind the hotel manager should,

(i) Do as much preregistration as possible.

(ii) Maintain a complaints book to cut down guest complaints.

(iii) A strategy for achieving the goal of increasing walk-in business to meet the objective of increasing occupancy percentage, may be installing an airport representative to fetch more and more business of those travellers who disembark at the airport without any prior reservation at any hotel.

An organisation chart is an illustrative presentation of the grouping of responsibilities and of some of the authorities and relations that arise among certain groups like managerial, supervisory and specialists. Such a chart may represent either position titles such as production manager, service manager, marketing and sales manager, and finance manager etc. or functions such as production, service, marketing and sales and finance etc. Organisation charts range from very simple drawings which merely outline the structure of major units to complex drawings which attempt to include all minor units as well as which purport to show minor variations in the levels of authority, cross relationship amongst departments and sometimes other features.

According to Pfiffner and Sherwood there are three main types of organisational charts.

A graphical presentation of the hierarchical framework. It contains of principal sub-units. These are arranged in levels of hierarchical status connected by lines suggesting the different types of authority. The line of communication is usually indicated by a solid black line, while a broken or hatched line represents staff or functional relationship.

Functional charts usually apply to sub-units showing smaller breakdowns into divisions, units or sections. Sometimes they go down far enough to depict every first line supervisor. Boxes are made to write down duties, activities or functions of that particular sub-unit executive or supervisor.

It is of the same graphic design as the functional chart but the boxes contain personal information. This may consist of the job title of the supervisor and each subordinate and in some cases the names of the incumbents are listed. Sometimes the authorized personnel are compared with the actual personnel on a given date.

Uses of Organisation Chart

(i) Gives a bird's eye view of the organisational structure.

(ii) Indicates line (direct) staff (lateral) and functional relationship.

(iii) Shows channels of communication.

(iv) Indicates the various job positions and levels of management.

Development of Organisation Culture

Corporate mission and strategic plan

(Giving birth to the culture)

↓

Human resources plan

(Defining the culture)

↓

Recruitment and selection

(Locating the bearers of the culture)

↓

Training and development

(Instilling the culture)

↓

Target setting and appraisal

(Enabling the culture)

↓

Reward management

(Reinforcing the culture)

↓

Succession planning and existing

(Maintaining the culture)

Number of factors such as location, type of hotel, type of service, structural layout, background and training of staff, policy of hotel, levels of management and type of ownership etc. are involved in hotel organisational plan.

Two divisions come under him. Each has four sub-sections:

(i) (a) Rooms sales

(b) Reservations

(c) Telephones

(d) Cash and bills office

(ii) (a) Bell desk
(b) Information
(c) Chauffeur and garage
(d) Rentals/Concessionaries etc.

Various kitchens and food production centres, executive chef, sous chef, commis, etc.

Various services outlets managers such as restaurants and bars, banquets and room service, etc. Manager restaurants, stewards and commis, etc.

Rooms public areas, provides vacant and clean rooms. Helps front office in keeping room status up to date.

Two sub-divisions (handles financial activities) :

(i) Cash
(ii) Credit

Paying all bills, sending outstation bills, receiving payments, computing pay rolls and making payroll cheques, computing income data (incomes and expenditures), making bank deposits, secure cash money, control and monitor revenue, compiling monthly income statement.

Three sub-sections :

(i) Energy
(ii) Power and Light
(iii) Temperature control

Responsible for keeping highest standards of appearance of interior and exterior and all equipment.

Looks after regular maintenance, preventive maintenance, breakdown maintenance, emergency work, special project assignments.

Plumber, mason, electrician, painter, polisher, carpenter, carpet repairer, etc.

Reports directly to G.M., Resident Manager. In-house or contracted service. Responsibilities include patrolling the property, monitoring surveillance cameras, guest, staff and property safety, maintaining relations with local law officials.

To attract guest to hotel. To find out sources of business, what they want knowledge of competitors, how you can beat them and finally to plan how you can get maximum revenue for your hotel. Designs brochures, billboards and other advertising material.

Looking after the welfare of staff and activities from recruitment to termination and retirement.

There is no other industry in world where the human resource is as important as it is in tourism and hotel industry. Although these days a lot of operations, such as forecasting and planning etc., can be done by automatic (computerized) system, yet the most important service of this industry i.e. the personal touch, can be given by a human being only—an employee who is well motivated and is willing to provide service. The personal functions are not of importance, but human resource management will always be an important issue. Hence the human resource department of a hotel is of great importance. The management of manpower working in the front office department is specially more important as the first and last impressions of the hotel are given by the staff working in this department of the hotel.

The function of human resource management and development is to find out that out of the employees working in the establishment who possess, and who lack the ability to deliver efficient and pleasant service to the guest and accordingly to be able to orient, train, motivate and evaluate, etc.

Many times the human resource managers are in conflicting pressure of organisational demands and employees concern and in this process develop elaborate structure and tightly controlled systems for managing people. With globalization, human resource is no longer confined to the culture and ethos of any single organisation as it has brought latest advances and management sciences, and has become more dynamic, flexible and creative. Now the ultimate goal of every human resource department should be to develop a linkage between the employee and organisation because the employee commitment to the organisation is crucial.

One of the major jobs of the front office manager is to manage the staff of his department. His job is to forecast the personnel needs of his department, determine desirable qualities in personnel, and communicate the same to the central personnel department.

The future need of staff by the front office department should be assessed and communicated to the personnel department so that the personnel department may arrange to fulfil this need of staff. For this it is very important that a near accurate forecast of the business i.e. the number of guest arrivals and departures, etc., is known. This will help in controlling labour cost. The future need of employee will also be affected by the pattern of employee turnover of the establishment (anticipate when an employee is unhappy and is about to leave, and plan his replacement well in time) and the effect of season on the business and not only the pattern of business on weekends but also during the week. An automatic system can be designed to tell as to what will be the requirement in terms of manpower and at the same time what will be the cost of labour involved for that requirement. This will make the budget of forecasted labour cost. This cost of labour budget should be studied against the forecasted sales budget.

Another factor that should be considered for determining the employee need is that they should be having the qualities and qualification needed for effectively completing the job for which they are required. For example you may need a front office staff who is an expert in upselling or a person who is efficient at record keeping etc. and hence the selection will be done accordingly. His previous experience, training and education will be helpful in selecting the right person.

Finally, after having forecasted the requirement of manpower and the attributes needed in them, it is important that the requirement of the department for future is communicated to the 'personnel' department to process the selection process and recruit, train and orient the selected staff well in time so that they may take up regular job position in the department and standard of services and goods provided to the guest does not suffer in quality.

To avoid any communication gap or miscommunication it is better that the need is communicated through a written job specification card which should specify : (i) educational qualification, (ii) technical qualification, (iii) relevant training, (iv)minimum experience of required job, (v) physical requirements like age, sex, height, etc. and (vi) condition and environment of work, etc.

Once the front office department communicates the requirement of employee to human resource department they start the selection and recruitment process which involve following basic steps: recruiting, testing, selecting, hiring, orienting, training, scheduling, evaluating, motivating including incentives, promotions, discipline and termination, etc.

Concept of Recruitment and Training : Recruitment can be called as the process of inviting and looking for correct and right applicant to fill up the job position (already vacant or going to be vacant in near future). It involves announcing the job vacancy position through proper sources, evaluating application and interviewing suitable person for job. For identifying the right prospects both internal and external sources should be contacted.

Filling up of a job internally refers to (i) promotions, (ii) transfers and (iii) referrals. This basically means finding out if there is any one capable of taking up the job from within. This is a very good way because the person is already well aware of the culture and systems of organisation and this is going to boost up the morale of the employee and motivate him highly. This is particularly true when higher positions such as assistant front office manager, deputy front office manager, deputy manager, lobby manager, reservation manager and front office managers are to be filled in. The process involves reviewing in-house staff for their competence.

Promotion is an incentive and reward and acknowledgement of good work and also an indication that the management has faith and confidence in the employee. Since he is from the department he is well versed with other staff members of the department. The orientation and training time will be reduced to almost zero and the employee shall be able to take up responsibility right from day one. All merits and demerits of the employee being considered for promotion must be considered before promoting him.

At times inter-department and intra-department promotions are also used to fill up a vacant or to-be-vacant post. The concept of multi-skilling of staff is very useful in such cases. Transfers may be done from one section of department to other section such as from reservation to front desk and vice versa or from one department to another department, from one unit of chain to another unit of chain within city or from one city to another city or from one country to another. Transfer may be motivational factors for employees e.g. the transfer of a bellboy from morning shift to night staff in those hotels which have heavy check-in and check-out in the night (a possibility of large amount of tips).

This is another internal recruiting source. Here the current employees recommend their relatives, friends and persons known to them to the management for the job. Although such persons may be easily available, and it will be an indirect obligation to the person who is recommending, yet it is important that these candidates must be thoroughly scrutinized and make sure that they fulfil all the requirements needed out of the candidate for the required job. Another important point in the case is that if many such candidates who are recommended by the staff working in the organisation are recruited they all may form their own lobby and may take the management to ransom at times.

Various external sources such as employment bureaus, schools, campus recruitment at various hotel management colleges and local agencies, both government and private, are good external sources of recruitment. Apart from these, advertisements in newspapers, trade magazines, periodicals, etc. will also give good prospective candidates for the job. A very carefully drafted advertisement in any of the above is given. The advertisement should include heading such as name of the organisation, job title, job profile, academic and technical qualification required (essential, necessary or desirable), level of training and required experience of the trade, duty hours, condition etc., physical requirements such as age, sex, height, etc. and remuneration, perks, etc.; also how to apply, last date of sending application etc. With globalization and fast modes of communication such as networking, the recruitment can be done through interviews on networking also. External recruiting helps in getting new employees who bring with them new ideas, new work culture etc. but it is important to test these new ideas etc. before implementing them in your organisation as they may not fit into your work culture. Private employment agencies such as placement consultant also can provide very useful employees. They usually charge a service fee. Media such as TV and radio are other sources through which the vacant job position can be advertised.

The HR department advertises in various newspapers/ magazines, etc. the vacant job position giving various details (as explained above) and invites applications from suitable candidates. Sufficient time should be given for receiving the application and also in order to get a wider choice advertisement should be given in various newspapers. Applicants may be asked to apply on a simple application form also.

Since media and newspapers etc. would cover a wide area, a large number of applications will be received by the personnel department of the hotel and it becomes necessary to scrutinize them and short-list only the most suitable candidates out of the total number of applications. Since screening involves technical knowledge of the advertised job it is important that the person involved in screening the application has good knowledge of the job or if required an expert from the front office department may be invited to assist. Job description which covers all the tasks and related information of the job and outlines responsibilities, reporting relationships, working conditions, equipment and material to be used, etc. is a very important selection tool. Another important selection tool is job specification which has been explained earlier. Screening also includes cross checking references given by the applicant in the application.

Next step after the screening of applications is fixing of interviews. The first step involved is formation of interview board which may include M.D/G.M./front office manager, personnel manager, a psychologist and a sectional head. Depending upon the job position, all of them or some of them may be on the interview panel. With the consent and availability of the members of the interview panel, a date and time is fixed and the same is intimated to all the short listed candidates, giving them sufficient time to prepare to reach on the schedule date and time. Further, depending upon the job profile, the interview technique should be decided. A written test, a trade test such as skill test, typing test, computer handling test, group discussion, communication skills test, stress test, etc. can be used.

Interview is not only an opportunity for the interviewer to judge the suitability of the applicant for the job but is also an opportunity for the applicant to know about the company, its profile, his job and position in the company and what it would be for him to work in this company and hence the interviewer should be well prepared to answer all questions the applicant asks him (about the job, salary, company growth etc.) during the interview and should be a skilful communicator. The interview must be conducted in a comfortable and relaxed atmosphere with no disturbances. The basic objective of the interview is to collect enough and accurate information from the applicant so as to make correct decisions, establish a basis for a working relationship, and to provide encugh information to the applicant about the company and job etc. so as to help him in deciding whether to take up the job or not. It must be kept in mind that the interview is able to create goodwill between the hotel and the applicant. Some important points that an interviewer should keep in mind are as follows.

- Interviewer should speak in a conversational tone i.e. his tone should be friendly and should treat the applicant with courtesy and respect.
- Interviewer should be patient with interviewees.
- Prepare a list of questions through which the interviewer shall allow the applicant to express himself fully without giving him a feeling that he is being interrogated and at the same time is able to find out whether the applicant has an outgoing personality, an eye for details, his attitude towards salesmanship, and whether he will be comfortable with computers or not.
- Begin interview with some small talk to make him feel at ease.
- Questions should be short but should give the applicant full opportunity to express himself.
- Interviewer should read the body language and expression etc. of the applicant during the interview.
- Reply to the queries of the applicant honestly and directly.
- Pursue the subject when responses seem unreasonable.
- Encourage the applicant to speak more and more (of course relevant) by using short affirmative responses.
- Suggest sample answers and reframe the questions if the applicant does not understand the question.

Another phase of the interview may be trade test through which his technical knowledge such as use of computer and other machines and how comfortable he feels with them can be carried out. To check his social skills such as communication he may be asked to speak extempore on some topic for 2 or 3 minutes. Similarly to find out if the applicant can work under pressure or stress, questions indicating his course of action in pressure situations such as fire or theft, etc. should be asked.

Every applicant has some weaknesses and strengths. An evaluation of interview of the applicant would highlight both. The weakness in one area (if not hampering the work) should not be a reason to reject the candidate but the strengths, although may not be directly related to the job profile, should be considered and ways to channelise them so that they become assets for the employee should be considered. Fair, unbiased and impartial assessment of all candidates should be done and the decision should not be done under any pressure. Generally a panel of selected candidates is made, and the job is offered to the person who tops the list. The panel usually remains valid for six months and in case the person who tops the list does not join or leaves the job the next person on the panel is called. The panel is submitted to the M.D. or G.M. or anyone who is authorized for approval.

It is a very useful practice followed by some organisations to intimate candidates who were not selected and thank them for showing interest in your organisation. This will be a goodwill gesture.

Once the panel is approved by the authority the next step is hiring, but before that it is important that labour laws and other legal requirements necessary for hiring are followed. After making sure that all legal formalities are completed a very carefully worded offer letter is prepared and given to the selected applicant. All clauses must be very clearly worded to eliminate misunderstanding. Give joining date and stick to that. Once the applicant accepts the offer, he should be assured that he has made the right decision. Current employees of the department, both senior to him and junior to him, should now be told about the new person's joining the establishment. This will prepare them mentally and psychologically to receive the new entrant. An orientation programme should be designed for the new entrant.

Orientation is also called induction and this is basically a process of interaction between the newly appointed employee and the organisation through its people, technology, structure, system and procedure with a view to facilitate his adjustment within the organisation. It is a systematic process of giving information to the new employee about his jobs, his colleagues, his boss, organisational structure and his role in the organisation, its policies and philosophies, systems and procedure, benefit and perks which he is entitled to, etc.

In order to ensure better discipline and performance from a new entrant to the organisational family, he is introduced and inducted in the organisation through a well designed programme to impart him with the essential information on various aspects of the organisation. Such systematic information help him to understand his own job functions, his role in the organisation, his reporting relationship with the boss and organisation for which he will now be working.

Contents of orientation programme and what should be included in the induction programme depends upon the management's philosophy, importance attached by it toward the development of human resources, the turnover rate of the employees, hotel's future plan and its work culture, etc. Educational background, past experience and level of recruitment are also very important considerations. Certified standing order of the establishment which include classification of workman, period of probation, and procedure for confirmation in the company, period of work, rest period, working day, weekly off, declared holidays and leave, conduct and misconduct, procedure for initiating disciplinary action, reward or punishment and grievances redressal system, etc. should also be included in the orientation programme. It should also include historical background of the company, future expansion and diversification plan, sales performance and marketing strength, annual plan, profitability records, pay scales, allowances, perks, personnel policies i.e. transfer, performance, placement, merit rating, etc., training facilities, growth avenues, safety schemes, channels of upward communication, role of the company in overall development of economy of the country, special achievement and contribution to the society as a whole. Much of this information may be included in the property's employees manual or hand book.

This includes all activities starting from deciding the number of new entrants to participate in the group, the contents of the programme, training aids to be used during the programme, the selection of who will conduct the orientation programme and receiving feedback from participants to further improve the standard of induction programme.

Preferably, the group of participants should be a maximum of 15 at a time. The induction equipment include equipment such as OHP, projector, T.V., VCR, films, chalkboard, white board, microphone, etc., organisational booklet and technique and seating arrangement, training room etc. Inductor should be preferably from the department or from HR department and should be well versed with the policies and working of the department. The content of programme should be as per the requirement already discussed. Feedback is also very important. Feedback from the participant can be obtained both in writing or verbal form. During the feedback session a panel consisting of HR manager, front office manager and the immediate boss of the employee will discuss the details of the feedback which may be both positive as well as negative.

Orientation programme boosts up the morale and ego of the employee, leads to a better understanding between him and the hotel and motivates him to perform better and brings in a sense of unity and belongingness in him.

Training is a method of imparting knowledge and information to the employee for improvement and upgradation of his skill, activities and potential for his own benefit as well as for the benefit of the organisation. Training and development is the process in which people are provided opportunity to learn the skills, knowledge, attitude and behaviour needed to perform their jobs effectively and prepare themselves for changing situations in present as well as in future. Training enables a person to learn the *what,* the *how,* and the *why* of a job.

It introduces individual employee to his job and company. It is a means for growth and development of the employee with a view to provide him faster career progression opportunities. Successful completion of training may be a prerequisite for promotion. It brings in confidence in the employee to take up the job without any fear or hesitation. It motivates the employee and gives satisfaction and pride to him as he is able to perform the task more efficiently and effectively through his skill and knowledge upgradation. It increases the productivity and profitability of the hotel. Training gives more job security to him. It reduces wastage of time and helps the employee in better time management. It improves interpersonal relation among the employee and supervisor and increases the disciplinary level in the employee.

Management is responsible for the development, progress and performance of their staff, and training is a way to carry out their responsibility. But how does the management know when or what type of training is needed? Following signs indicate when the staff needs training.

(i) When new methods or work procedure are introduced in the hotel.

(ii) When the production target are not met and there is a gradual decline.

(iii) When the cost of operations are increasing without any apparent reason and the complaints and grievances are increasing.

(iv) When the supervisor feels that the staff is becoming demotivated and workers do not seem to be satisfied and ask more and more question about their job, and the pride in job and company is missing.

(v) Accidents are increasing.

(vi) Quality of product is decreasing.

The management can determine the type of training required by direct supervision and observation, by counselling sessions, etc. Another important source can be the exit interview of employee when the labour turnover is high. Planning and development of a training programme for front office employees includes identifying the tasks performed and preparing step by step procedure and reviewing the steps involved in the training process. A job list, lists tasks that must be performed and should state what an employee must do in performing the job. Jobs are divided into tasks. Front office clerk has to perform many jobs. They are all put on the job list.

Step By Step Procedure Performance Sheet

Job	Knowledge	Assessment for 1st Quarter					
		Jan		Feb		March	
		Yes	No	Yes	No	Yes	No
Dealing with deposit for safe custody	(i) Company policy in relation to safe custody of money and valuables (ii) Legal aspects of safe custody (iii) Registering and labelling						

Skill	Assessment for 1st Quarter						Attitude	Assessment for 1st Quarter					
	Jan		Feb		March			Jan		Feb		March	
	Yes	No	Yes	No	Yes	No		Yes	No	Yes	No	Yes	No
(i) Read (ii) Write (iii) Communicate (iv) Calculate (v) Store items in an ordered and safe manner (vi) Operate safe locking Mechanism							(i) Integrity (ii) Helpfullness (iii) Security						

Training New Employees

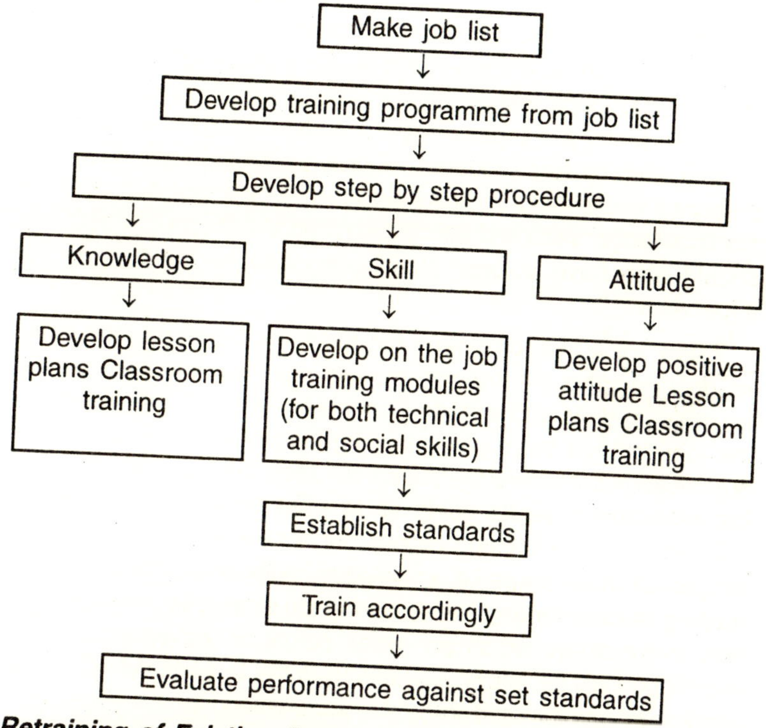

Retraining of Existing Staff

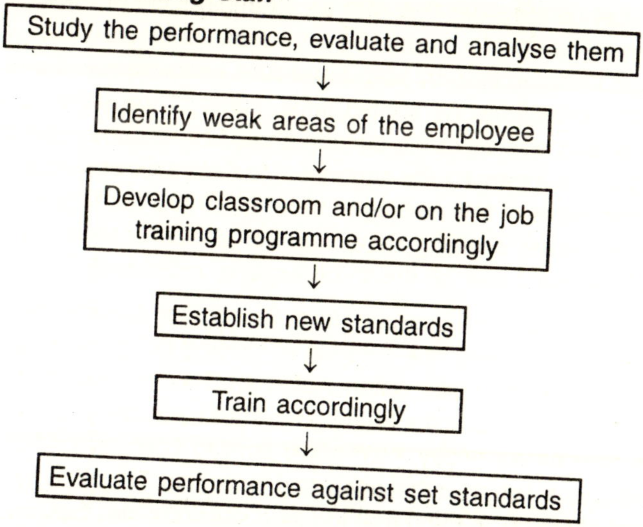

This job now can be divided into small tasks such as (a) greeting the guest, (b) assessing his requirement, (c) matching the product i.e. room to his requirement, (d) registering the guest, (e) getting his luggage installed in the room, (f) opening his folio, etc. All these tasks put together will complete the job i.e. *check-in.* Further, step by step procedure for each of these tasks should be prepared and should be recorded on a format which should list the knowledge, skills and attitude required to perform that task and should also have column of evaluation, to be filled in by the supervisor.

Now, for a new employee the training programme should be so designed that the training module will cover all three i.e. the knowledge, skills and attitude. For an employee who is already on the job and has been given training initially when he joined the organisation but where the supervisor feels the need of retraining, his assessment would guide as to what should be the training module. Hence a training module for a new entrant will have to include all three areas i.e. knowledge, skills and attitude, while a training module for an already on-the-job employee would include only those areas which are weak points of the employee (the information will be easily available from the last column of the job breakdown sheet, filled in by the supervisor).

Let us consider this with an example. One of the tasks of a front office cashier is dealing with deposits for safe custody. The sheet showing step by step procedure performance shows some of the knowledge he should have, some of the skills he should have, and also what his attitude should be. Column next to each of these is meant for the supervisor to record his observations and assessment of the employee while making a training module for an employee needing retraining. For a new entrant the training module will cover all the three aspects individually.

Develop a training plan from the job list. Decide the number of days of training, the duration of training on each day and then fit in all the job tasks within that span. Training plan must clearly define at what time the training will start each day and when it will be over on each day. Also make sure to keep tea/coffee breaks and lunch break in-between the sessions. The plan should be made keeping in mind that too long sessions may become boring and tiring. Develop lesson plans and decide on training method. Establish a time table.

Following is an example of designing (i) a job list for bell desk staff and (ii) a four days training module for the same.

Job list for Bell Desk

- Wear proper uniform and punch in.
- Luggage handling (arrival, change of room, storage and departure).
- Inducts the guest to room amenities and services.
- Paging.
- Mail and message handling (incoming and outgoing).
- Handling room keys (arrival and departure).
- Newspapers and magazine handling.
- Outside jobs.
- To arrange wake calls.
- Door and car parking area.
- Punch out.

Four Days Training Module

Day 1 (Monday)

- Wear uniform and punch in
- Appraisal of Bell Desk and its equipment
- Door area
- Punch out

Day 2 (Tuesday)

- Luggage handling (arrival)
- Handling room key
- Use of luggage trolley
- Use of elevator
- Escorting the guest to room
- Inducting him to room amenities

Day 3 (Wednesday)

- Luggage handling (departure and change of room)

- Handling room keys
- Paging
- Outside jobs
- Arranging wake calls
- Newspaper and magazine handling

Day 4 (Thursday)

- Luggage storage
- Mail handling (incoming and outgoing)
- Message handling
- Car parking
- Car valet
- Miscellaneous jobs
- Proformas and report making

Include field visits, on the job training etc. in addition to class room training. Select proper training location, time and season. The environment should be healthy. There should be proper lighting system, ventilation, audio-visual system, air conditioning, comfortable and proper seating arrangement, demonstration equipment, and an unobstructed view for the trainee. Assemble all training materials and equipment well in advance and before the commencement of training session. It is advisable to have a test run of all equipment and material before starting the session. Avoid using difficult jargon. Proceed slowly through training session as new employees are seeing and hearing most of the things for the first time.

A well planned training programme fully backed up with necessary requirement and ideal location may all be of no use if the trainer providing training is poor. Careful and proper consideration should be given to selecting the person who will train. He must be very well versed in the job procedures and training method and should have enough practical experience. He should have the ability to teach and shall have excellent communication skills. He should be not only familiar with modern systems but with the equipment needed for the system. The trainer should also be able to instill the advantages of training to the employee. The trainer should not discourage the trainee from asking questions. He should have patience. He should have professional and positive attitude. The trainer is greatly responsible in moulding the attitudes, skills and knowledge of a trainee. Any negative attitude shown by the trainer during training shall greatly demotivate the trainee.

Various methods of training are used. It is advisable to use a number of methods during the training session because if only one method is used the training session may tend to become boring, particularly class room lecture method. What methods should be used depends on various factors such as group, their social status, level of training and the job profile. Following methods are generally used.

It is the oldest method, but most commonly used. This mode of training is passive as only the lecturer speaks and other participants are only passive listeners. To make it more effective the lecturer should encourage more and more participation by trainees by asking more and relevant questions during the session.

It is used for senior management development programme. The method is used to develop better understanding amongst two departments. The managers from two departments are asked to play each other's role in front of the other participants. The dramatic conditions thus created involves interest of all the participants and leads to a high degree of learning.

Cases are prepared on the working of different aspects of a department and discussed during training session. This method of training is useful for middle and senior management. The method is effective in improving the power of analysis, decision making skills and techniques of participation apart from developing their skills to take group decision, interpersonal relation, human skills and respecting others' point of view.

It is a very effective and at the same time economical method for a new entrant. It is useful for technical skills development before being given independent charge. Periodic review by the supervisor is very important. Employee gets better opportunity to concentrate on his own efforts to improve his skills, technique and ability.

It is very effective for skill development. The trainer demonstrates to the trainee and the trainee can also participate. The trainer must have excellent skills. This method requires great deal of preparation before commencing the demonstration.

It is good for experienced staff. In itself, it can include various other methods such as lecture, discussion etc. But this is a time consuming method. Trainees can use role play and case study methods etc.

It is a problem solving approach by a group. It involves much trainee participation, but consensus can be obtained. At times it becomes difficult to control the group and consensus may not be achieved and conflicts may arise.

It is somewhat similar to role play and on the job training, and also to some extent to demonstration and hence good for full development. The trainee initiates action required in an almost real situation. These are time consuming methods.

The trainee is given a research project with an objective to understand how clear the concepts are to him. For example, he may be asked to study the existing problem of the lobby and design a new lobby. It helps to bring out the originality out of the trainee. But the project must be very analytically studied before approval.

It is a very effective method for developing employees at all levels. It is a concept of multi skilling where an employee is rotated to various sections of same department or to various departments with a view to utilize his ability in any section or department as per the need. It involves "Cross Training".

It is a new concept. Participants are given various types of games to play with—plastic blocks, drawing pictures, construction of some designs through blocks, etc. and while they are busy achieving the given objective they undergo interaction process with each other which helps them to solve the problem through team work.

Some Useful Tips for Improving Techniques of Communicating with Trainees during Training Session:

(a) Use an easy going approach. This will put the trainee at ease and relaxed.

(b) Speak the language the trainee speaks.

(c) Use words they speak and understand. Prefer short words to long words, simple words to complex words and short sentences to long sentences. Be clear.

(d) Keep emotions out of your style. Emotional ideas may cloud the issue for some listeners.

(e) Connect new ideas with old ones and modern procedure with outdated ones.

(f) Start with simple things first and explain the difficult ones later when the trainee's mind is better adjusted to it.

(g) Avoid negative approach to subject.

(h) Limit the number of ideas or points covered in a single session.

(i) Feedback should be encouraged. Promote questions to determine if you are getting through and to find out what you should repeat and where you may need to place emphasis.

Detent Approach : A detailed assessment and feedback is sought from the trainees after the training is completed. A well framed 'feedback form' should be used for this. The feedback is sought about the general arrangement, reading material supplied, video films and transparencies shown, lunch, tea and coffee served, training aids, coverage provided on the subject, usefulness of the training, quality of the trainers and whether such programmes are needed in future or not, etc. This will greatly help the HR department to design future training programmes.

Scheduling means assigning a schedule to the new entrant and it is one of the most difficult jobs. Although training prepares the new entrant to a great extent to take up the challenge of the new job, yet the front office manager will have to constantly observe the new entrant's performance. A person trained to do a specific job cannot be expected to do some other job with the same efficiency. Hence scheduling will largely be dependent upon the training given to him. An employee who has been given training for multi-skilling can be scheduled to any area wherever the need be. Some hotels schedule the employee as per their seniority. Employee's preferences and needs may also be considered which scheduling. Work schedule shall be made in such a way that no employee is neglected and no special favours are shown to any favourite employee. Generally schedules are made on weekly basis. Sufficient time notice should be given before changing the schedule for the next schedule period. Rescheduling can also be done in case of emergencies and anticipated business volume. If the anticipated volume of business demands, part time employee may be scheduled. Part time labour may prove to be economical. The most important point to be considered is that the front office manager is capable of scheduling the regular or part time staff to this maximum possible utilization and there is no wastage, and hence keeping the labour cost to minimum possible. Various concepts of flexible work hours or compressed work schedules and job sharing may be followed.

Motivation is creating an atmosphere and a conducive environment by the management for employee so that his interest in the work is maximum and the employee is continually attentive, observant, concerned and committed to his job and is able to give maximum output. This can also be called as finding out the needs and desires of the employees and to provide them within a reasonable framework return for the desired behaviour. Thus to motivate an employee you must first find out what he wants. A number of psychologists, such as Abraham Maslow, Elton Mayo, Douglas McGregor and Fredrick Herzberg, etc. have forwarded their motivational theories. These theories can be studied in detail in any management book. The main gist of these theories is that human beings dislike to work and hence most people must be coerced, controlled, directed, rewarded, threatened with punishment, etc. from time to time as per the demand of the situation. An employee's needs such as physiological, safety, love, affection, and belonging, self -esteem and esteem of others, self -actualization, self -realization and self-accomplishment, etc. should be identified and accordingly motivational programmes should be developed which may be designed on carrot and stick, or both theory basis. Promotions, transfers from one section to another (department to department), change of duty schedule (which might suit him), cash incentives (one selling rooms at higher rate, upselling of the room, selling rooms at rack rate etc.). His ability to convince the guest of the hotel to take and purchase hotel services such as food and beverages services, swimming pool and gift shop etc.

Mention the name of the dedicated worker of the month in the newsletter of the hotel. Applaud him in department meeting in front of other employees i.e. recognition of good work done by an employee. Announce paid holidays with family etc. The incentive programmes are designed after reviewing each employee's needs such as income, benefits, shift scheduling, vacation time, promotional goals etc. All departments and sections where sales increases because of the selling efforts and techniques of the front office staff will inform the same to the front office manager who will give appropriate incentives (usually cash) as per already designed policy of the hotel. Training is another way of motivation. Mention of marriages, births, engagements and promotion, etc. concerning the employee in the newsletter are also good incentives. Other rewards such as commendation letter, appreciation letter, complimentary dinner for him and family in hotel restaurant, gift certificate, discounted stay at other units of the same chain for employee and his family, etc. can also prove to be good incentives.

There is no motivational tool as powerful as praise. Usually giving something costs you money. But giving praise costs you nothing. In fact, it's the failure to praise that could cost you quite a lot in the long run. Its presence or absence are keenly felt. Following are six rules for using praise effectively to motivate staff.

Rule 1: Look for Things to Praise : Don't issue empty praise but do praise absolutely everything that deserves it. It is up to you to go out of your way to identify praiseworthy events, acts, ideas and works.

Rule 2 : Reinforce Praise : Praise is positive reinforcement. If you want your staffers to be more attentive to, say, customer service, praise them when they perform well in that area. Praise as many staffers as deserve it. As you reinforce the behaviour, you'll see results as the staffers produce more of the same.

Rule 3 : Deliver Timely Praise : It is important to associate positive reinforcement as closely as possible with a

desired behaviour. Time gap between the behaviour and reinforcement greatly reduces the effectiveness of reinforcement.

Rule 4 : Deliver Praise as Publicly as Possible *:* There is certainly some value in taking an employee aside and praising him privately, but the value is multiplied many times over if you praise in front of his colleagues. This heightens the effect of your kind words.

Rule 5 : Praise Specific Things : There is nothing wrong in telling someone that he is doing a great job. But the praise is much more powerful if it is tied to some specific events or actions.

Rule 6 : Look to the Future : Conclude your praise with a glance towards the future. "If you can keep satisfying customers like that, we ought to have a terrific year."

Many a times it is noted that in spite of several warnings an employee does not improve his performance, which reduces the output of the employee. Management may take strict actions such as transfer the employee from one section or department to another, reschedule his duties etc. At times management may decide to demote him. Hotel management must be very careful in taking these decisions. It is advisable that the management obtain legal opinion before taking any such decision. In India particularly this is more important where hotels have many labour unions and almost all the employees of the hotel are members of one or more such unions.

In some cases all the motivational efforts and disciplinary actions may yet not prove effective and in the interest of business the situation may demand that the management relieves the employee of his duties. In such cases the management should have a personal meeting with him and should suggest that the employee resigns from his job on his own rather than being terminated by the management. In case termination becomes unavoidable the supervisor must very tactfully and diplomatically communicate to the employee that his services are no more required by the organisation. Before submitting the termination letter to the employee, the management with the help of the legal advisor should keep all his dues ready and should hand them over to the employee with termination letter. The employee must be informed as to why his employment is being terminated. He should be then asked to appear for an exit interview with the HR manager.

Exit interview is conducted by the HR department. It may not always be in case of termination but it is a good practice to conduct the exit interview of all the employees who either leave the organisation on their own (either resign the job or retire after completing the tenure) or are terminated. It is particularly useful in case the labour turnover rate is high. The main idea of this interview is to determine views of the employee about the organisation in general and about his department/section in particular, including his co-workers, their nature, the degree of cooperation and coordination they offered to him during his tenure, equipment, systems, working conditions, motivational programmes, the difficulties he faced during his work tenure and also his suggestions on how these could be improved. Based on the analysis of this information record, for all exiting employees the HR department can reorganize and replan the policies and can restructure their various motivational programmes.

Key Terms

Organisation models	Strategies
Organisational mission	Orientation
Organisational objectives	Motivation
Goals	Training
Job lists	Job breakdown
Job analysis	Job specification

Management of In-House Activities

House Keeping : According to the World Tourism Organisation (WTO), there were about 13 million rooms worldwide in hotels, motels and similar establishments in 1996. The world's inventory of rooms was increasing by 3.8 per cent annually. The worldwide occupancy rates were averaging 66 per cent with some popular destinations, doing better than that.

Since 1990, there has been a rush to open new hotels in the new Republics of the erstwhile USSR and in the East European countries However, 72 per cent of the world's hotel and motel rooms are located in North America and Europe — Europe accounts for 44%. East Asia and Pacific had a share of 11.3 per cent.

In 1991, Europe offered 5.1 million rooms, USA 3.1 million and East Asia and Pacific 1.3 million. The city of New York alone had over 2,00,000 rooms in 1992 compared to only 10,000 in Delhi. In 1992, the total revenue of hotel industry in USA was US $ 66 billion compared to US $ 40 billion only five years ago. US $ 66 billion dollars was the revenue from regular hotels and motels but if you add the revenue from supplementary types of accommodations like condominiums and apartments, the revenue may be higher by another US $ 20 billion.

Welcome Courtesy : Besides the vast amounts generated in terms of revenue, hotels and motels create millions of jobs directly and thousands more indirectly for consultants, accountants and others who provide support services. Of the 9 million people employed directly in tourism related businesses, the USA hotel industry's share is over 3 million. Although no recent survey has been carried out in India on the employment directly provided by hotels and motels, a modest estimate would be one million in all types of tourist accommodations.

8

Modern Techniques

The telephone was invented in the late nineteenth century. That was four hundred years after America was discovered and the people of the Old World started moving to the New World in an attempt to widen their horizon. When the telephone appeared on the scene, people expected miracles to happen and some even predicted the end of travel in the world. But travel has expanded all over the world many times over. Whether we like it or not, we are now the citizens of cyberspace. We have instant access to any event in any part of the world—we can instantly convey our messages to anywhere. Stamped letters are being replaced by electronic mail, thanks to the computers as well internet. The computers have literally revolutionised communications. With the click of a mouse, we have access to a lot of advance information on countries and places we plan to visit. That means, we have fewer, if any, unpleasant surprises on our visit. We can embark on a trip with that much more confidence. It is interesting to note that virtual reality now heard so often, is creating the same kind of reaction about decrease in travel to other lands just as it happened when telephone was first invented. The travel, however, has no way of looking back. Our curiosity about other people and their countries increases, as new technology expands our knowledge.

In 1950, when CRS was first introduced to the airlines industry in its primitive form—the prophets of doom again questioned the cost-effectiveness of the computers and stated that the work could be done more effectively and economically by hiring a few additional hands for reservation purposes. However, there is no one today who questions the efficiency of CRS and speed they have brought to the travel transactions. With the expanding application of internet to link the closed-circuit network that used to link the airlines and travel agencies, is being transformed into web-based CRSs to the delight of the customers who want to make their own reservations with the airlines, hotels or the rental car companies, etc. Your personal computer can do these functions. The relatively limited scope of travel business that has been in place for one hundred and fifty years since Thomas Cook—is reaching unimaginable heights and is bound to grow further in the coming years.

A Milestone Start

The old-timers will recall how the airlines check-in staff operated at the airports with huge sheets of papers, manually matching the details of each passenger with the ticket and after satisfying themselves fully, issued the boarding pass. It took them a long time and the queues got even longer. Now, it takes only a minute or two, the staff at the counter takes your ticket and everything about the passenger comes on the screen—matched and the boarding pass is printed by the same machine instantly, telling you your seat number as well as the gate from where to board. The CRS is all about this—the details of all flights and millions of passengers are stored in the machine. It is called the Central Reservation System.

The breakthrough in technology took place three decades ago. In the fifties, some airlines began to use computers to keep track of number of seats available on some of their popular flights. First, it was to keep track of number of seats sold, a little later, the computer developed capacity to match passenger's name with each seat sold thus creating a record for the airlines. However, each airline had a different system. And, therefore, if one airline had to make reservation of a sector on a different airline, the two computers could not communicate with each other and they had to send teletype messages.

Till the seventies, both the carriers and the travel agents had to call the reservation system which was time-consuming as well as costly. Therefore, need arose for a Computer Reservation which could show the flight availability of all or most of the airlines and which should be small enough to be accommodated on a table of the travel agent, where they could themselves make reservations and order the computer to print the ticket as well as the itinerary.

Now, a few major airlines have developed these mega computers on their own or in partnership with other carriers. The travel agent can rent or lease one or more of such systems according to their requirements, and are now in a position to offer instant bookings and instant tickets to the customers. The travel agents put information directly in the system using their key-boards in a specified form acceptable to the carriers. The airlines can communicate with travel agents by issuing a queue format. The Reservation Systems have printers that produce tickets, invoices and itineraries. No tele-ticketing machines are required. In the USA and Europe, almost hundred per cent travel agents purchase or lease hardware from one or the other CRS vendor, occasionally from two. In India too, most of the IATA-approved travel agencies have a CRS, even in small towns. Indian Airlines and Air India schedules are represented in almost all the major CRS as they own no CRSs. We will talk about this in more details later in this chapter.

CRS and Marketing : The developments in computing and tele-communications technology have radically changed the way in which multinational organisations like international airlines and hotel chains do their business. New methods of storage, organisation, distribution, exploitation, analysis of product and consumer data have changed the marketing techniques and investment priorities of the airlines. Once an American Airlines, President, was asked—if he had a choice, what will he sell first—American Airlines or the SABRE CRS which the American Airlines then owned. His prompt reply was—airlines. It is a different matter that American Airlines have already sold the SABRE and it is now publicly traded. Surely, CRS today is the most important marketing tool of airlines. No need to hire an army of salesmen going around and visiting the travel agencies, explaining the product as well as the price. No need to buy a free lunch for travel agents to persuade them to give business to their airlines. All this can be done by a fax or e-mail message. Internet has opened new windows to sell your product directly to the consumers. That has made the travel agents running scared for the fear of getting eliminated in the distribution chain of airlines or hotels, etc.

CRS—An Assessment : CRSs are systems for information transfer. They store current information about all available travel service providers and have the necessary infrastructure to transfer such data. The systems also perform additional tasks related to service distribution, which in the area of goods, are typically performed by freight forwarders. Like an empty supermarket, the systems provide a sales area in the form of memory—a communications media. The service providers can fill the empty shelves by providing data to the CRS. The development of such systems was started in the early sixties. The principal objective at that time was to automate the seat reservation procedures of the airlines. Today, they are used primarily in this area though they offer information in other travel areas as well to make them more relevant to the consumers, as we will see from the detailed description of one of the major CRSs—SABRE. After several changes in the market, four major CRSs have emerged as leaders. Three of them are US-owned—SABRE, GALILEO, WORLDSPAN and one European-owned AMADEUS. The dominance of the US-owned CRSs led to resentment among European and Asian airlines for alleged discrimination or what is termed a 'halo' effect as the owning airlines could show Trias' in their own favour by displaying their flights first and the travel agents naturally preferred the flights which were shown first giving these airlines an advantage. In recent years, this bias is less visible in most of the Systems because of intense competition among CRSs to gain more users. Since European and Asian airlines did not want to be sidelined, some of them developed their own CRSs. Lufthansa, Air France, Iberia of Spain and SAS jointly developed AMADEUS—the name developed from restaurant where the executives of these airlines met in Madrid to plan the new CRS.

The British Airways, Swiss Air, KLM, Alitalia, Olympic of Greece and TAP of Portugal joined hands to develop GALILEO. Asian airlines have not remained far behind—Cathey Pacific of Hong Kong and Singapore Airlines have their own CRS ABACUS. All CRSs are joined together to some extent by various agreements between them because of intense competition and dependence on each other. All or most airlines are represented in major CRSs as they cannot ignore the travel agents who may be using the terminal of only one CRS. Although Air India and Indian Airlines have a tie-up with SABRE—which has a specially designed system for Indian Airlines and Air India branded SITAR— System Interface for Travel Agents Reservation—a customised version for the carriers to be distributed by them in India, both the Indian national carriers are represented in all other major CRSs paying a reservation fee to each for every booking effected. The new SITAR gives access to information on four hundred airlines, on several rail systems, car rentals companies, twenty-seven thousand hotels, and thirty-six tour wholesalers. SITAR was originally popular with all Indian travel agents, now other CRSs have got their foothold in the Indian market.

A brief description of SABRE and AMADEUS will give the readers an idea of the organisation and sophistication of the modern CRSs.

SABRE : SABRE is one of the largest privately-owned computer networks in the world. Its hardware is situated in Tulsa, USA, in a building specifically designed to make it virtually impregnable to terrorist and or criminal attacks and safe from natural disasters. It is difficult not to be impressed by SABRE's size and capacity.

- It uses six of the largest IBM computers, connected by hundred thousand kilometres of network data circuits to well over hundred thousand terminals all over the world.
- It contains flight and fare data on over thirty-five thousand city pairs throughout the world for more than seven hundred airlines.
- The database has more than fifty million domestic and international fares, with ability to construct many more, updated every business day at the rate of million a day.
- It can be used to book rooms in over thirty thousand hotel properties, rental cars from fifty companies and seats on

six railway systems. It contains details of sixty-five thousand vacation and recreation activities/spots. SABRE is more than thirty years old and is hundred per cent publicly traded since March 2000. They virtually invented E-Commerce for travel industry and run one of the most successful travel internet site, Travelocity.com—the first internet site for consumers where they can do business directly. Among the additional products they market are the SABRE Business Travel Solutions—it provides greater flexibility for business travellers and streamlined controls for their companies. Besides, airlines and transportation companies worldwide tap into SABRE strength for IT solutions—they provide products and services for streamlining operations and gaining efficiencies. They also claim to be world leaders in emerging technologies that save time and money.

AMADEUS : AMADEUS is a leading CRS—a market leader in Europe, Africa, Asia-Pacific with a strong presence in the USA and South America. It claims to have a worldwide network in sixty countries as a leading player. Founded in 1987, AMADEUS is a listed company with sixty per cent of its capital held by Air France, Iberia of Spain and Lufthansa of Germany. The company headquarter is located in Madrid, Spain; data-processing centre near Erding (Munich) and product development facilities at Sophia Antipolis near Nice in France. Marketing is shared by Madrid and Sophia Antipolis. It is truly an international company.

To service travel agencies in each local market, AMADEUS is represented by a National Marketing Company (NMC), responsible for local sales and marketing, including activities with service providers, local product definition and frontline training and support. AMADEUS has three regional offices—for Asia Pacific (Bangkok), North Central America (Miami) and for South America (Buenos Aires) to support the NMCs and to coordinate commercial relationships with that of the regional service providers. This includes twenty-four hour customer support.

The AMADEUS Global Network (AMANET) links providers and users—it is the largest civilian data centre in Europe.

Located at Erding near Munich it is built to support the massive, high speed transmission of data, voice and video, with numerous back-up and security mechanism. AMANET has fifteen computer groupings across Europe, North America and Asia that route, the data. It uses thirteen into two megabite data lines, numerous other data lines with standard transport speeds, and satellite services for backup.

AMADEUS provides travel agency customers with powerful software solutions to manage their sales processes and agency networks, including corporate travel management solutions. AMADEUS also works with business and technology partners to develop travel sales and management products, based on advanced network technologies and internet.

The following table will show the reach of our major CRSs in the world.

Global Reservation in Travel Industry

	AMADEUS	*GALILEO*	*SABRE*	*WORLD SPAN*
USA/Mexico/	U: 7.839	U: 13.347	U: 17.496	U: 9.200
Canada	T: 29.313	T: 59.980	T: 82.441	T: 41.106
Europe/Russia	U: 21.729	U: 12.561	U: 4.028	U: 5.474
	T: 59.804	T: 39.487	T: 11.477	T: 10.208
Latin America/	U: 4.631	U: 1.100	U: 1.985	U:53
Caribbean	T: 8.247	T: 1.918	T: 6.328	T:268
Far East/ Australia	U:920	U: 3.686	U: 4.113	U:0
	T: 2.034	T: 12.871	T: 14.246	T:0
Africa/Middle East	U:374	U: 1.632	U: 490	U:600
	T:768	T: 5.144	T: 1.452	T: 1.368
Total:	U: 35.493	U: 32.326	U: 28.112	U: 15.327
	T: 100.166	T: 119.400	T: 117.914	T: 47.950

Fig. Comparison between the number of users and the number of terminals of global systems (as at the beginning of 1996)

Computer's Role

The travel industry needs computers for following reasons:

- Direct access to an airlines' computer reservation system (CRS) to enable an agent to see the schedules and fares of airlines worldwide and make reservation immediately.
- The same CRS has access to data on hotels, car rentals companies, trains, cruises, buses, destinations, climate, currency, exchange rate, etc. With the push of a button, all arrangements are promptly confirmed.
- Besides reservations, the computer can perform routine functions at a lightning speed like changes in reservations, cancellations, etc.
- When linked to a printer, a computer can print complete tickets, itineraries and invoices, etc.
- The computer with appropriate software can summarise sales, commission income, etc. Such information enables the manager of the agency to monitor the performance of the company.
- Through a sophisticated backroom system, an agency can print invoices, maintain record of payments made by clients, keep track of receivable accounts, write cheques on the dates specified by the travel agency, keep an inventory of tour and group programmes, keep a record of commissions from car rental companies and hotels, maintain agencies' pay rolls, produce financial statements, compile employees' productivity reports, store mailing lists of companies' special clients, print address labels and undertake other functions. There is hardly any function that the computer cannot do for a travel agency.

How is an Airlines Reservation Made? : An airlines' reservation can be made in either of the two ways:

- By requesting the availability display and choosing from the display.
- By requesting space directly if the flight number and the airline to be booked is already determined.

After choosing the flight, the Passenger Name Record (PNR) appears on the screen. It contains the following mandatory bits of information—name of the airline, flight number, class of service, date of departure, departure city, destination city, desired number of seats.

As the necessary segments are confirmed, the following information is added—

(a) passenger's family name, initials and title

(b) passenger's home/business telephone number,

(c) Travel Agency's name, phone and agent's identification

(d) Ticketing information—date by which the passenger must pay and pick up the ticket or lose the reservation and the form of payment. Additional fields—hotels, cars, cruise, etc., can become a part of the record, if required.

To complete the PNR, the user must press the CTR to end the transaction. The key indicates that the transaction is now complete and the suppliers be informed. If the key is not pressed, the message will disappear and no record will be kept. Computer seldom loses a message unless it is malfunctioning.

Criticism of the CRS : In recent times, there has been a discussion about the CRSs. They have been called inflexible dinosaurs, not being able to fulfil the current or future market needs. Criticism relates mainly to the insufficient scope of services offered and the high distribution costs.

Scope not Sufficient

With most airlines, it is possible today to book a flight easily by pressing the required keys on the computer keyboard. However, there are numerous needs of travel industry which the present-day computers are ill-equipped to fulfil. With regard to product presentation, the CRSs adequately serves the airlines but other service providers such as hotels, rental car companies, charter airlines, tour operators, etc, cannot be served properly. Their reservation rate is low. Many of them cannot be displayed at all. In Europe, such functions are primarily performed by the national distribution systems and, hotel chains themselves.

Despite the current advance in CRS technology, it is easier to book a flight in a distant resort island than a hotel in the neighbouring city. While the reservation functions are working effectively on the basis of modern access technology, 'fare quoting' process is still complicated, confusing and incomprehensive.

Price transparency and even price negotiations are not supported by the System. One reason could be that airlines which own the CRSs are not interested in making prices comparable. However, some modifications are being made to make information about the best buy and negotiated fares known to the travel agents. Some more changes are contemplated to make computers more user-friendly for front office functions.

Rise in Distribution Costs

High distribution cost is another criticism of the CRSs. Optimal changes have already been made in the some of the airlines functions to make them competitive. Only areas where more economy and efficiency could be brought about are expenditure on personnel, fuel and the cost of distribution. Sales costs amount to some twenty to twenty-five per cent of the revenue, including travel agency commissions and the CRS reservation charges, which are on the high side.

There are two approaches to reduce sales costs—one, by providing effective on-line services to the end consumers. Many airlines now offer access to their internal service provider system via on-line services or via internet. This cuts the agents from the distribution system as well as saves the CRS fees. Lufthansa has introduced an innovative approach. Its interesting concept "Info-Highway" provides statistical information on CD-Rom and will make it possible to make direct reservation via an on-line interface. Moreover, some airlines now offer last-minute tickets at good prices in auctions via the internet. By using on-line services, it may be possible to reduce costs by eliminating travel agency and CRS commissions. This will, however, attract only a very small percentage of customers. In Europe, for instance, only three per cent of the population has, at present, access to on-line services and in Asia and India much less.

The so-called "no frill" carriers have gone a step forward to cut costs. Southwest Airlines of the US, for instance, have cut all unnecessary costs—services, meals, change of bookings, etc., and offer the basic service of transporting the passenger from point A to point B at the best possible price. They do not use CRSs for reservations and instead process all incoming bookings with the help of internal client/server system. As in the past, the customers now go back to the airline directly and pays there and then with their credit cards. This aggressive approach has made some other airlines also think of doing without the CRSs. Some carriers like the Swiss Air have come to agreements with a few major travel agency chains, to make their reservations directly in the system of the respective airlines. Some travel agency chains like the American Express offer the possibility to various airlines and hotels to display their services directly in the travel agents' internal systems. This can substitute the services provided by the CRSs and the cost of communication between the service provider and the travel agent can be reduced.

Crucial Cross Road

The CRS are at a crucial cross-road. On the one hand, the global CRSs have reached a high economic and technological level and travel agents can hardly do without these tools, while on the other hand, many service providers avoid using these tools due to high cost with its complicated functional requirements and worldwide networks. To remain in business, CRSs have to respond to the varied needs of the service providers or the worldwide electronic market will receive a severe jolt.

Regular Flying Programmes

An offshoot of the computer technology, is yet another marketing tool, introduced by most airlines of the world—the Frequent Flying Programmes. The objective is to create a brand loyalty for the airline. If you travel frequently on one particular airline, you earn some flying points after, for instance, every thousand kilometres from the airline you patronise. The programme has been made even more popular with the participation of some hotels and car rental companies. If you patronise a particular hotel or car rental company again and again, you gain some air-mileage points. Once you have adequate points accumulated, you can encash them into a free flight or upgradation of your existing flight. The essential thing is that you must seek the membership of the Frequent Flying Programme of an airline. Each airline has a different system to enable you to retrieve the mileage points in terms of free flights or upgradation.

International Networking

Internet has added new dimensions to the travel industry distribution worldwide. The system is very simple. Anyone owning a personal computer and having access to the internet, can reach a website where airline tickets or packaged holidays are on sale and buy whatever he prefers, by giving his credit card number. Jupiter Communications (www://jup.com) has done a study on the proliferation of travel related sites on the internet and worldwide web.

They estimated that on-line revenue for 1996 reached US$827 million which by 2002, exceeded US$8.9 billion. The revenue may even be on the higher side. In the US, some sixty-four million people were reported to have access to internet in 1998 (Source WTO) and the websites offered three hundred and twenty million pages of information on all subjects.

To make matters easier, there are a million websites of travel retailers, wholesalers and the consolidators as well as the national tourist offices of different countries, telling you the possibility of enormous options for bargains and deals in travel and holidays.

Internet is the largest and the fastest growing network in the world and represents a new challenge to the CRSs. Not only is the network registering twenty-five per cent growth annually, the people accessing it belong to a very high-income group with higher educational qualifications. The ease and low cost with which its users (consumers as well as travel retailers) can access it, has forced some of the CRSs to start their own websites, i.e., SABRE's Travelocity.com. Other important networks are— Microsoft Expedia, Internet Travel Network, Preview Travel, American Express and Travel Web which are full service mega-sites offering instant services.

While most airlines have their own schedules and fares, these sites rarely screen competitive rates. Some of these sites like Travelocity could give helpful information on schedules as well as comparative fares of different airlines.

Small to medium hotels and travel agency retailers are using the global reach of the web. It is serving as a great equaliser. A consumer can now select a modest hotel in Delhi or Paris as easily as five-star property in London. In Europe, many small hotels claim to be doing inbound business worth millions of dollars. Indian travel agents like Sita claim doing good inbound business from its newly launched website (www.Sitaindia.com). Other Indian travel agencies are not far behind.

Everyone in the tourism industry, from an airline giant to a lodging chain or a small retailer, has an equal chance. The principal challenge is to keep ones' information up-to-date. Any failure in this respect leads to disaster.

Limitation of Internet : Despite its great potential, internet has its limitations. It is hightech, but it is not high touch. Travel distribution uses technology, but travel is not all about technology—we buy travel services without seeing the product—on faith and trust. But travel is a complete service where the customer needs value. In the final analysis, the consumer value will prevail over technology.

Beyond the Internet : Although internet is the latest in the chain of technologies which seems to have an edge over any other at the moment, we have to look beyond the internet. How soon will the internet be an old technology? How soon will the travellers be able to book travel from all sorts of devices like the television set or an appliance that we do not know as yet in a networked home. Voice recognition systems are improving and the price of hardware and software to support them is declining. How soon will they become part of the automated system? The smart agent or digital robot, a computer application that can complete the job without human intervention—how soon? And how commonplace? Only the future will tell.

The day however is, not very far when large segments of market will communicate and transact business on the internet as routinely as we talk on the phone.

Technology in Prominent Role

Hospitality Industry is next only to airlines in the use of technology and has been enjoying the best of the both worlds. CRSs in the hotel industry, were first centralised by the Sheraton Group of the USA as early as 1956. These were further refined and developed by Holiday Inn in 1960s and since then have gone through generations of refinement. Every major hotel chain has its own Reservation System or the one based on readily available software in the market.

From computerised check-in to automatic wake-up calls, electronic locks to closed circuit TV, fire and security protection systems to teleconferencing, nothing is better organised than the modern-day hotels and resorts. One often wonders at the miracle that the present day hotels offer to the client. The modern hotels have integrated systems that the operational requirements including a reservation system which checks the availability of rooms for individuals and groups, assigns room types, tracks deposits, and prints managerial reports. The front-desk system handles registrations and check-outs, automatically posts guest accounts, provides telephone operators with room directory, updates accounts receivable and tracks house-keeping staff.

An accounting system handles guest accounting, night auditing and back office accounting functions. It can perform additional functions like energy management with more support.

An area in which technology has already advanced, is information processing. It includes the use of company-wide reservation network. At individual hotels the system provides for room management system, point of sales charging, computing, word-processing and personal computing. The second major category of information processing is the broad area of property management system. They ably and reliably perform not only reservation functions but also room management, front and back office-accounting and operational reporting. That includes guest reservation, and folio accounting (the record of the guest charges for room, food, beverage and telephone). Accounting includes night audit, city ledger, accounts payable, general ledger, travel agency accounts, daily and monthly operating reports, pay rolls and inventory.

As hotel operations need more options, the vendors go out of the way to meet their needs. The vendors will integrate their system with automated or non-automated parts of the hotel.

Point-of-sale systems have become commonplace in many food outlets, restaurants, clubs as well as hotels. A restaurant system allows the waiter to place order at the console located in the dining room, which prints it out in the kitchen for action. A restaurant system reduces errors in calculating and totalling the final check, immediately posts charges to the guests' room account and provides a variety of analysis including daily reports and food inventory.

What does technology mean to a well-run hotel and its guests? The interaction with technology starts at reservation itself where the Property Management System (PMS) confirms the guest booking as well as gives the history of guests and their likes and dislikes. The latter is useful specially to house-keeping and room service, to help them place required amenities in the room. When the guest checks-in, he or she is given the key-card rather than the traditional key. The key-card is swiped in at the time of check-in and is valid for the entire stay of the guest. His key-card also acts as the main electrical switch in the room. When the guest enters the room, the key-card can be put into the card slot next to the door, which switches on the lights and the TV in the room. When the guest checks-in, the PMS can be interfaced with paging device, so as to page room service and housekeeping with detail of the guest along with his preferences.

Inside the room, instead of switches, there can be control panels, conveniently placed at the bed-side table, which has small graphical icons representing various electrical appliances in the room. The panel can also have control for dimming the lights as well as for closing and opening of the curtains. The panels in all the rooms can then be linked to the control hub, which, in turn, can download the data from all the rooms to a central PC work-station. A simple programme will tell the house-keeping and front-office which rooms are occupied and which are vacant. Within the room, the TV can act as a wonderful tool for guest conveniences. It can be made interactive, helping the guests in a number of ways.

It can give information about various outlets of the hotel, business centre, health club, etc. It can be interfaced with the PMS and can be used to preview the bill before checkout, specially for those guests who want express check-outs. The biggest advantage is to use the TV for placing room service order. The guest can browse the menu on the TV and place the order from the TV itself. The KOT for the order will be printed in the service department, and the room service ordertaker can then call up the guest and customise the order to the guest's liking. TV can also be used by the guest to give feedback about the hotel, the feedback can be printed in the back-office for management scrutiny.

The same interactive TV can be used for the internet. For internet connectivity in each room, most hotels are using DSL technology. This technology uses the existing telephone lines (or CATS cabling if already laid down during the construction stage) and gives twenty-four hour connectivity in each room. The guests just have to plug in his or her laptop to work on the internet. If the guest does not have a PCMCIA network card in the laptop, or does not have the laptop at all, then the card or the laptop can be given on rent. The billing can be interfaced with the existing PMS.

Technology can help the housekeeping department also. The mini-bar billing which is the bane of every hotel can be made easy using the same interactive TV. Immediately after the check-out, as the room-boys go for room clearance, they can use the mini-bar remote and punch the consumption. The consumption will then be printed in the printer next to the cashier who will post it to the folio of the guest. So by the time the guest comes down, his mini-bar consumption is recorded in the bill. These are delightful experiences that enhance guest satisfaction in a hotel.

Indian Hotel Scene : The old school hotelier is dead, or at least on his last legs and his traditional skills, polished to perfection during his long climb to the corporate ladder, are now as outdated as his school tie. The perfect smile, practised handshake and patented sincerity, simply do not cut ice anymore. Today's hotel manager can never be set in his ways. He needs to constantly develop his skills, adapt fast to the changes and be a lot more business savvy than his twentieth century counterpart.

Although the hotel industry in India has been slow to adapt itself to the new technology, the hoteliers in the deluxe categories have moved faster than the west. The Indian chains like the Taj Group, the Oberoi and the Welcomgroup have in some ways, outdone the hotels in the western countries in guest satisfaction, using the latest technology, plus the personal touch. The IT technology is so important for the Indian hotels that at the Info tech Hotels Exp-2001-Conference, organised by the Hotels Association of India (HAI) in Delhi—the second in the series, there were over two hundred representatives of the hotel industry including the technology managers and chief executives of major hotels and hotel chains. Indian experts were more than a match for the foreign experts in knowledge and skills.

The Taj and Oberoi operate hotels in many western countries, so the technology changes in India occur almost simultaneously. The fact that India is now a leader in information technology has helped leading Indian hotels to bring about necessary changes.

Referring to technology change in the hospitality industry of India, Mr R.K. Krishan Kumar, Managing Director of the Taj Group of hotels wrote in the Infotech Hotels Guide-2001, "Technology in the hospitality industry of India is playing an increasingly important role. Annual investments in technology account for 3.4 per cent of the annual revenue." Commenting on internet, he said, "The internet holds a very large potential for hoteliers, apart from enabling websites that will take bookings and instantly confirm rooms with on-line payments, hotels will be able to conduct business to business (B2B) and will be able to tie-up with suppliers to maintain an effective supply chain management. Large chains are bound to gain and improve their bottom-lines through such system." Mr Ravi Bhothlingam, President of the Oberoi Group, echoed the sentiment, "Intelligent hotels will come up in a big way in India. Hotel rooms will not only have temperature control facility but would have control for lighting of the room to control the colours, change different light effects, sound effects and change the ambience as per the choice of the guests." The registration procedure will be extremely simplified, he added.

Need of Technology

Technology will totally change the way marketing is done by the NTAs all over the world. Gone are the days of marketing destinations by distribution of tourism brochure to stray visitors coming to offices, film shows or the desk-bound officials sitting cozily in their chairs and disseminating information from their moth-eaten files. It is now an age of websites as well as internet-instant updated information on the websites and on-line purchase of holiday packages. A slow but perceptible change is in the pipeline to the delight of the consumers. Several countries have taken steps to reduce the number of their tourist offices overseas or have pruned the strength. They are investing more in technology and media advertising. Here also they advertise the website identity to encourage the readers to probe further about their destination.

WTO has strongly recommended to their members to adopt internet technology for the promotion of their respective destinations. Addressing a WTO seminar in Madrid in early 2001, Mr Pedro Ortun, European Union, Director Services, Trade and Tourism, said that internet represents "great opportunities, but also great risks for those who do not adopt it."

The decision to purchase a destination by a visitor, is based solely on the basis of recommendations from friends, a brochure supplied by the national tourist office or perhaps an advertisement in the media. Increasingly, however, the prospective visitors are tapping the wealth of destination material on the worldwide web of a country, using it as their primary source. The new truth for destination marketing is that if you are not on-line then you are not on sale within your key markets. If your destination is not on the web, it may then be ignored by millions of people who have access to internet and they are the more educated and people with higher incomes. These people expect that every destination will have a comprehensive presence on the web.

Participation in the web is essential but not a daunting task. A good presence on the web can be achieved by a surprisingly low-cost.

The worldwide web is the ideal channel for promotion of destinations—a global medium. It costs no more to distribute your information to a continent on the other side of the globe than it does to the neighbouring region. It is a multimedia experience.

Multimedia is a term used to describe information presented in a variety of formats. The most commonly used formats on the web are text and images, graphics and photographs. However, the web can also deliver sound and video and the media is becoming increasingly popular to provide rich audio-visual experience.

If one NTA can represent its destination better than another, then it may win the tourist who is uncertain about where to travel.

One of the key challenges for an NTA is to build a database of multimedia destination information that can be used for on-line promotion. Once a suitable depth of information is available electronically, this can be used to build a website. It can also be made available to tourist information centres within your region or the country. Thus, the NTA begins to build an integrated information system strategy, whereby a single source of information is used both internally for the Destination Marketing Organisation and externally on the web and in partnership with the third parties, interested in promoting your destination like the specialised travel agencies, tour operators, national airlines from the country, interested in the information—without infringing the copyrights. The challenge for the NTA is to assist private sector organisations to promote its destination in the best possible way.

As more and more consumers worldwide adopt on-line distribution channel as their preferred way of buying travel products, industry will change. A new breed of global travel vendors has entered the market. The new electronic distribution channels are a boon for the new entrants. They need not invest in physical infrastructure of the traditional high street retail agent and, in theory, can operate from a spare room of the house or a motor garage. All they need is access to customers. The new players may be internet search directories like Yahoo, Excite or Lycos or software companies like Microsoft and Netscape. They have on-line customer relationships worldwide. There are also new ways of selling. Many new sites have emerged—auction sites where the customer sets the price—they are becoming increasingly popular.

Having experienced the effectiveness of the websites as

marketing tools, many countries have launched their websites and India is one of them. The quality and the depth of information may vary. USA, for instance, has the most numbers from that of the Travel Industry Association of America (TIA) to numerous others representing the various State Tourism Organisations as well as the airlines of the country, etc.

Indian Profile

Being the nodal agency overseeing the development of tourism for India, the Ministry of Tourism, has taken an initiative and launched its portal—www.tourismofindia.com—providing information about the country. The portal provides the facility of two-way communications, etc. In the near future, the Ministry plans to provide e-commerce facilities on their website. To assist the tourists coming to the Indian shores, the Ministry has not only setup information offices at the airports, but has also sixty tourist information kiosks at airports and other public places in the country.

The information on hotels and hotel bookings is being provided through kiosks at the domestic and international airports. A pilot project has been started in Delhi and soon the facility will be extended to other major airports of the country.

In the four regional tourist offices, there is Interactive Voice Response System (IVRS)—this facility provides twenty-four hour information to tourists, on the phone.

The Ministry has created a new technology called HARK (solid state random tourist guidance access system) in collaboration with NUT. It has already been introduced in the Red Fort—a visitor to the Red Fort could listen to the authentic commentary as he moves within the Fort, looking at different buildings. At the moment, this technology has been limited to the monument scale, later it will cover the entire city.

Another innovation, first of its kind in the world—the new project enabling a tourist to view the entire video view of the Qutab Minar from the top, without ever climbing the tower.

The Ministry has also come up with ten CDs on different aspects of Indian tourism. Among them are the walk-through CDs on the Taj Mahal, Khajuraho, Hampi and Konark.

The Ministry, however, is of the view that technology cannot replace the human touch. It can only help the travel industry to improve its efficiency and service.

Worldwide, tourism is ten per cent of the GDP—providing employment to millions of people. In India, it is three per cent of the GDP, with great potential for the future. If we can tap it a little more, tourism earnings will be enough to meet our trade deficits.

To summarise, automation has changed the face of travel industry in less than three decades. Information technology in travel industry was first initiated by airlines and they have been the major beneficiaries in terms of business, efficiency, speed and economy. Since the travel agents were integral part of the travel industry distribution chain, the automation in the airlines sector was passed on to the travel agencies by the airlines.

The new technology manifested itself in the form of Central Reservation Systems (CRSs). First developed by the American Airlines, its SABRE System is still one of the world's largest. Soon, other US airlines also joined hands for developing their own CRSs—Apollo, Worldspan and System One. Not to be left behind and discriminated by US airlines, some of the European carriers set up their own CRSs—AMADEUS and GALILEO. Some Asian airlines like Singapore Airlines and Cathey Pacific of Hong Kong, developed their own CRS called ABACUS. They all work together through arrangements with each other in different parts of the world.

Airlines like Air India and Indian Airlines own no CRS. They are, however, represented in all major CRSs and pay fee to the owning companies for every reservation received through their CRS. Air India and Indian Airlines, however, distribute in India a specially designed version developed by SABRE, suited to India. It is branded as SITAR.

The internet is a recent phenomenon adding a new channel to travel industry distribution chain. The consumer can buy travel products directly, eliminating the travel agent as well as the CRS. Some airlines now offer access to their systems to the internet users. Besides, some CRS like SABRE have set up their own websites for bargain hunters and low-price tickets. Some websites offer last minute auction of the air seats on their portals.

Apart from storing data for some seven hundred airlines of the world, the CRSs store information about thousands of hotels, car rental companies, railway systems, cruise lines, etc. But, the reservation ratio is low.

Major hotel chains and leading hotels have developed their own reservation systems to accept bookings from travel agents, and consumers directly. Hotel chains have made excellent use of the new technology. The traditional hotel managers are no more in demand. Instead, it is the business and computer-savvy gentleman who is in command. Large hotels even have their own Technology Managers.

National Tourist Administrations (NTAs) too have caught the technology bug. The focus is now on multimedia websites promoting their destinations. The tourist offices are becoming redundant as millions of well-educated and affluent people with internet access, are seeking information from such websites. India is one of those nations which has an excellent portal and the Ministry of Tourism plans to soon make it accessible for e-marketing.

Bibliography

Abani, K.M. : *Tourism in Asia and Europe*, Peacock Pub., 2003.

Addison, William : *English Spas,* Batsford, London, 1951.

Aldous, T. : *Battle for the Environment,* Collins, London, 1972.

Alfred Joh : *Tourism Development,* Star Publication, Sydney, 2003.

Andrew Vladimir : *The Complete Travel Marketing Handbook,* NTC Business Book, Lincolnwood, USA, 1989.

Andrews, S.: *Food and Beverage Science*, Tata McGraw Hill, Publishing Co. Ltd., New Delhi, 1980.

Arora, K.: *Theory of Cooking*, K.N. Gupta & Co., Delhi, 1982.

Ashworth, G. : *Recreation and Tourism,* Bell and Hyman, London, 1984.

Baron, Raphael Raymond, V.: *Seasonalty in Tourism: A Guide to Seasonality and Trends for Policy-making*, The Economist Intelligence Unit, 1975.

Bernecker, Paul : *Methods and Media of Tourist Publicity,* Austrian National Tourist Office, Vienna, 1961.

Birch, G.G., J.G. Prennan and K.J. Parker : *The Sensory Properties of Foods*, Applied Science Publication Ltd., London, 1977.

Bland, J.W. : *Clinical Metabolism of Body Water and Electrolytes*, U.B. Saunders Company, Philadelphia, 1962.

Board, R.G.: *A Modern Introduction to Food Microbiology*, Blackwell Scientific Publications, Oxford, 1983.

Boniface, B. and Cooper, C. : *The Geography of Travel and Tourism* Heinemann, London, 1987.

Boniface, Brain G. : *The Geography of Travel and Tourism*, Butterworth-Heinmann, Oxford, 1991.

Burkart & Medlik : *Tourism — Past, Present and Future*, Heinemann Professional, London, 1990.

Burkart, A.J. : *The Management of Tourism*, Heinemann, London, 1975.

Burkart, A.J. and Medlik, S. : *Tourism: Past, Present and Future*, Heinemann, London, 1976.

Checchi and Co. : *The Future of Tourism in the Far East* (1961).

Cherry, G.E. : *Town Planning and its Social Context*, Hill, London, 1970.

Clayne, R. Jensen : *Leisure and Recreation: Introduction and Overview*, Lea and Febiger, Philadelphia, 1977.

Coltman, Michael M. : *Introduction of Travel and Tourism*, Van Nostrand Reinhold, New York, 1989.

Coltman, Michael M. : *Introduction to Travel and Tourism—An International Approach*, Van Nostrand Reinhold, New York, 1989.

Cooper, C. : *Tourism Principles and Practices*, Pitman, London, 1993.

Copson, D. A.: *Microwave Heating*, The AVI Publishing Co., Connecticut, 1975.

Cosgrove, Isabel and Jackson, R. : *The Geography of Recreation and Leisure*, Hutchinson, London, 1972.

Dale, E. : *Management Theory and Practice*, McGraw Hill, New York, 1983.

David Off, Phillips and Doris : *Sales and Marketing for Travel and Tourism*, Blackhill, USA, 1990.

David, R. Yale : *The Publicity Hand Book*, Bantam Books, Toronto, 1992.

David, Stewar : *The Theory and Practice of Transport*, Heinmann, London, 1980.

Davidson, E.A.: *Carbohydrate Chemistry*, Holt, New York, 1967.

Doswell, Royer : *Case Studies in Tourism*, Berrie and Jenkins, London, 1978.

Douglas Pearce : *Tourism Today: A Geographical-Analysis,* Longman, New York, 1987.

Duckworth, R.B.: *Fruits andVegetables,*Ptrgamon Press, New York, 1966.

Edmunds : *Environmental Administration,* McGraw-Hill, New York, 1973.

Edward, J Mayo : *The Psychology of Leisure Travel,* CBI Publishing Company, Boston, 1981.

Edwards, Francis, G. : *How to Focus ? Your Marketing Efforts,* Louis A. Allen Associates, London, 1976.

Edwards, Francis, G. : *How to Focus Your Marketing Efforts,* Louis A. Alien Associates, London, 1976.

Eisenberg, D. and H. Kauzmann : *The Structure and Properties of Water,* Clarendon, Oxford, 1969.

Eley, G.: *Wild Fruits and Nuts,* E.P. Publishing Ltd., Yorkshire, 1976.

Fersht, A. : *Enzyme Structure and Mechanism,* W.H. Freeman & Co., 1977.

Forster, John : *"The Sociological Consequences of Tourism",* International Journal of Comparative Sociology, 1964.

Foster, D. : *Travel and Tourism Management,* MacMillan, London, 1985.

Foster, Kerr Pannell : *Trends in Hotel Industry,* Houston, USA, Pannell Kerr Foster, 1984.

Frank, R.E. : *Market Segmentation,* Prentice-Hall, New Jersey, 1972.

Furia, T.E.: *Hand Book of Food Additives,* C.R.C. Press, T.C. Ohio, 1977.

Godwin, Nadin : *Complete Guide to Travel Agency,* Automation, Albanj, Delmer, 1987.

Goeldner, Erent and McIntosh : *Tourism, Principles, Practices and Philosophies,* John Wiley and Sons, New York, 2000.

Gurr, M.E. and A.T. James : *Lipid Biochemistry—An Introduction,* Cornell, Ithaca, New York, 1975.

Hawkins, Donald : *Tourism Planning and Development Issues,* George Washington University, 1980.

Heath, E. : *Marketing Tourism Destinations,* Wiley, New York, 1992.

Hibbert, Christopher : *The Grand Tour,* Weidenfel and Nicolson, London, 1969.

Hilditch, T.P. and P.N. Williams: *The Chemical Constitution of Natural Fats*, Chapman and Hall, London, 1964.

Hiller, Herbet L. : "*The Development of Tourism in the Caribbean Region*" Air Travel and Tourism, 1972.

Holman, R.T. : *The Progress in the Chemistry of Fats and other Lipids*, Pergamon Press, New York, 1971.

Hosansky, M. : *The 27 Billion Meeting Industry—Meetings and Conventions,* New York, 1983.

Jafferson, Alan and Lickorish, Leonard : *Marketing Tourism,* Longman, UK, 1983.

Jarari, J. :. *Role of Tourism in Socio-Economic Transformation of Developing Countries*, 1973.

John, Lea : *Tourism Development in the Third World,* Routledge, New York, 1988.

Joseph, D. Firdgen : *Dimensions of Tourism,* East Lansing, American Hotel and Motel Association, Michigan, 1991.

Kernan, J. B. : *Promotion,* McGraw-Hill, New York, 1970.

Kerry Godrey and Jackie Clarke : *The Tourism Development Handbook,* Cassell, London, 2000.

Kotler P. : *Introduction to Marketing Management: Marketing Management Analysis*, Planning and Control, Prentice Hall, 1990.

Kotler P. : *Principles of Marketing,* Prentice-Hall, New York, 1999.

Kusuma D.L. : *Profile of Nutrition of Rural Adolescent Girls*, Discovery Publishing House, New Delhi, 2001.

Lal, G., G.S. Siddappa and G.L. Tandon : *Preservation of Fruits and Vegetables*, Indian Council of Agricultural Research, New Delhi, 1960.

Marks, J., A : *Guide to the Vitamins: Their Role in Health and Disease*, University Park Press, Baltimore, 1975.

Marton, I.D. and A.J.Macbod : *Food Flavours*, Elesvier Scientific Publishing Co., New York, 1982.

Mate, S. A.: *Bakery Technology and Engineering*, The AVI Publishing Co., Connecticut, 1972.

Medlik, S. : *Profile of the Hotel and Catering Industry,* Heinemann, London, 1972.

Medlik, S. and Middleton V.T.C. : *"The Tourist Product and its Marketing Implications"*, International Tourism Quarterly, 1973.

Meridith, George and Fried, Robert P. : *Incentives in Marketing,* NPSC Education Fund Union, New Jersey, 1977.

Meyer, L.H. : *Food Chemistry*, Reinhold Publishing Corporation, New York, 1961.

Michael Eskin, N.A. : *Plant Pigments, Flavours and Textures,* Academic Presss, New York, 1979.

Murphy, Peter E. : *Tourism : A Community Approach,* Methuen, 1985.

Murthy, R.B.: *Breeding Procedures in Pearl Millet,* ICAR, New Delhi, 1977.

Norval, A.J. : *The Tourist Industry,* Issac Pitman and Sons Ltd., London, 1936.

Ogilvie, F.W. : *The Tourist Movement: An Economic Study,* Staples Press, London, 1933.

Ogilvy David : *Confessions of an Advertising Man,* Ballantine Books, New York, 1976.

Ogilvy, F.W. : *The Tourist Movement—An Economic Study*, Staples Press, London, 1997.

Parry, J.W. : *Spices,* Chemical Publishing Co., New York, 1969.

Pearce, Sales, J. : *Travel and Tourism Encyclopedia,* Blandford, London, 1959.

Peckham, G.G. and J.H. Freeland-Graves : *Foundations of Food Preparation*, Macmillan Publishing Co., New York, 1979.

Peters, Michael : *International Tourism: "The Economics and Development of the International Tourist Trade",* Hutchinson, London, 1969.

Pimlott, J.A.R. : *The Englishman's Holiday,* Faber, London, 1947.

Potter,N.M. : *Food Science,*The AVI Publishing Co., Connecticut, 1978.

Prasad, A.S. and D. Oberleas : *Trace Elements in Health and Disease*, Academic Press, New York, 1976.

Ranganna, K.S. and K.T. Achaya : *Indian Dairy Products,* Asia Publishing House, Bangalore, 1974.

Ranganna, S. : *Manual of Analysis of Fruit and Vegetable Products*, Tata McGraw-Hill Publishing Co. Ltd., New Delhi, 1984.

Rao D. B. : *Woman and family Health*, Discovery Publishing House, New Delhi, 1999.

Robinson, G.W.S. : *"The Recreation Geography of South Asia,"* Geographical Review, (October 1972).

Runeckles, V.C. : *Recent Advances in Phytochemistry*, Academic Press, New York, 1972.

Russell Williams : *The Nutrition and Health,* Discovery CBS Publishers, New Delhi.

Ryan, C. : *Recreational Tourism :A Social Science Perspective,* Routledge, London, 1991.

Sakumaran, P.S. : *Perental Involvement in the Education of Mentally Handicapped Children,*Discovery Publishers, New Delhi, 2000.

Smartt, J.: *Tropical Pulses*, Longman Group Ltd., London, 1976.

Sultan, W. J.: *Modem Pastry Cheff*, The AVI Publishing Co., Connecticut, 1977.

Susan Homer : *Marketing Tourism Hospitality and Leisure in Europe,* International Thomson Business Press, London, 1996.

Sutton, Geoffrey : *How to Sell Travel ?,* Travel Topics, London, 1959.

Sutton, W.A. : *"Travel and Understanding Notes on the Social Structure of Touring",* International Journal of Comparative Sociology, 1967.

Tata, J.R.D. : *"The Story of Indian Air Transport"*, Journal of Royal Aeronautical Society, London, 1961.

Trease, Geoffrey : *The Grand Tour,* Heinemann, London, 1967.

Tull, D. S. : *Marketing Research: Measurements and Methods,* Prentice-Hall, London, 1993.

Urry, John : *The Tourist Gaze — Leisure and Travel in Contemporary Societies*, Sage Publications, New Delhi, 1990.

Usha Rani, D. : *Nutrition and Religion*, discovery Publishing House, New Delhi. 2003.

Wahab Salah : *Tourism Management,* Tourism International Press, London, 1975.

Whitaker, J.R. : *Principles of Enzymology for Food Science*, Marcel Dekker Inc., New York, 1977.

White, J. : *History of Tourism,* Leisure Art, London, 1967.

Whiteley, P.P. : *Biscuit Manufacture*, Elsevier Publishing Co. Ltd., London, 1971.

Williams, A, : *Bread Making*, Hutchinson, Benhan, London, 1975.

Williams, J., R. E. Eakin, E. Beersteeker, and W. Shine : *The Biochemistry of Vitamins*, Reinhold, New York, 1950.

Yukic, T.S. : *Fundamentals of Recreation,* Harper Row, London, 1963.

Zeithaml, V.A. : *Services Marketing,* McGraw-Hill, London, 1996.